YES IS MORE

AN ARCHICOMIC ON ARCHITECTURAL EVOLUTION

EVERGREEN

LESS IS MORE

LUDWIG MIES VAN DER ROHE
Architect

Quote mid-20th century

Modernism, Minimalism:
One of the founding fathers of Modern architecture (along with Le Corbusier), Mies van der Rohe's architecture was like an architectural revolution. Liberating the architectural vocabulary from stylistic exercises through the consistent elimination of excess ornament and redundant form, he created a tabula rasa from which pure concepts and spaces could emerge.
For his followers (and to some degree for himself) the revolutionary movement gradually degenerated as the liberating mantra became a starvation of the imagination, turning the freedom from style into a stylistic straightjacket itself. The result is the relentless repetition of identical anonymous boxes that dominate vast areas of the contemporary city.

ROBERT CHARLES VENTURI JR
Architect

Quote 1970s

Postmodernism:
As a counterrevolution against the limited choice of vocabulary for the orthodox
modern architect, Robert Venturi and
Denise Scott Brown started looking at
the contemporary city outside the realm
of modern architecture. By "Learning
from Las Vegas", they reintroduced
symbolism and signs in the architectural palette, offering "complexity and
contradiction" in place of simplicity and
consistency.
The counterrevolution against the
monotony of strictly functional modern
architecture, in turn led to its own epi-
demic of indistinguishable Postmodern
towers no more varied nor interesting
than their Modern siblings.

PHILIP CORTELYOU JOHNSON
Architect

Quote 1982

Opportunism and Eclecticism:
Like a curator rather than a creator,
Philip Johnson has been capable of iden-
tifying and assimilating a broad history of
styles and architectures. Curator of the
Modern Architecture show in 1932 and
then again the Deconstructivist show in
1988, both at MoMA, he has had a capacity
to nail the spirit of the moment.
And subsequently incorporate the latest
forms, materials, vocabularies into his
own work. His Glass House estate in New
Canaan, Connecticut is like an Expo of 20th
century architecture history: like a collection of exotic species of various 'isms
and epochs, they are all his own original
designs.

REM KOOLHAAS
Architect & founder of OMA & AMO
at BIG HQ, 2006

Quote 2001

Dirty Realism:
Rem Koolhaas, nicknamed the Le Corbusier of our times*, is often misunderstood
as being a protagonist of the conditions
he investigates.
In essays (not manifestoes) he has explored phenomena such as the Berlin Wall,
the Generic City, Size, China, Globalization,
Shopping, etc., attempting to suspend
judgment and prejudice in order to fully
appreciate and comprehend the world as
it actually is.
As such, "more is more" is not a manifesto, rather an observation that in Junk-
space (the residue that mankind leaves
on this planet), accumulation and addition
has replaced higher forms of organization
such as hierarchy and composition.
Understanding precedes action.
* Jeffrey Kipnis, "Recent Koolhaas", El
Croquis 79, 1996

BARACK HUSSEIN OBAMA II
44th President of the United States of America

Quote 2007

Unity and Optimism:
Resisting the political opposition's
default strategy of contradiction
and conflict, Barack Obama offered
change through unity. Why choose between red states or blue states, when
you can choose the United States of
America?

YES IS MORE

BJARKE INGELS
Founder of BIG ApS

Quote 2009

Pragmatic Utopianism:
Historically the field of architecture
has been dominated by two opposing
extremes. On one side an avant-garde
of wild ideas, often so detached from
reality that they fail to become something other than eccentric curiosities.
On the other side there are well-
organized corporate consultants that
build predictable and boring boxes
of high standard. Architecture seems
entrenched between two equally
unfertile fronts: either naively utopian or petrifyingly pragmatic. Rather
than choosing one over the other, BIG
operates in the fertile overlap between the two opposites. A pragmatic
utopian architecture that takes on the
creation of socially, economically and
environmentally perfect places as a
practical objective.

YES IS MORE!
– A THEORY OF EVOLUTION

The traditional image of the radical architect is the angry young man rebelling against the establishment. The avantgarde is defined by what it is against rather than what it is for.

This leads to an oedipal succession of contradictions where each generation says the opposite of the previous. And if your agenda is dependent on being the opposite of someone else's - you are simply a follower in reverse.

Rather than being radical by saying fuck the context, - the establishment, - the neighbours, - the budget, or - gravity, we want to try to turn pleasing into a radical agenda.

The Danish welfare state is the culture of consensus. The socially most egalitarian country in the world, it is ruled by the good principles that everybody has the same rights, every point of view the same value.

Besides the obvious societal virtues, these principles have had a significant side effect in the realm of architecture: a gray goo of sameness accounting for the vast majority of the urban tissue, where most attempts to stick out have been beaten down into the same non-offensive generic box, and all libido invested in polishing and perfecting the ever finer details. The sum of all the little concerns seems to have blocked the view of the big picture.

What if trying to make everybody happy did not have to lead to compromise or the lowest common denominator? It could be a way to find the ever elusive summersault that twists and turns in order to fulfill every desire and avoid stepping on anyone's toes.

Rather than revolution, we are interested in evolution. Like Darwin describes creation as a process of excess and selection, we propose to let the forces of society, the multiple interests of everyone, decide which of our ideas can live, and which must die. Surviving ideas evolve through mutation and crossbreeding into an entirely new species of architecture.

Human life evolved through adaptation to changes in the natural environment. With the invention of architecture and technology we have seized the power to adapt our surroundings to the way we want to live, rather than the other way around.

This is what makes it interesting to be an architect: as life evolves, our cities and our architecture need to evolve with it. Our cities are not polluted or congested because they have to be. They are what they are because that's how we made them. So when something doesn't fit anymore, we architects have the ability - and responsibility - to make sure that our cities don't force us to adapt to outdated leftovers from the past, but actually fit to the way we want to live.

Viewed in this way we architects don't have to remain misunderstood geniuses, frustrated by the lack of understanding, appreciation or funding. We won't even be the creators of architecture but rather the midwives of the continuous birth of architectural species shaped by the countless criteria of multiple interests.

The whole world insists on conflict. The media craves conflict, and the politicians craving media presence need to engage in conflict to get there. Currently the biggest conflict in Danish politics is that the social democrats and the liberals (left and right) promote identical political programs which in any other context would be the very definition of harmony! In politics, it's the opposite.

What if design could be the opposite of politics? Not by ignoring conflict, but by feeding from it. A way to incorporate and integrate differences, not through compromise or by choosing sides, but by tying conflicting interests into a Gordian knot of new ideas.

An inclusive rather than exclusive architecture. An architecture unburdened by the conceptual monogamy of commitment to a single interest or idea. An architecture where you don't have to choose between public or private, dense or open, urban or suburban, atheist or Muslim, affordable flats or football fields. An architecture that allows you to say yes to all aspects of human life, no matter how contradicting! An architectural form of bigamy, where you don't need to chose one over the other, but you get to have both.

A pragmatic utopian architecture that takes on the creation of socially, economically and environmentally perfect places as a practical objective.

Yes is More, Viva la Evolucíon!

IT IS NOT THE STRONGEST OF THE SPECIES THAT SURVIVES, NOR THE MOST INTELLIGENT. IT IS THE ONE THAT IS THE MOST ADAPTABLE TO CHANGE.

CHARLES ROBERT DARWIN
Naturalist

Quote 1987, Clarence Darrow

PEOPLE'S BUILDING
人 REN

FOUND IN TRANSLATION

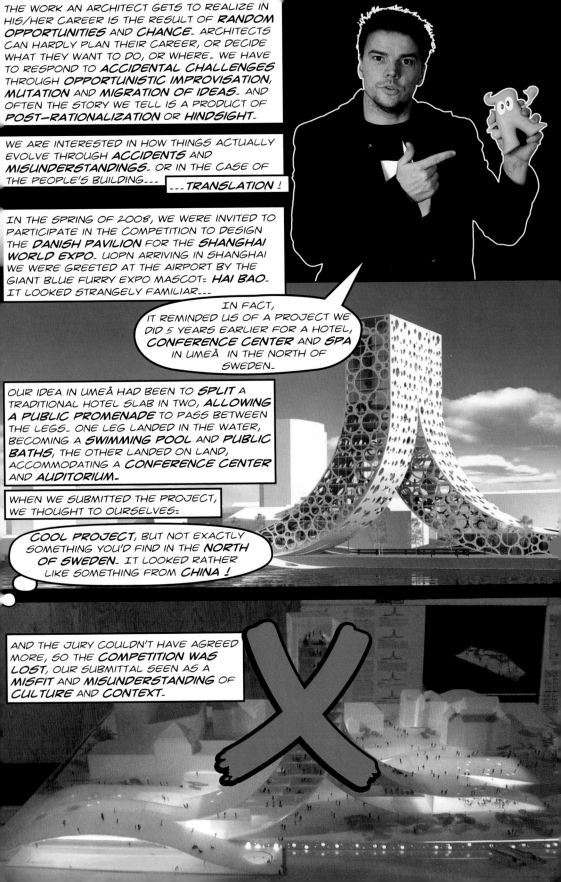

THE WORK AN ARCHITECT GETS TO REALIZE IN HIS/HER CAREER IS THE RESULT OF **RANDOM OPPORTUNITIES** AND **CHANCE.** ARCHITECTS CAN HARDLY PLAN THEIR CAREER, OR DECIDE WHAT THEY WANT TO DO, OR WHERE. WE HAVE TO RESPOND TO **ACCIDENTAL CHALLENGES** THROUGH **OPPORTUNISTIC IMPROVISATION, MUTATION** AND **MIGRATION OF IDEAS.** AND OFTEN THE STORY WE TELL IS A PRODUCT OF **POST-RATIONALIZATION** OR **HINDSIGHT.**

WE ARE INTERESTED IN HOW THINGS ACTUALLY EVOLVE THROUGH **ACCIDENTS** AND **MISUNDERSTANDINGS.** OR IN THE CASE OF THE PEOPLE'S BUILDING---

---**TRANSLATION !**

IN THE SPRING OF 2008, WE WERE INVITED TO PARTICIPATE IN THE COMPETITION TO DESIGN THE **DANISH PAVILION** FOR THE **SHANGHAI WORLD EXPO.** UOPN ARRIVING IN SHANGHAI WE WERE GREETED AT THE AIRPORT BY THE GIANT BLUE FURRY EXPO MASCOT: **HAI BAO.** IT LOOKED STRANGELY FAMILIAR---

IN FACT, IT REMINDED US OF A PROJECT WE DID 5 YEARS EARLIER FOR A HOTEL, **CONFERENCE CENTER** AND **SPA** IN UMEÅ IN THE NORTH OF SWEDEN.

OUR IDEA IN UMEÅ HAD BEEN TO **SPLIT** A TRADITIONAL HOTEL SLAB IN TWO, **ALLOWING A PUBLIC PROMENADE** TO PASS BETWEEN THE LEGS. ONE LEG LANDED IN THE WATER, BECOMING A **SWIMMING POOL** AND **PUBLIC BATHS**, THE OTHER LANDED ON LAND, ACCOMMODATING A **CONFERENCE CENTER** AND **AUDITORIUM.**

WHEN WE SUBMITTED THE PROJECT, WE THOUGHT TO OURSELVES:

COOL PROJECT, BUT NOT EXACTLY SOMETHING YOU'D FIND IN THE **NORTH OF SWEDEN.** IT LOOKED RATHER LIKE SOMETHING FROM **CHINA !**

AND THE JURY COULDN'T HAVE AGREED MORE, SO THE **COMPETITION WAS LOST,** OUR SUBMITTAL SEEN AS A **MISFIT** AND **MISUNDERSTANDING** OF **CULTURE** AND **CONTEXT.**

WE WOULD HAVE LEFT IT AT THAT IF WE HADN'T HAD A MEETING WITH A BUSINESSMAN FROM THE **GUANGXI PROVINCE** WHO WAS LOOKING FOR SCANDINAVIAN ARCHITECTS.

HE SAW THE MODEL, AND SAID...

WOW! THAT'S THE CHINESE CHARACTER FOR THE WORD **"PEOPLE"** !

人

AS A MATTER OF FACT, THIS IS HOW YOU WRITE **"PEOPLE"** IN CHINESE ! AS IN "THE **PEOPLE'S** REPUBLIC OF CHINA" !!! WE EVEN DOUBLE CHECKED !

people /ˈpiːpl/ *n* **1** [pl] 人 rén:

AT THE SAME TIME, WE RECEIVED A LETTER FROM SHANGHAI INVITING US TO EXHIBIT AT THE **SHANGHAI CREATIVE INDUSTRY WEEK.**

WE THOUGHT: "THIS IS TOO GOOD TO BE TRUE ! WE STUMBLE UPON WHAT COULD BE THE **LANDMARK** OF THE PEOPLE'S REPUBLIC OF CHINA AND THEN GET THIS INVITATION **ON THE SAME DAY** !"

SO WE **SCALED THE BUILDING UP 3 TIMES** TO CHINESE PROPORTIONS, HIRED A FENG SHUI MASTER AND WENT TO CHINA.

REN

UMEÅ

3X UMEÅ = REN !!!

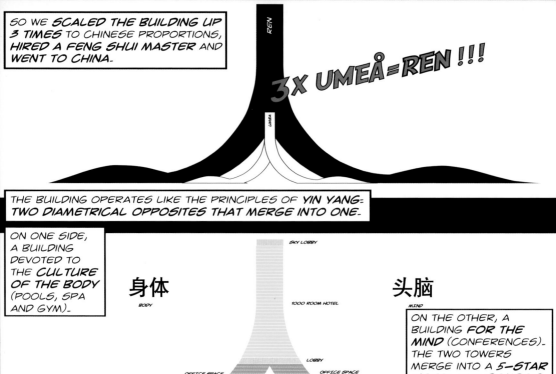

THE BUILDING OPERATES LIKE THE PRINCIPLES OF **YIN YANG**: TWO DIAMETRICAL OPPOSITES THAT MERGE INTO ONE.

ON ONE SIDE, A BUILDING DEVOTED TO THE **CULTURE OF THE BODY** (POOLS, SPA AND GYM).

身体
BODY

头脑
MIND

ON THE OTHER, A BUILDING **FOR THE MIND** (CONFERENCES). THE TWO TOWERS MERGE INTO A **5-STAR HOTEL** AND **CONDOS**.

SKY LOBBY

1000 ROOM HOTEL

LOBBY

OFFICE SPACE

OFFICE SPACE

WATER CULTURE HOUSE

SPORTS FACILITIES

LOBBY

CONFERENCE FACILITIES

CONFERENCE CENTER

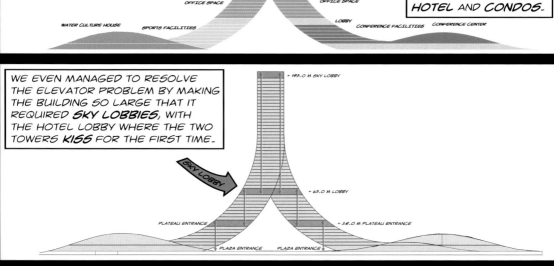

WE EVEN MANAGED TO RESOLVE THE ELEVATOR PROBLEM BY MAKING THE BUILDING SO LARGE THAT IT REQUIRED **SKY LOBBIES**, WITH THE HOTEL LOBBY WHERE THE TWO TOWERS **KISS** FOR THE FIRST TIME.

+ 193.0 M SKY LOBBY

SKY LOBBY

+ 63.0 M LOBBY

PLATEAU ENTRANCE

+ 28.0 M PLATEAU ENTRANCE

PLAZA ENTRANCE

PLAZA ENTRANCE

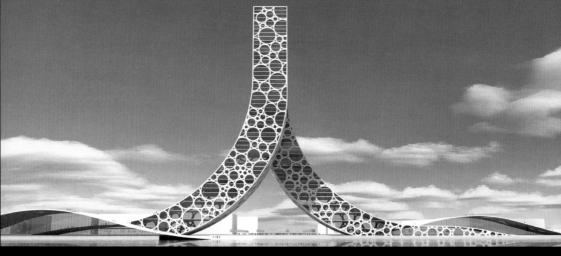

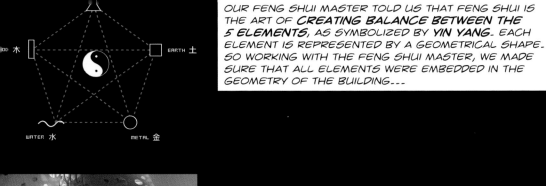

OUR FENG SHUI MASTER TOLD US THAT FENG SHUI IS THE ART OF **CREATING BALANCE BETWEEN THE 5 ELEMENTS**, AS SYMBOLIZED BY **YIN YANG**. EACH ELEMENT IS REPRESENTED BY A GEOMETRICAL SHAPE. SO WORKING WITH THE FENG SHUI MASTER, WE MADE SURE THAT ALL ELEMENTS WERE EMBEDDED IN THE GEOMETRY OF THE BUILDING...

FIRE 火

THE SYMBOL FOR **FIRE** IS A **TRIANGLE** = THE GATE FROM THE CITY TO THE WATER.

EARTH 土

EARTH IS A **PERFECT SQUARE** = THE PUBLIC SQUARE IN THE SHADE OF THE MERGING TOWERS

METAL 金

MY FAVORITE MOMENT OF FENG SHUI IS THE FACT THAT THE SYMBOL FOR **METAL** IS A **CIRCLE** = OUR CIRCULAR MESH OF RING BEAMS FORMING THE LOAD-BEARING EXOSKELETON MAKING THE TOWER FLOAT.

WATER 水

WATER IS A **WAVE** = THE GENTLE SILHOUETTES OF CONFERENCE HALL AND POOL COMPLEX.

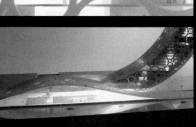

WOOD 木

FINALLY **WOOD** IS A **VERTICAL RECTANGLE** —THE ACTUAL SILHOUETTE OF THE TOWER ALONG THE EMBANKMENT.

AS A SCANDINAVIAN ARCHITECT, YOU AREN'T USED TO DEALING WITH **SYMBOLISM** AT SUCH A **BLATANT LEVEL**. IN A CHINESE CONTEXT HOWEVER, **FENG SHUI** IS AS SERIOUS AN ISSUE AS **DAYLIGHT**, FUNCTIONALITY OR **GRAVITY**. AND WE STARTED TO LIKE IT !

IN SHANGHAI, OUR TWO INTERPRETERS INSTANTLY STARTED DIGGING THE PEOPLE'S BUILDING, AND THE MORNING AFTER IT WENT STRAIGHT ON THE *COVER OF WEN HUI BAO*...

OMG...

WTF ?

..."SHANGHAI EXPO 2010"...

..."PEOPLE"...

AT THE TIME, NONE OF US ACTUALLY UNDERSTOOD CHINESE, BUT WE WERE ABLE TO RECOGNIZE THE CHARACTERS FOR "SHANGHAI", "EXPO 2010" AND "PEOPLE" SO WE WERE CONFIDENT THAT IT HAD BEEN UNDERSTOOD.

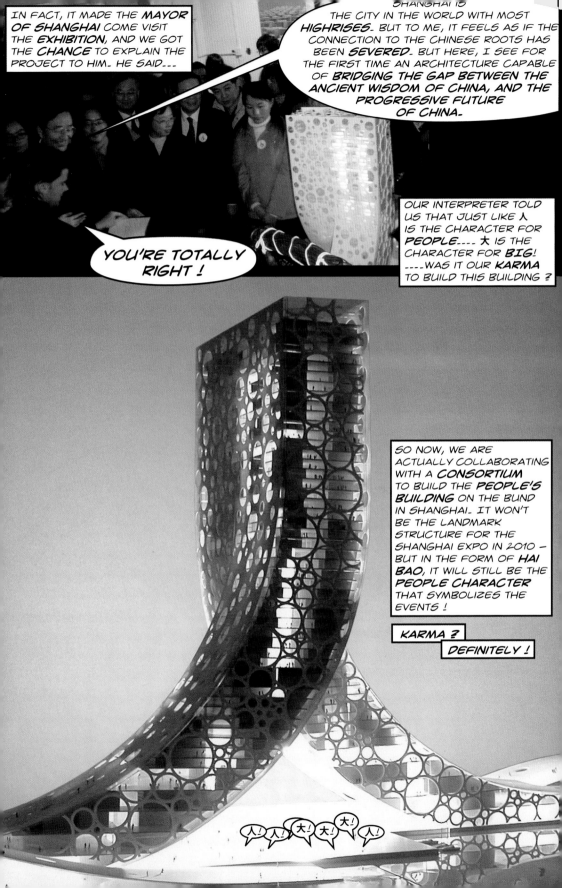

THE DANISH PAVILION / SHANGHAI EXPO 2010

HAI BAO – AKA THE **CHINESE CHARACTER FOR "PEOPLE"** – HAS BEEN CHOSEN AS THE MASCOT FOR THE SHANGHAI WORLD EXPO IN 2010, TO MATCH THE **SUSTAINABILITY THEME** OF THE EXPO UNDER THE MOTTO:

> **BETTER CITY BETTER LIFE !**

SUSTAINABILITY IS OFTEN ASSOCIATED WITH SOME **PURITAN CONCEPT** WHERE YOU'RE NOT SUPPOSED TO TAKE LONG WARM SHOWERS OR TAKE LONG DISTANCE FLIGHTS FOR HOLIDAYS – **BECAUSE IT'S NOT GOOD FOR THE ENVIRONMENT.** SO GRADUALLY, YOU GET THE IDEA THAT **SUSTAINABLE LIFE IS LESS FUN THAN "NORMAL" LIFE !**

> WHAT IF WE COULD FOCUS ON EXAMPLES WHERE **SUSTAINABILITY ACTUALLY INCREASES THE QUALITY OF LIFE ?** WHERE A SUSTAINABLE LIFESTYLE ISN'T PAIN – BUT **PLEASURE !**

WE ALSO ASKED OURSELVES: WHAT COULD **DENMARK** POSSIBLY SHOW THAT WOULD BE **RELEVANT** TO THE **CHINESE ?** SO WE MADE A LITTLE **COMPARISON** BETWEEN THE TWO COUNTRIES...

ONE OF THE WORLD'S **BIGGEST** COUNTRIES.

9 596 960 KM²

ONE OF THE **SMALLEST.**

43 094 KM²

VS

A **SOCIALIST PLAN ECONOMY.**

MAO ZEDONG, FOUNDER OF PEOPLE'S REPUBLIC

A **SOCIAL DEMOCRATIC WELFARE STATE.**

THORVALD STAUNING FATHER OF THE DANISH WELFARE STATE

CHINA'S NATIONAL SYMBOL IS THE **DRAGON.**

IN DENMARK, WE HAVE A NATIONAL BIRD: **THE SWAN** (THE BIRD FORMERLY KNOWN AS **THE UGLY DUCKLING**).

CHINA IS KNOWN FOR ITS MANY **POETS,** ESPECIALLY **LI PO.**

TO OUR SURPRISE, WE DISCOVERED THAT THE PEOPLE'S REPUBLIC'S PRIMARY SCHOOL CURRICULUM CONTAINS 3 FAIRYTALES BY THE POET **AN TU SHUNG AKA HANS CHRISTIAN ANDERSEN,** THE DANISH POET.

SO IN FACT, ALL 1,3 BILLION CHINESE HAVE GROWN UP ON A LITERARY DIET OF THE **EMPEROR'S NEW CLOTHES, THE LITTLE MATCH GIRL** AND **THE LITTLE MERMAID.** IT IS ALMOST LIKE A **SMALL PART OF DANISH CULTURE** THAT HAS BEEN INTEGRATED INTO **CHINESE CULTURE.**

THE BIGGEST TOURIST ATTRACTION IS **THE GREAT WALL,** THE ONLY MANMADE STRUCTURE THAT CAN BE SEEN FROM **OUTER SPACE.**

VS

AND THE BIGGEST TOURIST ATTRACTION IS **THE LITTLE MERMAID** (WHICH CAN HARDLY BE SEEN FROM THE CANAL TOURS).

BOTH SHANGHAI AND COPENHAGEN ARE **PORT CITIES...**

...BUT OF **RADICALLY DIFFERENT SCALES.**

AND THE URBAN FABRICS ARE EQUALLY DIFFERENT — **SKYSCRAPERS AMONG HIGHWAYS...**

...VS EUROPEAN CITY BLOCKS.

IN FACT, THE GREATEST DANISH WORK OF ARCHITECTURE, **THE SYDNEY OPERA** BY JØRN UTZON,...

...IS A **SCANDINAVIAN INTERPRETATION** OF A **CHINESE TYPOLOGY** — THE **PAGODA ON A PLINTH.**

BUT WE WEREN'T REALLY FINDING AN OBVIOUS HOOK FOR OUR PAVILION UNTIL WE STARTED LOOKING AT *THE RECENT URBAN DEVELOPMENT OF SHANGHAI AND COPENHAGEN.*

THIS IS A PHOTO OF SHANGHAI FROM 30 YEARS AGO: *BROAD BOULEVARDS JAM-PACKED WITH BICYCLES.* ONLY 2 KINDS OF CARS IN SHANGHAI BACK THEN: SHANGHAI NO 1 AND SHANGHAI NO 2.

WITH THE *MASSIVE ECONOMIC BOOM* AND *URBAN EXPLOSION*, EVERYBODY WANTS A CAR, THE STREETS ARE CONGESTED WITH *TRAFFIC JAMS,* AND THE BICYCLE HAS EVEN BEEN *FORBIDDEN* IN SOME PARTS OF TOWN.

IN THE SAME PERIOD OF TIME, COPENHAGEN HAS BEEN CREATING *MORE BICYCLE LANES* AND *REDUCING CAR TRAFFIC.* THE BICYCLE HAS BECOME *A SYMBOL OF A SUSTAINABLE CITY AND A HEALTHY LIFESTYLE.*

I ♥ CPH

WE HAVE DEVELOPED *MULTIPLE SPECIES OF BIKES* TO MOVE NOT ONLY OURSELVES, BUT *OUR KIDS* AND *OUR STUFF AROUND* AS WELL.

WE EVEN HAVE A SO-CALLED *CITY BIKE* THAT VISITORS *CAN BORROW FOR FREE* AND MOVE AROUND TOWN BEFORE THEY RETURN.

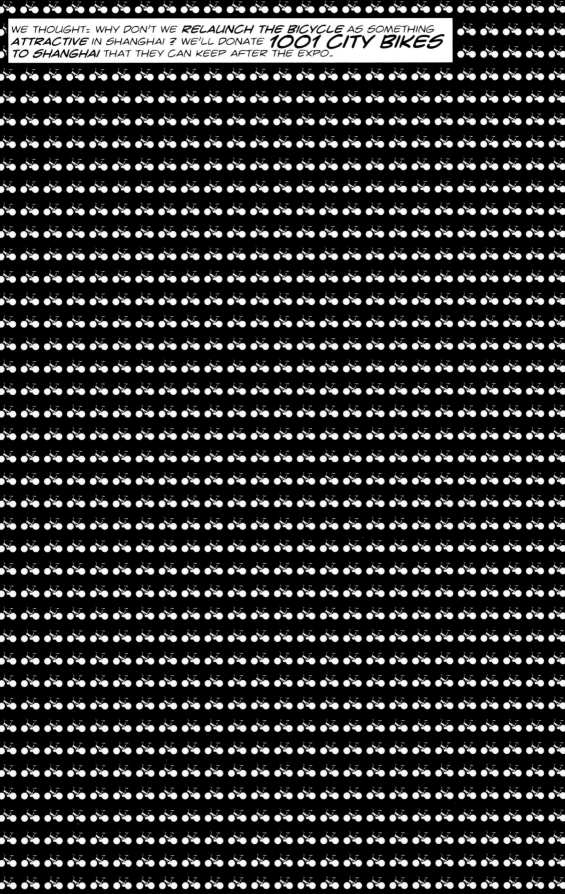

WE THOUGHT: WHY DON'T WE **RELAUNCH THE BICYCLE** AS SOMETHING *ATTRACTIVE* IN SHANGHAI ? WE'LL DONATE **1001 CITY BIKES** TO **SHANGHAI** THAT THEY CAN KEEP AFTER THE EXPO.

SO WHEN YOU ARRIVE AT THE EXPO, YOU GO STRAIGHT TO THE **DANISH PAVILION**, GET YOUR **CITY BIKE**...

...AND THEN YOU RIDE TO THE SWEDISH, KOREAN OR AZERBAIJANI PAVILIONS ON YOUR **DANISH BIKE**.

SO WE IMAGINED THE DANISH PAVILION **AS AN INFRASTRUCTURE FOR BICYCLES**. LIKE A **BICYCLE LANE, LOOPED AROUND ITSELF**.

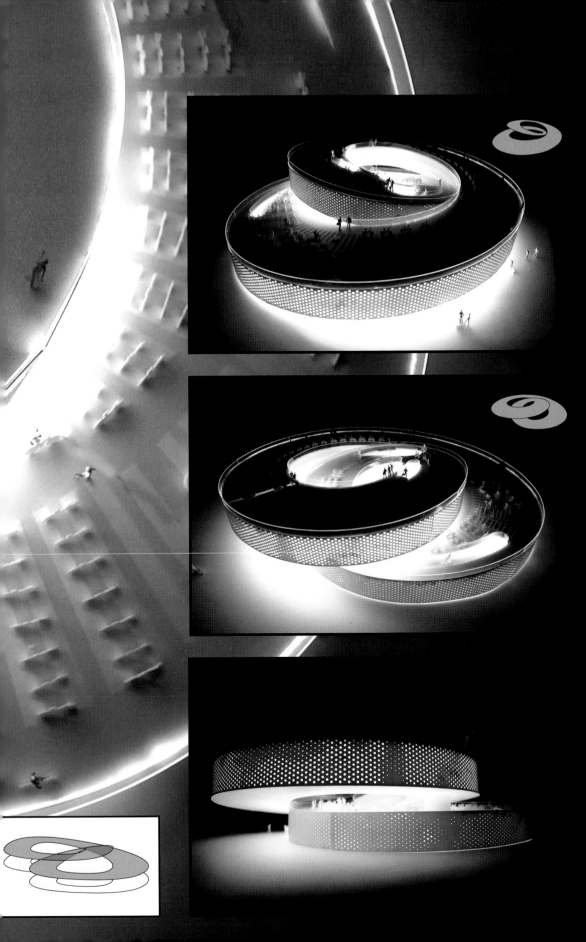

AS MENTIONED, BOTH SHANGHAI AND COPENHAGEN ARE **PORT CITIES.** BUT IN COPENHAGEN, THE **INDUSTRY** HAS BEEN **MOVED AWAY** OR **MADE CLEAN.** FORMER **INDUSTRIAL SITES** HAVE TURNED INTO **PARKS,** AND THE WATER HAS BECOME **SO CLEAN THAT YOU CAN SWIM IN IT.**

IN FACT, ONE OF THE **FIRST PROJECTS** WE EVER DID WAS THE **ISLANDS BRYGGE HARBOR BATH** THAT SIMPLY **EXTENDS THE URBAN LIFE FROM DRY LAND INTO THE WATER.**

SO WE PROPOSED TO SHIP **1 MILLION LITERS OF HARBOR WATER FROM COPENHAGEN HARBOR** TO SHANGHAI IN A TANKER.

IN THE HEART OF THE PAVILION, WE WOULD **CREATE A HARBOR BATH** WHERE ALL THE VISITORS WITH THE COURAGE TO DO SO COULD BORROW A PAIR OF RED AND WHITE SWIM SHORTS OR A SWIMSUIT AND TAKE A SWIM IN **REAL COPENHAGEN HARBOR WATER.**

AND IN THE MIDDLE OF THIS LITTLE PIECE OF COPENHAGEN HARBOR, JUST LIKE IN THE REAL COPENHAGEN HARBOR, WE PROPOSED TO CREATE A PILE OF ROCKS AND **PLACE THE ACTUAL LITTLE MERMAID. NOT A COPY, BUT THE REAL DEAL.**

DON'T YOU THINK CHINA ALREADY HAS ITS SHARE OF COPIES ?!

H.-C.-ANDERSEN'S MOTTO WAS: **"TO TRAVEL IS TO LIVE".** NOW THE MERMAID WOULD FINALLY **COME TO LIFE !**

SO WHERE NATIONAL PAVILIONS NORMALLY COME ACROSS AS FULL OF **STATE-FUNDED PROPAGANDA, EMPTY WORDS** AND **SUPERFICIAL IMAGES,** WE WANTED TO DELIVER **THE REAL DEAL.** THE CHINESE WOULD BE ABLE TO **RIDE THE CITY BIKE, SWIM IN THE HARBOR WATER** AND **SEE THE ACTUAL LITTLE MERMAID** THAT THEY HAD KNOWN SINCE ELEMENTARY SCHOOL.

IN THE ABSENCE OF THE MERMAID, WE WOULD INVITE A **HANDFUL OF CHINESE ARTISTS** TO **REINTERPRET THE LITTLE MERMAID** ON THE SPOT WHERE SHE NORMALLY SITS.

IN COPENHAGEN, DANES RARELY CHECK OUT THE MERMAID — IT'S MOSTLY THE DOMAIN OF ... WELL ... CHINESE TOURISTS ! SO FOR 6 MONTHS, WE WOULD ACTUALLY HAVE **A NEW EXCUSE** TO GO THERE — AND **PERHAPS ANOTHER ONE TO SEE HER COME HOME.**

THE PAVILION ITSELF IS A *LINEAR EXHIBITION CURLED UP IN A DOUBLE LOOP* WITH THE *HARBOR BATH IN THE CENTER* AND *THE BICYCLES ON THE ROOF.*

HARBOR BATH

EXHIBITION SPACES

BICYCLE ROOF

PEOPLE WILL *ARRIVE AT THE BATH...*

...MOVE THROUGH THE *EXHIBITION...*

... AND REACH THE ROOF WHERE THEY'LL GO *BROWSING FOR A BIKE.*

MOUNTED, THEY'LL *RIDE* THROUGH THE LAST PART OF THE EXHIBITION...

...AND OUT INTO THE *EXPO AREA.*

STRUCTURALLY, THE PAVILION IS CONCEIVED AS **ONE GIANT SELF-SUPPORTING TUBULAR TRUSS**...

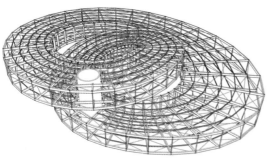

...SIMILAR TO THE HULL OF A **STEEL SHIP**.

THE FACADE NEEDS **PERFORATION** FOR **DAYLIGHT** AND **VENTILATION**, BUT DUE TO THE STRUCTURAL PERFORMANCE OF THE TRUSS...

...THE DEGREE OF PERFORATION VARIES WITH THE **STRUCTURAL STRESS**.

AS A RESULT, THE FACADE OF THE PAVILION BECOMES **THIS ABSTRACT PATTERN OF LIGHT AND DARKNESS** REFLECTING **THE FLOW OF PEOPLE AND BICYCLES WITHIN THE PAVILION** AS WELL AS **THE FLOW OF FORCES INSIDE THE STEEL WALL**.

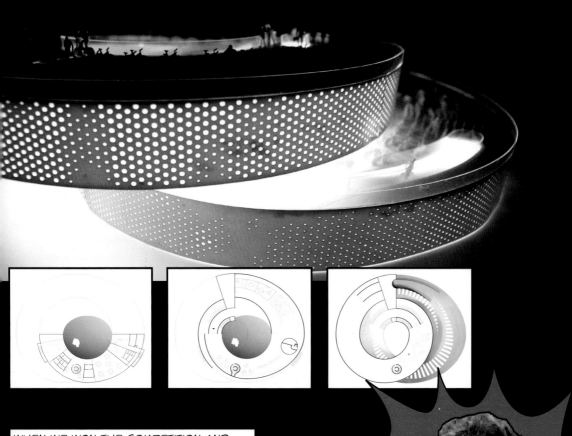

THE NATIONALIST PEOPLE'S PARTY ATTEMPTED TO INVENT **A LAW SPECIFICALLY AGAINST IT.** AS A RESULT, WE WERE INVITED FOR THE FIRST TIME TO SPEAK AT THE **NATIONAL ASSEMBLY.** MOVED BY THE CHINESE AFFINITY FOR H.C. ANDERSEN AND AROUSED BY THE GENEROSITY OF THE GESTURE, ALL PARTIES EXCEPT TWO WERE **IN FAVOR OF SENDING HER AWAY:** THE RIGHT-WING NATIONALISTS BECAUSE THEY WANTED TO **KEEP HER FOR THEMSELVES,** THE LEFT-WING UNITY PARTY BECAUSE THEY PREFERRED SENDING **A WINDMILL** INSTEAD !

THE FINAL DEBATE WAS HELD ON THE **SAME DAY** THAT PARLIAMENT WAS DISCUSSING THE BAILOUT PACKAGE FOR **THE GLOBAL CREDIT CRUNCH** !!

9.00 TO 11.00: GLOBAL FINANCIAL CRISIS.

11.30 TO 13.30: MER—MAIDEN VOYAGE TO CHINA .

FOR ONCE, I MANAGED TO CONSUME **THE ENTIRE MEETING MINUTES** OF A TWO—HOUR POLITICAL DEBATE BECAUSE SOME OF THE POLITICIANS, LIKE **HANS CHRISTIAN THONING**, HAD REALLY **PUT THEIR HEARTS IN IT:**

"THE FAIRYTALE OF "THE LITTLE MERMAID" IS A TALE ABOUT **LEAVING YOUR HOME** IN ORDER TO **MEET ANOTHER WORLD**, ABOUT **UNITING TWO CULTURES**, AND PERHAPS MOSTLY, IT IS A TALE ABOUT THE BELIEF THAT BY GIVING UP A PART OF YOURSELF, YOU WILL GET SO MUCH MORE IN RETURN."

WE HAD FOUND A WAY TO TURN POLITICS INTO POETRY !

NOW THAT'S A WELFAIRYTALE...

WE RECENTLY EXHIBITED THE DANISH PAVILION AT SHANGHAI URBAN CENTER. KNOWN FOR SOMETIMES EXERTING **PUBLIC CENSORSHIP**, IT WAS NO SURPRISE WHEN THE CHINESE AUTHORITIES INTERVENED.

1. WE HAD USED **DATED PHOTOS OF CHINESE PARTY MEMBERS** – THEY WERE REPLACED BY CURRENT ONES.

2. WE SHOWED THE MAP OF CHINA **WITHOUT TAIWAN** – IT WAS AUTOMATICALLY ADDED.

3. THE IMAGE OF THE **FIERCE CHINESE DRAGON** WAS SUGGESTED TO BE REPLACED WITH THAT OF A **BAMBOO-MUNCHING PANDA !**

LEARNING FROM LOMBORG

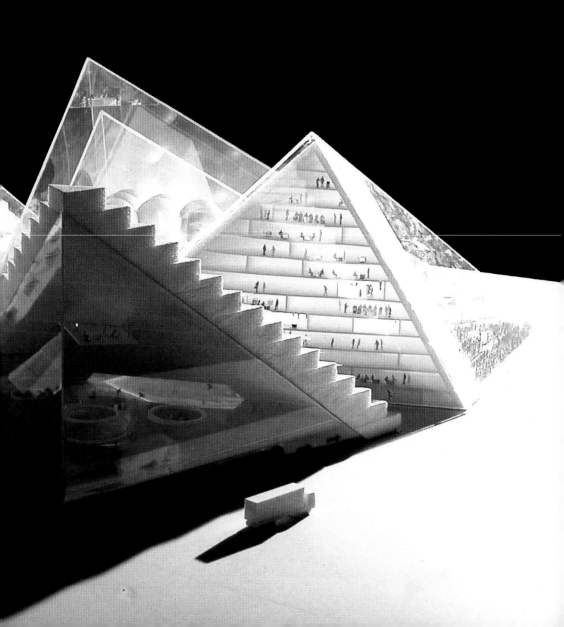

WHAT IF ECOLOGY WASN'T ABOUT **REGRESSION** – BUT ABOUT **PROGRESS** ?

WHAT IF SUSTAINABLE LIVING WASN'T ABOUT CHANGING YOUR LIFESTYLE AND TURNING OFF THE LIGHTS, TURNING DOWN THE HEAT AND SLOWING DOWN ?

WHAT IF WE DIDN'T HAVE TO **ADAPT OUR LIFESTYLE TO SUSTAINABILITY**, BUT **ADJUSTED OUR SUSTAINABLE DESIGNS TO THE WAY WE WANT TO LIVE** ? INSTEAD OF TRYING TO **CHANGE PEOPLE**, WE COULD **CHANGE THE WORLD**.

WHAT IF WE COULD DESIGN A SOCIETY WHERE **THE MORE ENERGY YOU SPEND, THE MORE ENERGY YOU GET** ?

WE NEED A NEW MANIFESTO FOR HEDONISTIC SUSTAINABILITY !

THE 10 COMMANDMENTS OF GOOD CONSUMPTION !!!

USE
1# REDUCE, REUSE, RECYCLE
HIT THE ROAD
2# STAY CLOSE TO HOME
MAXIMIZE HYDROGEN
3# MINIMIZE USE OF COMBUSTION ENGINES
PRODUCE ENERGY WHILE DRIVING
4# REDUCE FUEL CONSUMPTION
SUPPORT YOUR OWN HOUSEHOLD WITH ENERGY
5# SUPPORT GOVERNMENT REGULATION WITH POLITICAL CHOICES

6# SUPPORT THOUGHTFUL INNOVATIONS !!!
THE MORE YOU USE – THE MORE YOU GET
7# PRIORITIZE
WASTE
8# VOTE
Don't
9# FEEL GUILTY
ENJOY MORE
10# ENJOY WHAT YOU HAVE

THE HEATED DEBATE TRIGGERED BY "COPENHAGEN CONSENSUS" – **BJØRN LOMBORG'S** (THE MARTIN LUTHER OF THE ENVIRONMENTALISTS) INITIATIVE TO PUT A PRICE TAG AND A PRIORITY ON EARTH'S GREATEST SOCIAL AND ENVIRONMENTAL CHALLENGES – **UNCOVERS A FUNDAMENTAL MISUNDERSTANDING THAT PITS ECOLOGY AGAINST ECONOMY AS GOOD VS EVIL**.

IN FACT, THEY ARE NOT DIAMETRIC OPPOSITES, BUT RATHER **TWO SIDES OF THE SAME STORY**.

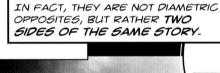

ECOLOGICAL INITIATIVES **WILL ONLY PROSPER IN THE REAL WORLD** IF THEY **WORK AS VIABLE ECONOMIC MODELS**. AND BUSINESS MODELS BASED ON WEARING DOWN OUR NATURAL RESOURCES ARE **NOT VIABLE** MODELS **FOR LONG TERM GROWTH**.

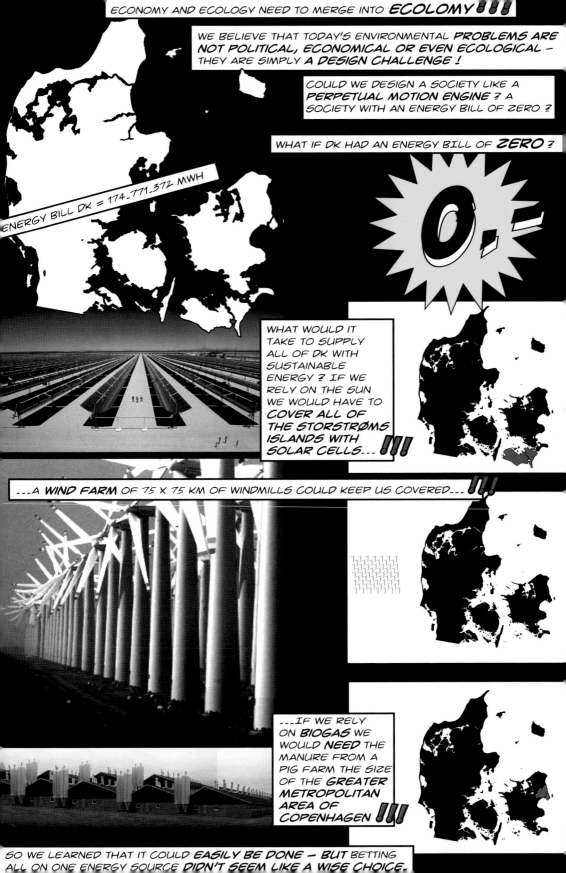

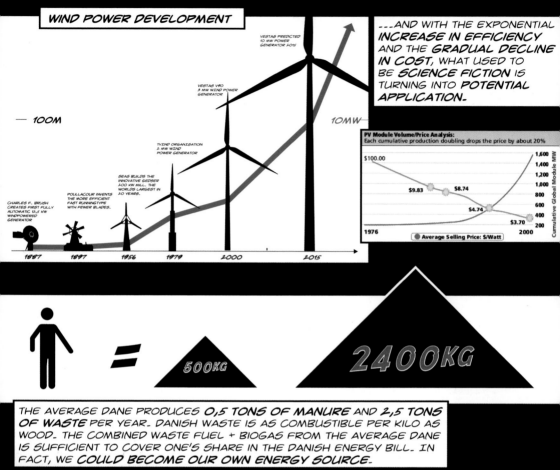

WIND POWER DEVELOPMENT

VESTAS PREDICTED 10 MW POWER GENERATOR 2015

VESTAS V90 3 MW WIND POWER GENERATOR

— 100M

10MW—

TVIND ORGANISATION 2 MW WIND POWER GENERATOR

SEAS BUILDS THE INNOVATIVE GEDSER 200 KW MILL. THE WORLDS LARGEST IN 20 YEARS.

POULLACOUR INVENTS THE MORE EFFICIENT FAST RUNNINGTYPE WITH FEWER BLADES.

CHARLES F. BRUSH CREATES FIRST FULLY AUTOMATIC 12,5 KW WINDPOWERED GENERATOR

1887   1897   1956   1979   2000   2015

...AND WITH THE EXPONENTIAL **INCREASE IN EFFICIENCY** AND THE **GRADUAL DECLINE IN COST**, WHAT USED TO BE **SCIENCE FICTION** IS TURNING INTO **POTENTIAL APPLICATION.**

PV Module Volume/Price Analysis:
Each cumulative production doubling drops the price by about 20%

$100.00

$9.83 $8.74

$4.74

$3.70

1976   2000

1,600 / 1,400 / 1,200 / 1,000 / 800 / 600 / 400 / 200

Cumulative Global Module MW

Average Selling Price: $/Watt

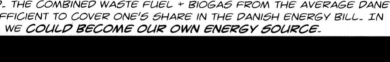

500KG   2400KG

THE AVERAGE DANE PRODUCES *0,5 TONS OF MANURE* AND *2,5 TONS OF WASTE* PER YEAR. DANISH WASTE IS AS COMBUSTIBLE PER KILO AS WOOD. THE COMBINED WASTE FUEL + BIOGAS FROM THE AVERAGE DANE IS SUFFICIENT TO COVER ONE'S SHARE IN THE DANISH ENERGY BILL. IN FACT, WE *COULD BECOME OUR OWN ENERGY SOURCE.*

IN ARCHITECTURE *90% OF OUR ENERGY IS SPENT ON HEATING OR COOLING OUR HOUSES!* ONLY *10% IS SPENT ON ELECTRICAL APPLIANCES.* BY SIMPLY ORGANIZING OUR RESIDENCES AND WORKPLACES IN MORE OPTIMAL WAYS *WE COULD REDUCE THE ENERGY BILL OF THE BUILT ENVIRONMENT TO 1/10 !*

90%

10%

COOLING

EXCESS HEAT

DIFFERENT ACTIVITIES HAVE DIFFERENT *ENERGY CONSUMPTION PATTERNS.* HOUSES SPEND ENERGY ON HEATING. OFFICES SPEND ENERGY ON COOLING. WE CAN *ANALYZE THE CONSUMPTION PATTERN* OF EACH PROGRAM IN OUR SOCIETY AND *GET AN OVERVIEW* OF THE PARTICULAR NEEDS AND EXCESSES OF ENERGY, HEAT AND WATER.

THE **REFRIGERATORS OF A SUPERMARKET** PRODUCE SO MUCH **EXCESS HEAT,** THAT THEY COULD **HEAT** THE WATER OF AN **ENTIRE PUBLIC SWIMMING POOL... FOR FREE !**

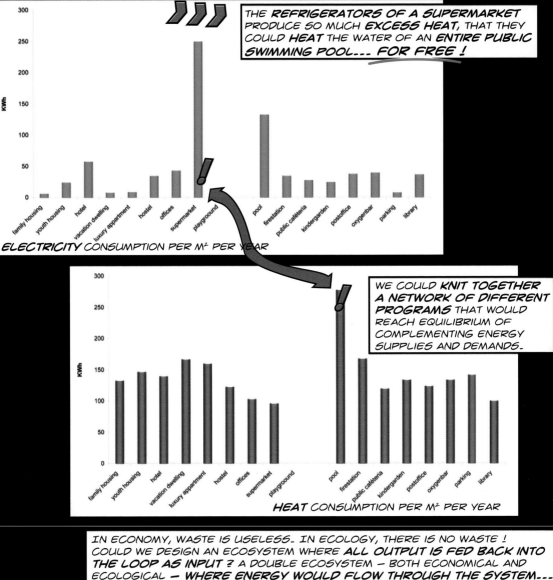

ELECTRICITY CONSUMPTION PER M² PER YEAR

WE COULD **KNIT TOGETHER A NETWORK OF DIFFERENT PROGRAMS** THAT WOULD REACH EQUILIBRIUM OF COMPLEMENTING ENERGY SUPPLIES AND DEMANDS.

HEAT CONSUMPTION PER M² PER YEAR

IN ECONOMY, WASTE IS USELESS. IN ECOLOGY, THERE IS NO WASTE ! COULD WE DESIGN AN ECOSYSTEM WHERE **ALL OUTPUT IS FED BACK INTO THE LOOP AS INPUT ?** A DOUBLE ECOSYSTEM — BOTH ECONOMICAL AND ECOLOGICAL — **WHERE ENERGY WOULD FLOW THROUGH THE SYSTEM...**

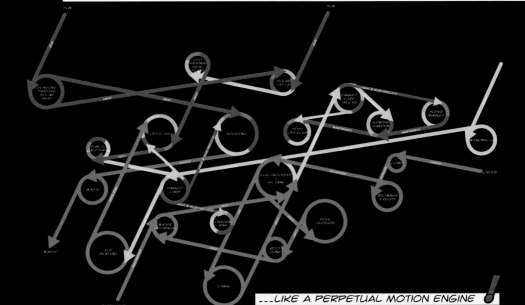

...LIKE A PERPETUAL MOTION ENGINE

ALL OF DENMARK WOULD BE LIKE A SINGLE HOUSEHOLD WHERE NO RESOURCE IS WASTED, NO BYPRODUCT A DEAD END. A SOCIETY IN ECOLOMICAL SYMBIOSIS.

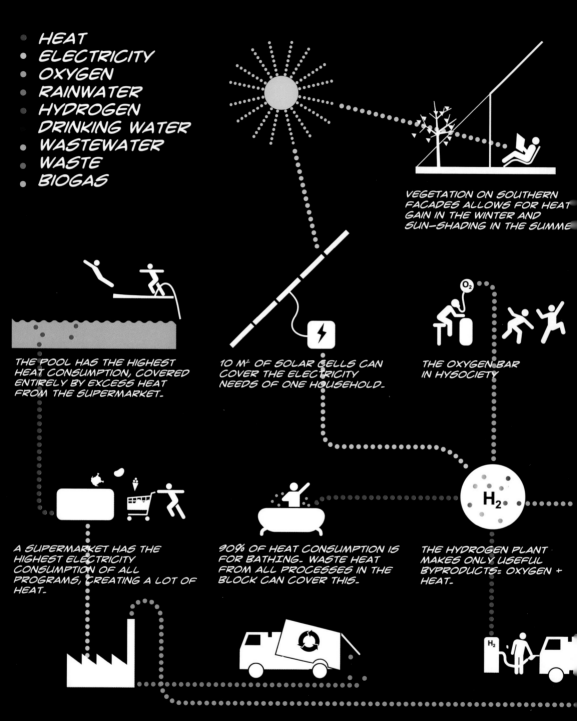

- HEAT
- ELECTRICITY
- OXYGEN
- RAINWATER
- HYDROGEN
- DRINKING WATER
- WASTEWATER
- WASTE
- BIOGAS

VEGETATION ON SOUTHERN FACADES ALLOWS FOR HEAT GAIN IN THE WINTER AND SUN-SHADING IN THE SUMME

THE POOL HAS THE HIGHEST HEAT CONSUMPTION, COVERED ENTIRELY BY EXCESS HEAT FROM THE SUPERMARKET.

10 M² OF SOLAR CELLS CAN COVER THE ELECTRICITY NEEDS OF ONE HOUSEHOLD.

THE OXYGEN BAR IN HYSOCIETY

A SUPERMARKET HAS THE HIGHEST ELECTRICITY CONSUMPTION OF ALL PROGRAMS, CREATING A LOT OF HEAT.

90% OF HEAT CONSUMPTION IS FOR BATHING. WASTE HEAT FROM ALL PROCESSES IN THE BLOCK CAN COVER THIS.

THE HYDROGEN PLANT MAKES ONLY USEFUL BYPRODUCTS: OXYGEN + HEAT.

THE INCINERATION PLANT FEEDS ENERGY FROM THE WASTE BACK INTO THE SYSTEM, WHILE SUPPLYING GREENHOUSES WITH HEAT.

THE BLOCK PRODUCES ENOUGH HYDROGEN TO FUEL 100 CARS.

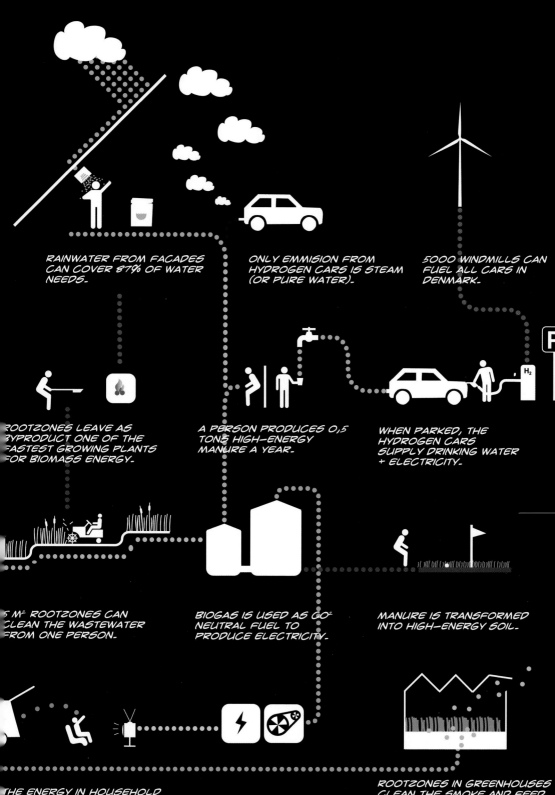

RAINWATER FROM FACADES CAN COVER 87% OF WATER NEEDS.

ONLY EMMISION FROM HYDROGEN CARS IS STEAM (OR PURE WATER).

5000 WINDMILLS CAN FUEL ALL CARS IN DENMARK.

ROOTZONES LEAVE AS BYPRODUCT ONE OF THE FASTEST GROWING PLANTS FOR BIOMASS ENERGY.

A PERSON PRODUCES 0,5 TONS HIGH-ENERGY MANURE A YEAR.

WHEN PARKED, THE HYDROGEN CARS SUPPLY DRINKING WATER + ELECTRICITY.

5 M² ROOTZONES CAN CLEAN THE WASTEWATER FROM ONE PERSON.

BIOGAS IS USED AS CO_2 NEUTRAL FUEL TO PRODUCE ELECTRICITY.

MANURE IS TRANSFORMED INTO HIGH-ENERGY SOIL.

THE ENERGY IN HOUSEHOLD WASTE IS THE SAME AS IN PURE WOOD.

ROOTZONES IN GREENHOUSES CLEAN THE SMOKE AND FEED FLOWERS WITH PURE CO_2.

THE IDEA OF **TURNING ALL OF DK INTO AN ECONOMICAL AND ECOLOGICAL ECOSYSTEM** SEEMS UTOPIAN BECAUSE OF ITS MAGNITUDE. ALL CONCRETE PROPOSALS WILL APPEAR LIKE ABSTRACT PRINCIPLES BECAUSE WE CAN'T GRASP THEM.

THEREFORE WE HAVE **BOILED THE COMPONENTS OF DK DOWN TO THE SIZE OF AN ARCHITECTURAL PROJECT:** ALL OF DENMARK'S DIFFERENT PROGRAMS COMPRESSED PROPORTIONALLY INTO A 100.000M² URBAN BLOCK — LIKE A BIOPSY OF THE DANISH URBAN TISSUE.

AT THIS SCALE, THE CHALLENGE BECOMES AS TANGIBLE AS ANY OTHER COMMISSION — SOLVE THE PROGRAM AND KEEP COUNT OF THE FLOW OF RESOURCES AND ENERGY LIKE WE DO WITH THE SQUARE METERS AND THE CONSTRUCTION COSTS.

ALL WE NEED IS A SITE: EVER SINCE THE NATIONAL ARCHIVE WAS CANCELLED, ØRESTAD NORTH IS MISSING ITS LANDMARK, AND NOUVEL'S CONCERT HALL IS MISSING ITS **NEW NEIGHBOR.**

THE RIGSARKIV SITE COULD BE AN **OBVIOUS TESTING GROUND FOR NEW ECOLOMICAL FORMS OF URBANITY.** THE SITE COULD BE THE TRANSFER HUB BETWEEN ØRESTAD NORTH AND "URBANPARKEN" **CRISS—CROSSED BY SHORTCUTS ALLOWING MAXIMUM CONNECTIVITY.**

DK

640.2 MIL M² DK
334.3 MIL M² HOUSING
131.5 MIL M² AGRICULTURE
61.1 MIL M² SERVICE
58.8 MIL M² INDUSTRY
40.2 MIL M² INSTITUTIONS & CULTURE
13.9 MIL M² SUMMER HOUSES
2.292.268 CARS

MINI DK

100.000 M² DK
51.000 M² HOUSING
20.000 M² AGRICULTURE
10.000 M² SERVICE
9.000 M² INDUSTRY
7.000 M² INSTITUTIONS & CULTURE
3.000 M² SUMMER HOUSES
348 CARS

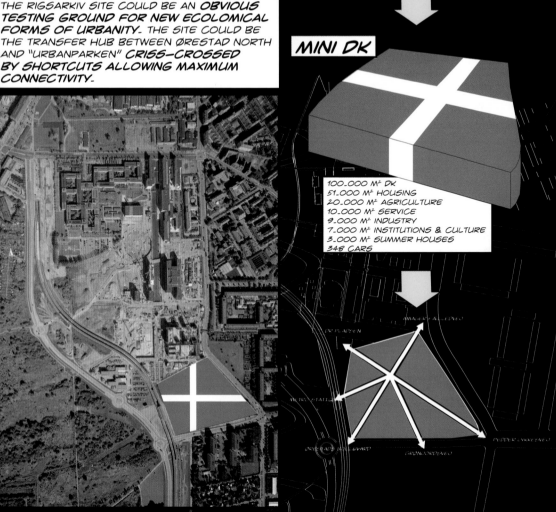

SO NOW THAT ALL THE THEORY AND TECHNOLOGY WAS IN PLACE, WE REALIZED THAT TURNING THEORY INTO PRAXIS, OR TECHNOLOGY INTO FORM, WAS HARDER THAN WE HAD THOUGHT. **WE TRIED VARIOUS MODELS OF PREVIOUS REGIMES:**

PHARAOH...

...NUCLEAR...

...MAXIMUM CONTENT WITH MINIMAL ENVELOPE...

...GREENHOUSES ALL OVER.

NOTHING REALLY OBVIOUS **EMERGED** UNTIL WE DISCOVERED THIS **GRAPH** FOR HOW TO **OPTIMIZE THE INCLINATION** OF A FACADE TO **MAXIMIZE THE SOLAR GAIN.**

TOTAL IRRADIATION IN A YEAR, COPENHAGEN

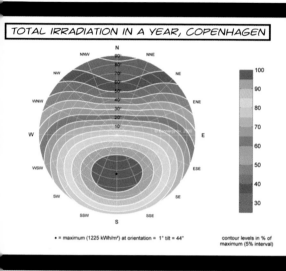

• = maximum (1225 kWh/m²) at orientation = 1° tilt = 44°

contour levels in % of maximum (5% interval)

SOLAR-OPTIMIZED FACADE ANGLES

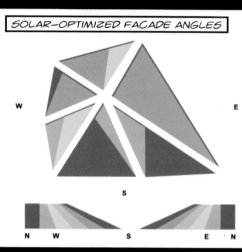

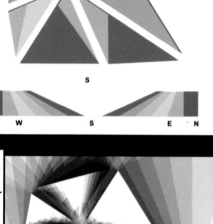

TOWARDS THE SOUTH, THE SUN IS RELATIVELY HIGH ON THE SKY, GIVING A RATHER **INCLINED ANGLE** OF ALMOST 45 DEGREES – TO THE EAST OR WEST, THE SUN ANGLE IS GRADUALLY LOWER, MAKING THE OPTIMAL FACADE **MORE VERTICAL.** TO THE NORTH, THERE IS NEVER SUN, SO **VERTICAL FACADES MAKE PERFECT SENSE.**

APPLIED TO OUR SITE, CRISS-CROSSED BY SHORTCUTS, THE FORMULA PRODUCED A **CLUSTER OF TILTING PYRAMIDS OF VARIOUS SIZES** – THE OPTIMAL BUILDING ENVELOPE FOR **MAXIMUM SOLAR HEAT GAIN !**

FACADE EXPOSURE: PYRAMIDS CAST SHADOWS ON EACH OTHER

WE MEASURED THE IMPACT OF SUN ON THE RESPECTIVE FACES OF THE PYRAMIDS. OBVIOUSLY THE PYRAMIDS WERE **CASTING SHADOWS ON EACH OTHER.**

THE PLACES THAT **NEVER RECEIVED SHADOW** WERE **IDEAL FOR INTEGRATION OF SOLAR PANELS AND PV'S.**

THE PLACES THAT RECEIVED A MAXIMUM OF **2 HOURS OF SHADOW PER DAY** WOULD STILL BE GREAT **FOR HOUSING.**

THE AREAS THAT WERE SUBJECT TO **MORE THAN 2 HOURS IN THE SHADE WERE SIMPLY ELIMINATED** – CREATING AN INTRIGUING HYBRID BETWEEN CRYSTALLINE AND SOFT FORMAL LANGUAGES.

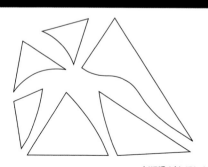

SHADED AREAS

THE **HARD ANGLES** GENERATED BY THE **SUN,** THE **SOFT CURVES** DELINEATED BY THE **SHADOWS.**

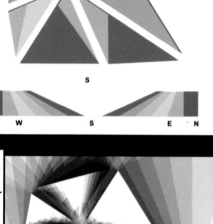

URBAN PLAN

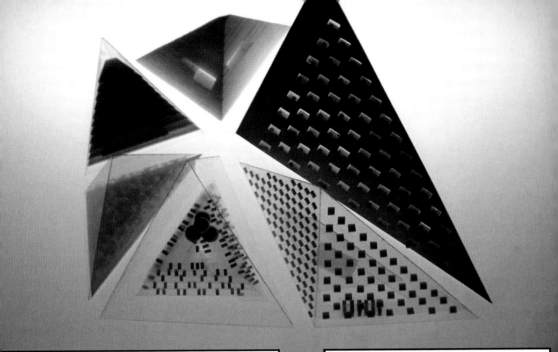

EACH PYRAMID CONTAINS A MIX OF PROGRAMS. SINCE **HOUSING LIKES SUN** ON THE TERRACE AND PASSIVE SOLAR HEATING, THEY OCCUPY THE SUN ORIENTED SLOPES. THE **OFFICES THAT LIKE DAYLIGHT BUT HATE SUNSHINE** DUE TO THE EXCESS HEAT AND GLARE OCCUPY THE VERTICAL NORTH FACADES. **THE CENTRAL SPACES**, WHICH PHARAOH WOULD NORMALLY OCCUPY WITH HIS TOMB, IS **RESERVED FOR PUBLIC PROGRAMS AND PARKING**, WHICH CAN EXPLOIT BIG DEEP INTERIOR SPACES.

VOLUMES

OFFICES

HOUSING

PARKING

SPORTS & CULTURE

ONE PYRAMID WAS DESIGNED LIKE A STACK OF **OFFICES** AND A PILE OF **RESIDENTIAL ENTITIES** WRAPPED AROUND A **SPORTS HALL.**

ANOTHER, SIMPLY A SOLID OF WORK AND LIVING SPACES...

...WITH A **MALL** AND **FOOD COURT** CARVED OUT OF IT.

THEN THERE WAS THE NEW *CITY LIBRARY AND PARKING GARAGE* COVERED BY A SLOPING ROOF OF TERRACE HOUSES.

THE LIBRARY WAS CONCEIVED AS A *SINGLE CONTINUOUS SLOPE OF BOOKS AND READING ROOMS.* THE FLOOR SLAB OF THE LIBRARY WAS 3 METERS THICK, LEAVING *SPACE FOR CONTINUOUS PARKING INSIDE.*

THE APARTMENTS ABOVE ALL WOULD HAVE A *SOUTH-FACING TERRACE WITH A TREE GROWING ON IT.* IN THE SUMMER, WHEN SOUTH FACING GLASS FACADES WOULD MAKE YOU FRY, THE *NATURAL SHADE* FROM THE TREE WOULD *PROTECT THE INHABITANTS.* BUT IN THE WINTER, WHEN THE SUN WOULD BE WELCOME, THE *LEAVES WOULD BE GONE* TO LET IT ALL THE WAY IN. *A FORM OF NATURE'S OWN ECO-TECH !*

FINALLY, A **HOTEL WITH A SWIMMING POOL AND SUPERMARKET** – WHERE **REFRIGERATORS AND SWIMMING POOL WOULD BE EACH OTHER'S HEAT EXCHANGE.** THE DIVING POOLS WOULD CONTINUE ALL THE WAY DOWN INTO THE SUPERMARKET, PROVIDING A SOCIAL EXCHANGE BETWEEN THE TWO PROGRAMS.

SUPERMARKET

SWIMMING...

---DIVING---

---SHOPPING.

THE **ECOLOMICAL PYRAMIDS** ARE PROOF THAT SUSTAINABILITY ISN'T THE DOMAIN OF TREEHUGGERS OR HIGH-TECH, AND NEITHER IS IT SOME SUSTAINABLE ICING THAT YOU APPLY TO THE USUAL RECIPE. LIKE LOMBORG HAS TAUGHT US, YOU NEED TO PUT A PRICE AND A PRIORITY ON THE ENVIRONMENT SO **YOU CAN START TREATING SUSTAINABILITY SPENDINGS LIKE AN INVESTMENT RATHER THAN AN EXPENSE !**

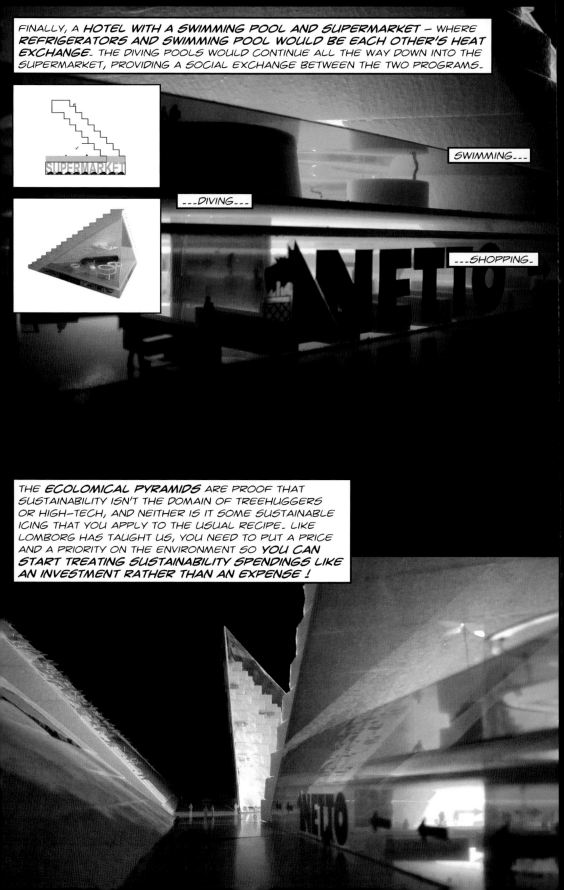

LE CORBUSIER DESIGNED BUILDINGS LIKE MACHINES FOR LIVING, AND IT TRIGGERED A WHOLE NEW AND LIBERATING AESTHETIC: AN *ESPRIT NOUVEAU* ! *ECOLOMICAL DESIGN* TEACHES US TO DESIGN BUILDINGS LIKE ECOSYSTEMS FOR LIVING, ORCHESTRATING THE FLOW OF WATER, HEAT AND ENERGY, FINANCIAL AND HUMAN RESOURCES THROUGH THE BUILDING.

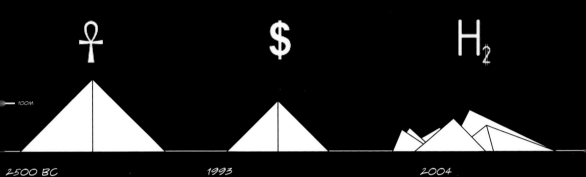

— 100M

2500 BC
THE CHEOPS PYRAMID, EGYPT

1993
LUXOR HOTEL, LAS VEGAS

2004
LITTLE DENMARK, CPH

THE *AZTECS AND PHARAOHS* DESIGNED PYRAMIDS IN WORSHIP OF THE SUN. 3000 YEARS LATER, ATTENTION TO THE POWER OF THE SUN LED US TO *REINVENT THE DESIGN IN THE NAME OF ECOLOMY.*

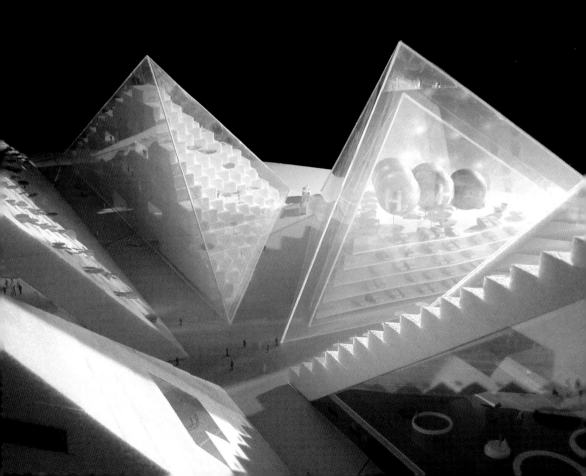

THE VM HOUSES

VM

66

SINCE THIS IS THE FIRST BUILDING IN A GHOST TOWN YET TO COME, WE ASKED OURSELVES **WHAT WILL MAKE PEOPLE GO HERE ?** EVERYBODY WE KNOW WHO HAS JUST PURCHASED A FLAT HAS SPENT THE FIRST MONTHS KNOCKING DOWN WALLS TO JOIN SPACES. WE DECIDED **TO MAKE NO WALLS**, JUST ONE ROOM APARTMENTS.

MOST FLATS ARE... WELL... FLAT ! WE DECIDED TO CREATE **DUPLEXES** AND **TRIPLEXES**.

MEOWWW !

MOST APARTMENTS HAVE LITTLE WINDOWS AND NO VIEWS. WE OPENED THE FLATS WITH **GLASS**...

---FROM CEILING TO FLOOR.

BUT AS THE BUILDING WAS REACHING COMPLETION, IT BECAME EVIDENT THAT THE TWO MAIN ENTRANCES NEEDED A **FACELIFT**. COMING HOME TO A WINDOWLESS 80 M² LARGE BLANK WALL OF ALUMINIUM WAS SIMPLY GOING TO BE **TOO COLD**.

HAVING JUST RETURNED FROM A TRIP TO BRASILIA WHERE **COOL MODERNISM** IS COMBINED WITH **COLOURFUL CERAMICS**, I PROPOSED TO OUR CLIENT THE IDEA OF MAKING AN INTEGRATED ARTWORK. HIS RESPONSE WAS "I'M A DEVELOPER, NOT A GALLERIST – SO GO WITH ALUMINIUM."

...A FEW DAYS LATER I HAD DINNER AT ALBERTO K – THE RESTAURANT AT THE TOP OF **ARNE JACOBSEN'S HOTEL ROYAL**, AND I NOTICED A PAINTING ON THE WALL. I ASKED THE WAITER WHO IT WAS.

IT IS A PORTRAIT OF **ALBERTO K** – THE DIRECTOR OF THE HOTEL AT THE TIME OF CONSTRUCTION. IT'S PAINTED BY **ARNE JACOBSEN** HIMSELF !

SO I TOLD OUR CLIENTS – PER HØPFNER AND AXEL FREDERIKSEN – THAT IT WAS A DANISH **MODERNIST TRADITION** FOR ARCHITECTS TO PAY TRIBUTE TO THEIR CLIENTS WITH A PORTRAIT. BUT SINCE I'M NOT AN ARTIST, AND OUR CANVAS WAS MUCH BIGGER, WE ENDED UP USING **10X10 CM BATHROOM TILES** IN **10 DIFFERENT STANDARD COLOURS** TO CREATE THUMBNAIL RESOLUTION PORTRAITS OF **OUR HANDSOME CLIENTS**. AND SUDDENLY THERE WAS MONEY IN THE BUDGET FOR THE ARTWORK !

Nyt makkerpar bygger i Ørestad

WITH THIS IDEA WE LITERALLY TURNED **ASS-KISSING** INTO **AN ARTFORM** !

THIS IS THE ENTRANCE TO THE KINDERGARTEN. ONE MORNING, I HEARD A KID ASK HIS MOM WHO WAS ON THE PORTRAIT. SHE REPLIED **"THAT'S ELVIS"** – SO NOW HE HAS ALSO BEEN SPOTTED IN ØRESTAD !

WHEN THE CITY OF COPENHAGEN AWARDED VM THE **BEST BUILDING OF THE YEAR**, WE DECIDED TO INSERT THE 10X10 CM BRASS PLATE INTO THE PORTRAIT LIKE A **GOLD TOOTH IN PER HØPFNER'S SMILE** !

PRÆMIERET AF KØBENHAVNS KOMMUNE 2006

PS

IF YOU PLAY THE DANISH VERSION OF **MONOPOLY**, YOU CAN NOW BUY THE VM HOUSES FOR 1,4 MILLION KR – **WHICH MAKES IT THE CHEAPEST PROPERTY IN THE GAME** !

World
Architecture
Festival
Category Winner
2008

ovmålvej

VERTICAL SUBURBIA

THIS USED TO BE THE VIEW FROM MY APARTMENT...

...AND IT USED TO BE THE SITE OF MY **THESIS PROJECT** AT THE ROYAL DANISH ACADEMY OF FINE ARTS.

IN 1999 ØRESTAD HAD ALREADY BEEN PLANNED, BUT NOTHING HAD YET MATERIALISED. IT WAS EASY TO SEE FROM THE SKETCHES THAT IT WOULD BE A **BORING MASTER PLAN POPULATED BY SQUARE BLOCKS.**

I WANTED TO FIND A WAY TO ESCAPE THE STRAIGHTJACKET OF A **COURTYARD INCARCERATED BY A WALL OF PROGRAM**, WHERE EVERY PROGRAM REGARDLESS OF SCALE OR ACTIVITY WOULD BE **WEDGED INTO THE SAME MOULD.**

THE POLITICAL VISION FOR ØRESTAD WAS TO CREATE AN INTEGRATED CITY, WHERE **LIVING** AND **WORKING, PUBLIC** AND **COMMERCIAL**, WOULD BE **MIXED FREELY.** I THOUGHT PERHAPS THIS IDEA OF INTEGRATION COULD BE A WAY TO ESCAPE THE UNIFORMITY OF THE MASTER PLAN. I DECIDED TO DESIGN AN **ØRESTAD BIOPSY**: LIKE A TISSUE SAMPLE, THE PROJECT WOULD CONTAIN THE SAME PROGRAMMATIC MIX AS THE CITY ITSELF.

FUNCTIONALISM STILL RULES IN SCANDINAVIA, SO **DIFFERENT PROGRAMS** ARE BELIEVED TO HAVE DIFFERENT NEEDS, AND ARE SEPARATED INTO TAILORED STRUCTURES. BUT EXACTLY BECAUSE OF THEIR DIFFERENCE, THEY CAN FORM A SORT OF **ARCHITECTURAL SYMBIOSIS WHERE EACH PROGRAM GRAVITATES TOWARDS ITS IDEAL LOCATION.**

THE RESULT WAS A MIXED-USE BLOCK COMBINING AMONG OTHER THINGS **HOUSING** AND A **SPORTS HALL.** THE HOUSING WAS TRANSFORMED INTO **A MOUNTAIN OF TERRACE HOUSES,** AND THE SPORTS HALL WAS EXCAVATED FROM THE MASSIF OF APARTMENTS TO CREATE **A KIND OF SPORTS CAVE ENVELOPED IN LIVING UNITS.**

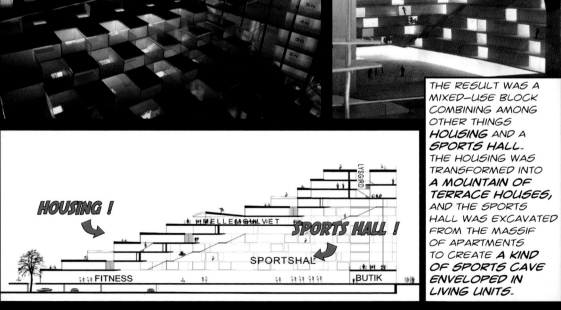

HOUSING !

SPORTS HALL !

LYSGRD

MELLEMGULVET

SPORTSHAL

FITNESS

BUTIK

MANAGED TO GRADUATE WITH THE PROJECT. BUT DESPITE AGGRESSIVE ATTEMPTS TO GET DEVELOPERS TO BUILD IT, THE PROJECT ENDED UP IN THE BOTTOM DRAWER. THERE IT RESTED FOR 6 YEARS IN SILENCE, UNTIL ONE DAY WHEN OUR VM CLIENT PER HØPFNER ACQUIRED THE VERY SAME SITE !

HELLO BJARKE ! IT'S ME AGAIN !

WHEN ASKED TO DESIGN A NEW PROJECT NEXT TO THE JUST-COMPLETED VM HOUSES — FOR THE SAME CLIENT, OF THE SAME SIZE AND ON THE SAME STREET — WE DECIDED TO CONCEIVE IT AS AN **EVIL TWIN** AND EXPLORE NEW TERRITORY.

I WANT TWO SEPARATE BUILDINGS: A 10.000M² **CONDOMINIUM** NEXT TO A 20.000M² **PARKING STRUCTURE.**

PROGRAMMATIC SYMBIOSIS STRIKES AGAIN !

RATHER THAN ERECTING **A STANDARD APARTMENT SLAB** NEXT TO **A BORING PARKING BLOCK**---

---WE DECIDED TO TURN THE PARKING INTO **A PODIUM FOR LIVING.**

THE PARKING STRUCTURE IS SLOPING UPWARDS IN A **SERPENTINE ZIGZAG** FROM SOUTH TO NORTH.

THE HOUSING IS **SMEARED** IN AN EVEN LAYER OVER THE TOP---

---SO THE APARTMENTS ARE TRANS-FORMED INTO COURTYARD HOUSES WIT BIG GARDEN AND GENER-OUS VIEWS.

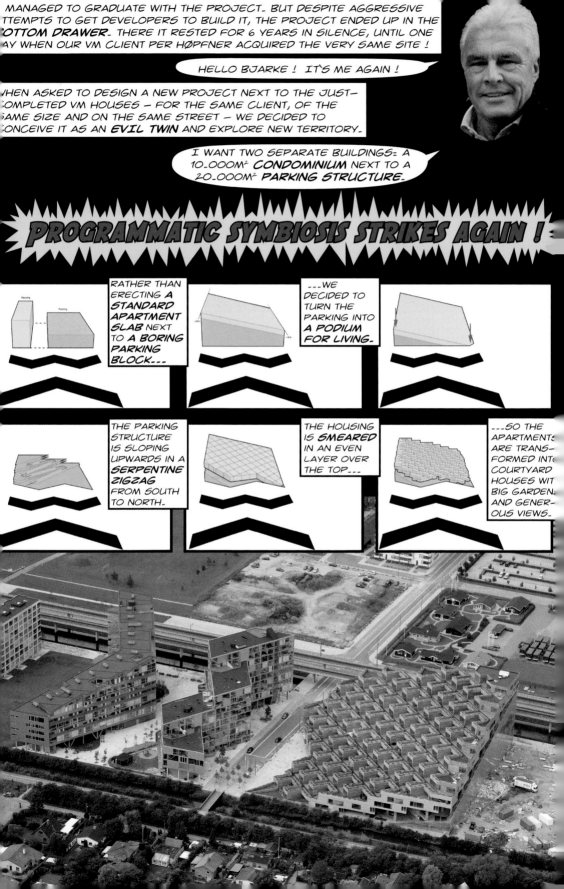

IT'S LIKE THE **NEIGHBOURING SUBURB** IS CROSSING THE CANAL AND **OVERFLOWING THE PARKING BLOCK** ALL THE WAY FROM THE GROUND...

...TO THE 11TH FLOOR.

THE SOUTH SIDE OF THE BUILDING IS A **STEPPED HILLSIDE** OF PRIVATE BACKYARDS.

THE TERRACE HOUSES ARE BASED ON JØRN UTZON'S L-SHAPED COURTYARD TYPOLOGY, AND COMBINE ALL THE **SPLENDOURS OF A SUBURBAN LIFESTYLE**...

...A HOUSE WITH A *LARGE GARDEN*...

...WITH *URBAN DENSITY*...

...AND A *PENTHOUSE VIEW*.

A SLOPING ELEVATOR (DENMARK'S FIRST) GIVES ACCESS TO THE HOUSES FROM *UNDERNEATH.*

WHILE THE SOUTH FACADE IS A CASCADE OF BARBEQUES AND DECK CHAIRS, THE NORTH FACADE, FACING THE CITY, IS *A DAZZLING OPEN PARKING STRUCTURE.*

THE NATURALLY VENTILATED PARKING REQUIRES *A PERFORATED FACADE* TO ALLOW AIR TO PASS WHILE KEEPING RAIN AND SNOW OUT.

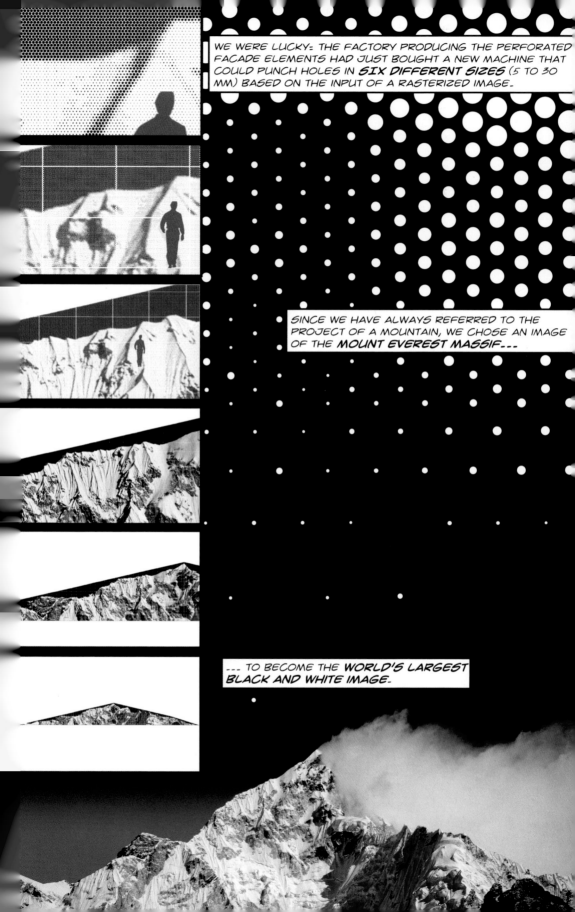

WE WERE LUCKY: THE FACTORY PRODUCING THE PERFORATED FACADE ELEMENTS HAD JUST BOUGHT A NEW MACHINE THAT COULD PUNCH HOLES IN **SIX DIFFERENT SIZES** (5 TO 30 MM) BASED ON THE INPUT OF A RASTERIZED IMAGE.

SINCE WE HAVE ALWAYS REFERRED TO THE PROJECT OF A MOUNTAIN, WE CHOSE AN IMAGE OF THE **MOUNT EVEREST MASSIF**...

... TO BECOME THE **WORLD'S LARGEST BLACK AND WHITE IMAGE.**

NOW THIS IS WHAT IT LOOKS LIKE FROM MY APARTMENT !

DANISH POET SØREN ULRIK THOMSEN WROTE AN ESSAY CALLED "COPENHAGEN THE SUBURBAN NEIGHBOURHOOD IN UPRIGHT POSITION" AS A CRITICISM OF THE GENTRIFICATION AND SUBURBANISATION OF THE INNER CITY.

THE MOUNTAIN IS A LITERAL EMBODIMENT OF THE UNINTENDED POTENTIAL OF THAT METAPHOR.

8-HOUSE AND LITTLE TOWER

INFINITY LOOP

BEING A COPENHAGEN TOWER DEFINED BY THE CITY'S TRADITIONAL SPIRES, THIS SHOULD NOT BE A GIANT SKYSCRAPER BUT A TALL, *SLENDER* TOWER.

THE FOOTPRINT IS ONLY *160 SQUARE METER* — EQUIVALENT TO A TYPICAL SINGLE FAMILY HOUSE — BUT IN OUR CASE SINGLE FAMILY HOUSE OF 16 FLOORS.

THE PROPORTIONS ARE ALSO FIXED: 10 X 16 METERS, FACING SOUTH.

AT THE TOP OF THE BUILDING, IT WORKS PERFECTLY. THE RESIDENCES HAVE A *VIEW* OVERLOOKING THE ROOFSCAPE OF OUR BLOCK.

BUT THE LOWER FLOORS LOOK STRAIGHT INTO THE BACK OF THE BLOCK.

SO WE SIMPLY *TWIST* THE BOTTOM PART, LIKE THIS...

CRUNCH!

AND THE RESIDENCES FACE SOUTHWEST TOWARD THE PLAZA.

ARCHITECTONICALLY, THE RESULT IS A *FACETTED TRIANGULAR GABLE* MOTIF. HERE IT ACTUALLY REMINDS US OF A TRADITIONAL MERCHANT'S ESTATE — A POINTED GABLE WITH A PITCHED ROOF, IN THIS OTHERWISE MODERN TOWER.

THE RESULT IS A TWISTED TOWER WITH THE SAME FORMAL LANGUAGE AS A *CRUSHED MILK CARTON.*

WHOOSH!!

WHAM!!

WE THEREFORE PLACE THE WHOLE COMMERCIAL PART IN THE **BOTTOM** OF THE BUILDING.

THE OPPOSITE GOES FOR HOUSING, WHICH **LOVES SUNSHINE** BUT HATES A GROUND FLOOR LOCATION WHERE PEOPLE CAN LOOK STRAIGHT INTO THE APARTMENT.

WE THEREFORE PLACE ALL THE DWELLINGS ON TOP OF THE COMMERCIAL FUNCTIONS. BUT SHOPS AND OFFICES HAVE DEEPER FLOORS THAN HOUSING.

ALONG THE LOWEST RESIDENCES A PATH, OR ROOF GARDEN, APPEARS AS IT WOULD IN DANISH **POTATO ROW HOUSING.**

IMAGINE IF WE COULD CREATE A MODERN VERSION OF THE POTATO ROWS BY TURNING THE BOTTOM RESIDENCES INTO **TWO-STORY ROWHOUSES** WITH FRONT GARDENS AND A CONNECTING PATH SO THE KIDS CAN GO VISIT EACH OTHER ?

ON TOP OF THE ROWHOUSES, WE THROW A LAYER OF **TRADITIONAL APARTMENTS**, WHERE THE LOWEST ONE IS LOCATED ON THE 3RD OR 4TH LEVEL.

CLUNK!!

FINALLY, ON TOP, WE ADD TWO FLOORS OF **ROOFTOP ROWHOUSES**...

...WITH BOTH **FRONT GARDENS** AND **ROOF GARDENS.**

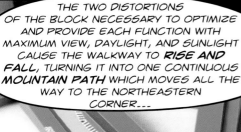

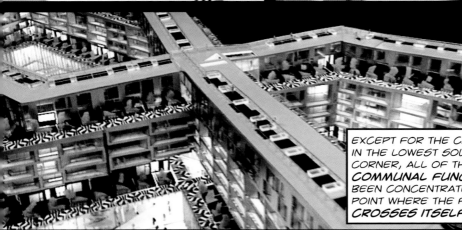

SCALA TOWER

SP<del>ANISH</del>
D<del>ANISH</del>
STEPS

COPENHAGEN USED TO BE CALLED **THE CITY OF TOWERS**. THE CITY'S COAT OF ARMS PORTRAYS THREE TOWERS RISING ABOVE THE WATER.

IF YOU LOOK AT THIS PHOTO, THE ONLY ADDITIONS WE'VE MADE TO THE SKYLINE IN THE LAST 100 YEARS ARE THE CHIMNEYS OF TWO POWER PLANTS AND THE GOLDEN TOWER OF TIVOLI.

BUT THE CITY'S LOVE FOR TOWERS SEEMS TO HAVE **FADED AWAY**...

DUTCH ARCHITECT **ERICK VAN EGERAAT** RECENTLY WON AN INTERNATIONAL COMPETITION FOR A WATERFRONT RESIDENTIAL DEVELOPMENT WITH A SCHEME OF **SIX SLENDER URBAN VILLAS**. SMALL IN FOOTPRINT BUT STRETCHED BEYOND THE NORMAL PROPORTIONS OF A VILLA, THE TALLEST TOWER ROSE TO A DIZZYING HEIGHT OF **55 METERS** !

FOR THAT IT WON THE (UN)POPULAR NAME **'MINI MANHATTAN'**, AND TRIGGERED A NEW COPENHAGEN COMMUNITY: **"THE SOCIETY AGAINST MISPLACED HIGH-RISES"**.

THIS SOCIETY IS FOUNDED ON THE PRINCIPLE THAT NOTHING IN COPENHAGEN IS SUPPOSED TO BE **TALLER THAN 21 METERS** (AN AESTHETIC RULE DATING BACK TO THE HEIGHT OF THE FIRE DEPARTMENT'S LADDERS AT THE TURN OF LAST CENTURY). HIGH-RISES ARE CONDEMNED TO A LIFE IN THE **OUTSKIRTS**.

THE SOCIETY LAUNCHED A **POLITICAL BATTLE AGAINST THE PROJECT** BY COLLECTING SIGNATURES AGAINST IT.

WHEN THEY REACHED 20.000+ SIGNATURES, THE POLITICIANS **PANICKED** AND **CANCELLED** THE PROJECT.

THE CORE OF THE SKYSCRAPER **SKEPTICS** IS VOICED IN THE MEDIA BY PROFESSOR OF URBANISM **JENS KVORNING** FROM THE ROYAL DANISH ACADEMY OF ARTS, SCHOOL OF ARCHITECTURE IN COPENHAGEN:

SOME PEOPLE THINK THAT TOWERS ONLY BELONG IN...

BEIJING...

---OR NEW YORK...

"UNFORTUNATELY, MOST HIGH-RISES ARE ONLY CONCERNED WITH **SYMBOLIC VALUE**. YOU MIGHT HAVE YOUR OPINIONS ON THE TURNING TORSO IN MALMO, BUT SEEN FROM A DISTANCE IT IS A KIND OF **NICE SCULPTURAL STICK**. BUT I DON'T KNOW IF YOU'VE BEEN STANDING AT THE FOOT OF THAT TOWER? IT IS **VERY UNPLEASANT**. NOTHING HAS BEEN DONE TO MAKE THE TOWER PART OF THE SURROUNDING CITY. IT IS MERELY A **MONUMENT** THAT SHOULD **LOOK GOOD AT A DISTANCE**."

---OR DUBAI...

---BUT **NOT** IN COPENHAGEN !

O WHEN WE WERE ASKED O DO A PROJECT IN FRONT F TIVOLI'S MAIN ENTRANCE, OMPRISING **SHOPS**, INEMAS, THE **CITY LIBRARY**, CONFERENCE CENTRE AND LUXURY HOTEL...

...WE KNEW WE HAD TO SOMEHOW CIRCUMVENT THE **TOWERPHOBIC PUBLIC OBSESSION**.

WE STARTED OUR INVESTIGATION BY TAKING A QUICK GLANCE AT **COPENHAGEN'S SKYLINE**. IT REVEALED A CHANGE FROM **TRADITIONAL** TO **MODERN TOWERS**.

WHERE THE **TRADITIONAL TOWERS** ARE **SPIRES EMERGING FROM URBAN BLOCKS** WELL-INTEGRATED IN THE CITY FABRIC, THE **MODERN TOWERS** ARE GENERIC EXTRUSIONS OF **RECTANGULAR FLOOR PLANS**...

WE THEN PROPOSED A **REINTERPRETATION** OF THE HISTORICAL COPENHAGEN TOWER, CONSISTING OF **TWO ELEMENTS**:

A **SLIM TOWER** TAKING PART OF THE SKYLINE...

...AND A **BASE** RELATING TO THE SCALE OF THE SURROUNDING BUILDINGS.

THE TOWER IS A **HOTEL** AND **ROOFTOP SPA**, AND THE **BASE** COMPRISES ALL THE **PUBLIC PARTS** OF THE BUILDING.

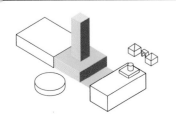

HEALTH CLUB
HOTEL
OFFICE
CONFERENCE
LIBRARY
SHOPS

THE TOWER AND THE BASE ARE **MORPHED TOGETHER IN A SPIRAL-SHAPED CASCADE OF STAIRS** CLIMBING THE FACADES...

...TO A **NEW PUBLIC ROOFTOP PLAZA** OVERLOOKING THE TOWN SQUARE AND THE TIVOLI GARDENS.

COPENHAGEN IS A CITY MATERIALIZED ALMOST EXCLUSIVELY IN **BRICK.** THE FACADES OF THE SCALA TOWER ARE AN INTERPRETATION OF THE **PATTERN** RATHER THAN THE MATERIAL OF THE BRICK.

THE REGULARITY OF THE BRICK PATTERN **INTERACTS** WITH THE TRANSFORMING OUTLINE OF THE WARPED TOWER---

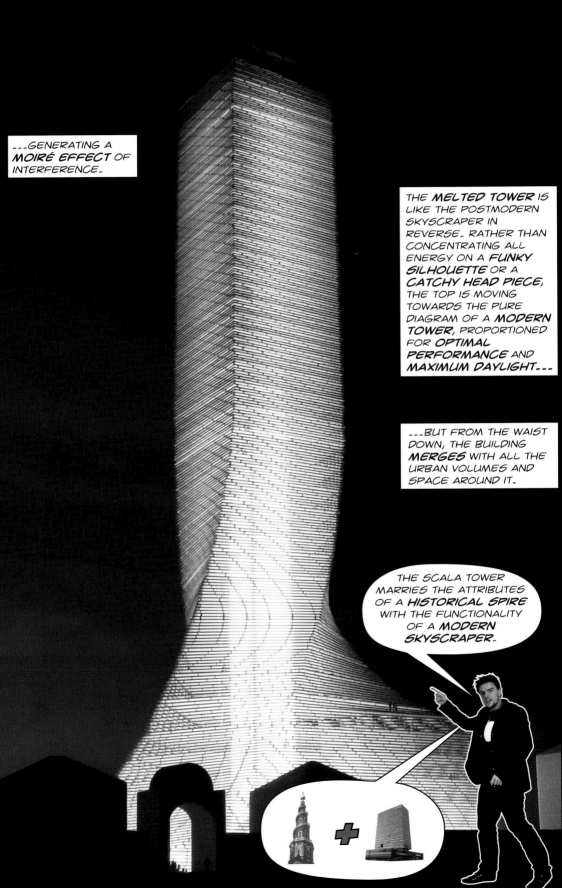

...AS WELL AS ON THE **INSIDE**.

LIKE A **DANISH VERSION**...

...OF THE **SPANISH STEPS** IN ROME.

LEGO TOWERS

⬧ LEGO

MODULAR MANIA

DURING THE **MARSHALL YEARS** WHEN POSTWAR DENMARK WAS BEING REBUILT, THE STATE CHOSE TO FAVOUR **PREFABRICATED CONCRETE** OVER ALL OTHER FORMS OF CONSTRUCTION.

AS A RESULT, THE IN-SITU CAST CONCRETE INDUSTRY HAS ALMOST VANISHED, LEAVING THE ENTIRE BUILDING INDUSTRY BASED ON **PREFABRICATED MODULES** AND **CONCRETE ELEMENTS**.

CONTEMPORARY DENMARK HAS BECOME A COUNTRY ENTIRELY MADE FROM **CONCRETE LEGO SLABS**.

LEGOLAND IN BILLUND

110

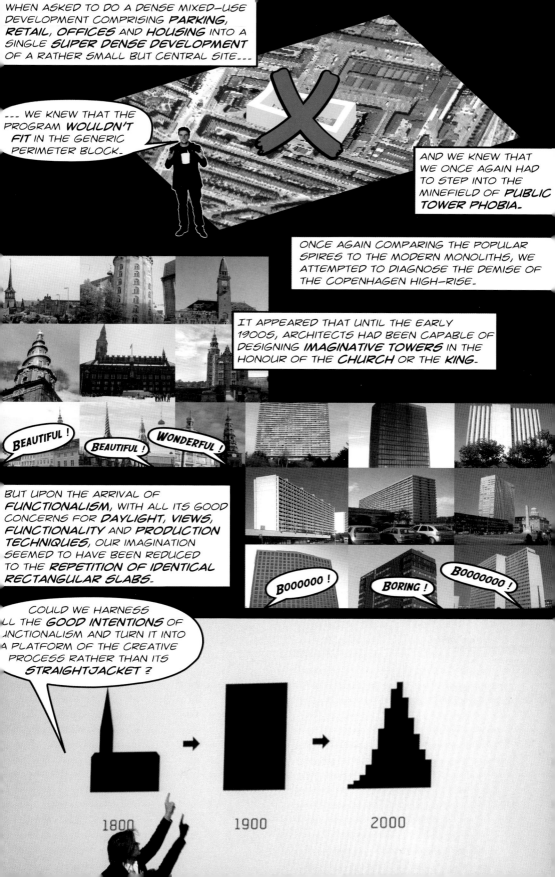

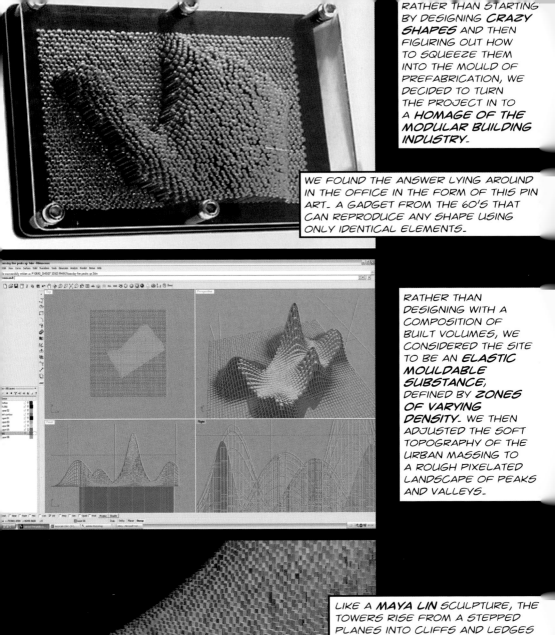

RATHER THAN STARTING BY DESIGNING **CRAZY SHAPES** AND THEN FIGURING OUT HOW TO SQUEEZE THEM INTO THE MOULD OF PREFABRICATION, WE DECIDED TO TURN THE PROJECT IN TO A **HOMAGE OF THE MODULAR BUILDING INDUSTRY.**

WE FOUND THE ANSWER LYING AROUND IN THE OFFICE IN THE FORM OF THIS PIN ART. A GADGET FROM THE 60'S THAT CAN REPRODUCE ANY SHAPE USING ONLY IDENTICAL ELEMENTS.

RATHER THAN DESIGNING WITH A COMPOSITION OF BUILT VOLUMES, WE CONSIDERED THE SITE TO BE AN **ELASTIC MOULDABLE SUBSTANCE,** DEFINED BY **ZONES OF VARYING DENSITY.** WE THEN ADJUSTED THE SOFT TOPOGRAPHY OF THE URBAN MASSING TO A ROUGH PIXELATED LANDSCAPE OF PEAKS AND VALLEYS.

LIKE A **MAYA LIN** SCULPTURE, THE TOWERS RISE FROM A STEPPED PLANES INTO CLIFFS AND LEDGES OF HUMAN OCCUPATION, A MODULAR WET DREAM...

SO TO PROVE THAT THIS WAS REALLY AFFORDABLE WITH STANDARD TECHNIQUES, WE DECIDED THAT NOTHING WOULD BE MORE CONVINCING THAN IF *YOU COULD BUILD IT IN LEGO.* IT HAPPENED THAT ON THE 1:500 SCALE MODEL OF THE BUILDING, THE SIZE OF A SINGLE PIXEL WAS IDENTICAL TO THE SIZE OF *THE SMALLEST ONE-DOT LEGO BRICK.*

WHEN YOU ARE DONE, YOU CLICK SUBMIT, GET A PRICE QUOTE AND THREE DAYS LATER YOU RECEIVE A BOX FROM 'LEGO FACTORY' *WITH AN IMAGE OF YOUR DESIGN ON THE COVER AND ALL THE BRICKS TO BUILD IT INSIDE !*

ONE OF OUR ARCHITECTS SPENT TWO DAYS OF HIS LIFE BUILDING IT *ONLINE,* AND ANOTHER TWO TO REPEAT THE TRICK IN *REAL-LIFE !*

SO AT THE END OF THE PRESENTATION, WE GAVE THE CLIENT HIS OWN LEGO-PROJECT (PREASSEMBLED). HE PASSED IT ON TO HIS SON, AND GAVE US THE *COMMISSION* TO DO IT.

IT EVEN TURNED OUT THAT *LEGO* HAD A WEBSITE WHERE YOU CAN DOWNLOAD FREE SOFTWARE AND *BUILD VIRTUALLY WITH ALL THE LEGO PIECES AVAILABLE.*

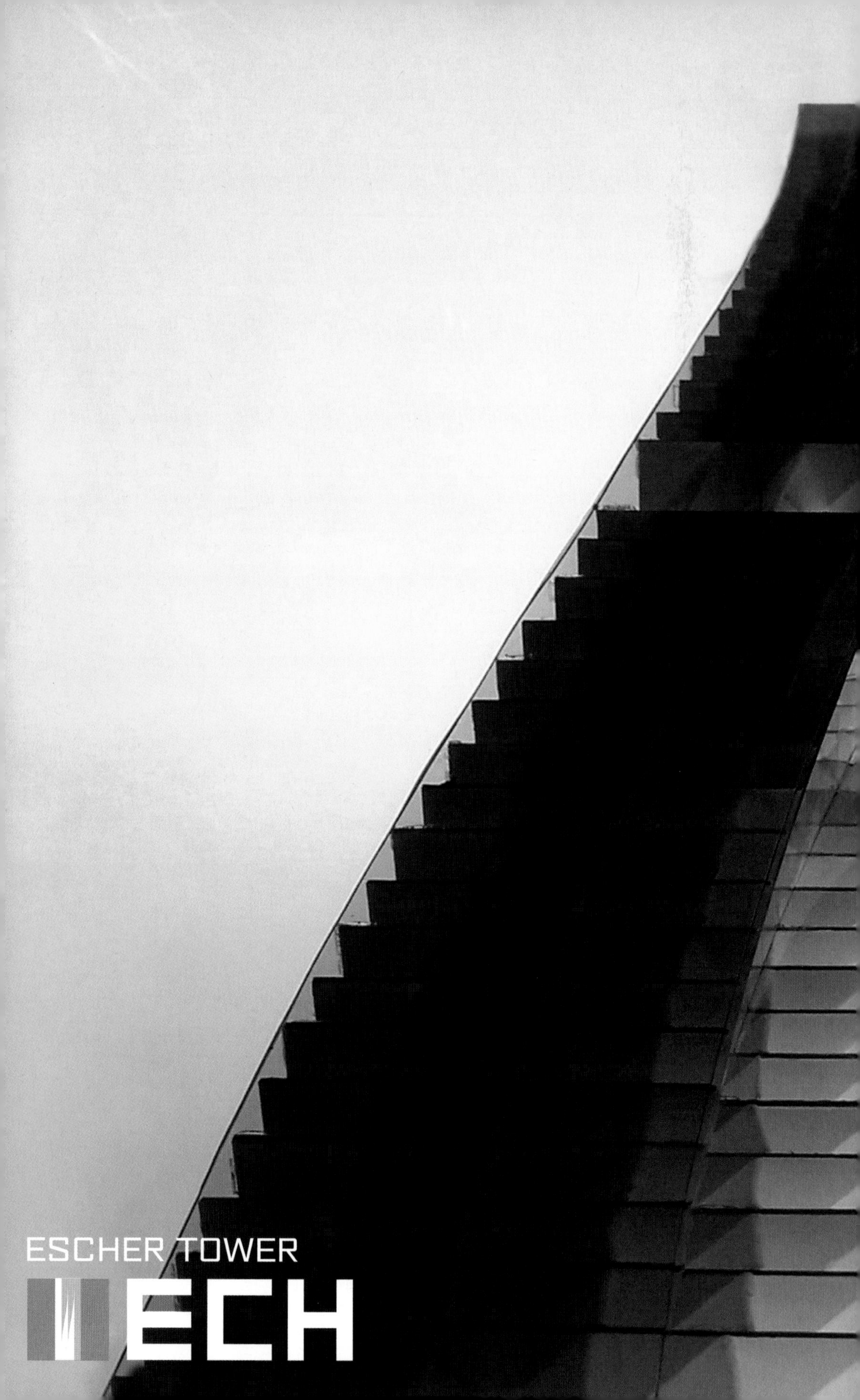
ESCHER TOWER
ECH

SCANDINAVIAN SKYSCRAPER

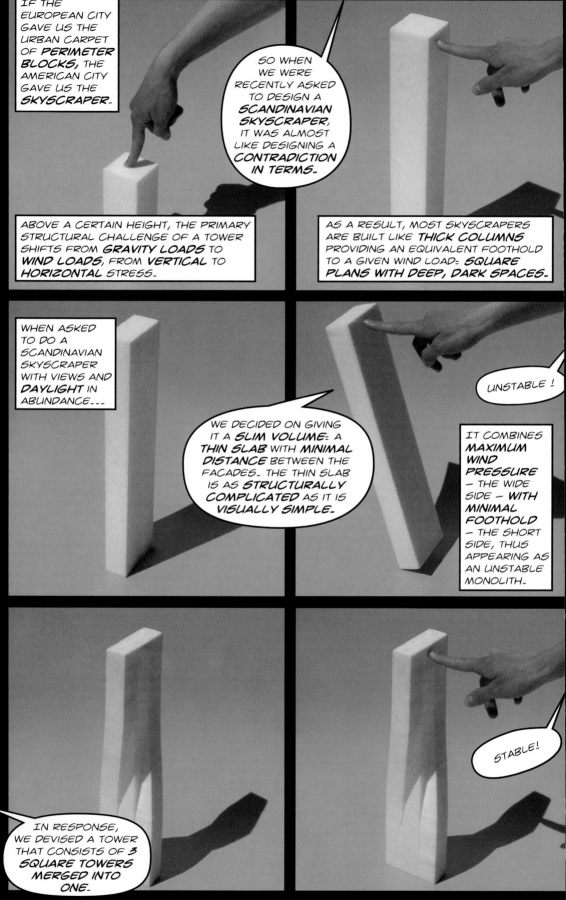

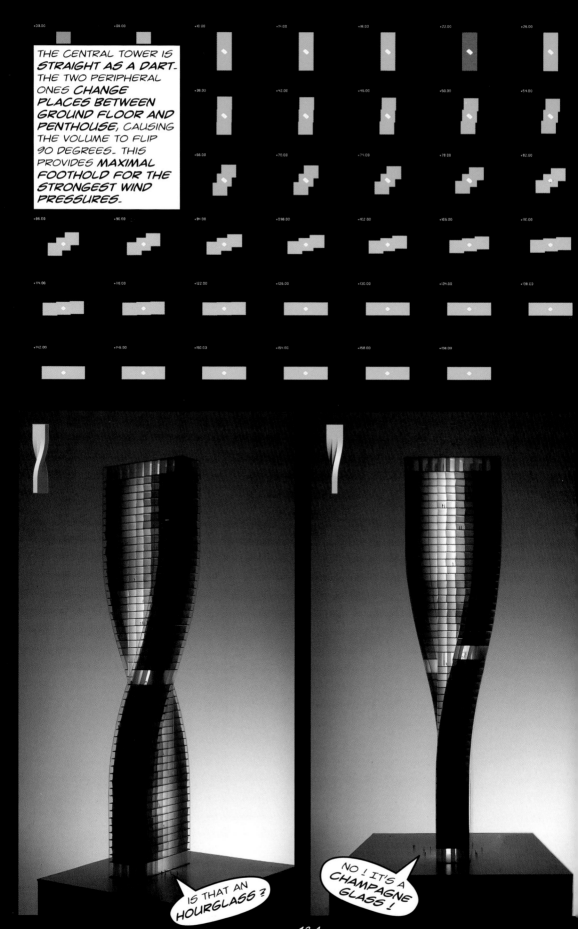

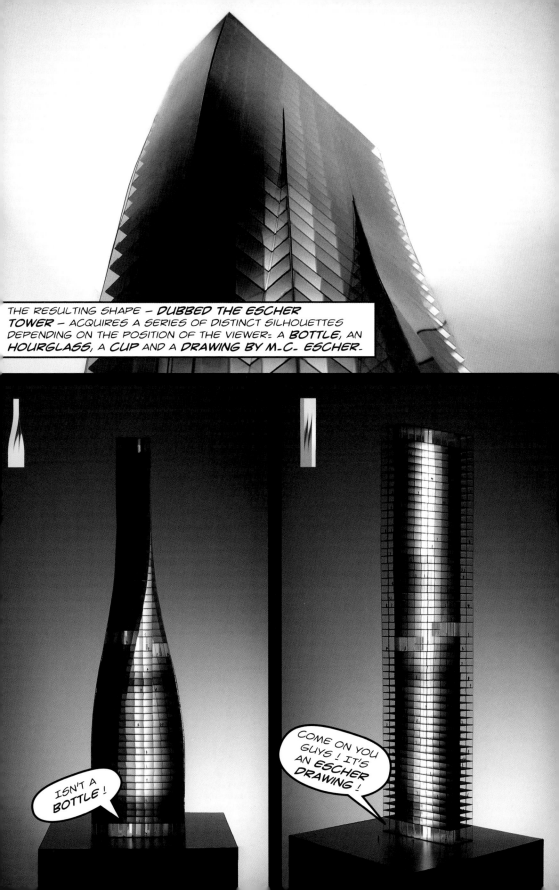

THE RESULTING SHAPE — *DUBBED THE ESCHER TOWER* — ACQUIRES A SERIES OF DISTINCT SILHOUETTES DEPENDING ON THE POSITION OF THE VIEWER: A *BOTTLE*, AN *HOURGLASS*, A *CUP* AND A *DRAWING BY M.C. ESCHER.*

ISN'T A *BOTTLE* !

COME ON YOU GUYS ! IT'S AN *ESCHER DRAWING* !

M.C. ESCHER
"BELVEDERE" 1958

THE DIFFERENCE FROM ESCHER IS THAT HIS ART DEPICTS BUILDINGS THAT **SEEM TO FUNCTION** BUT ARE IN **REALITY IMPOSSIBLE CONSTRUCTIONS.** THE ESCHER TOWER IS THE **OPPOSITE:** **IT LOOKS CRAZY** BUT IS IN FACT A CREATION OF **COMMON SENSE.**

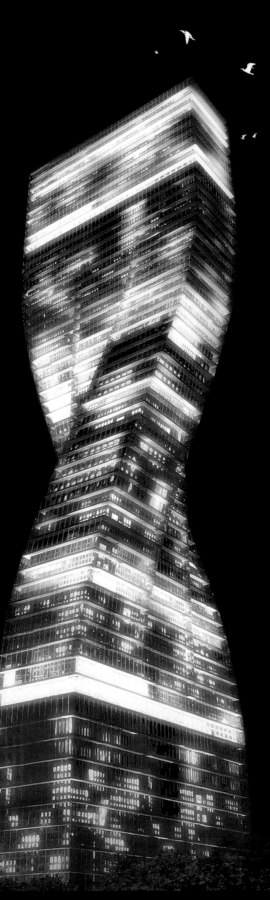

TØJHUSET

TØJ

BUREAUCRATIC
BEAUTY

URBAN DEVELOPMENT IS GENERATED IN A **COMPLEX INTERPLAY OF PUBLIC AND PRIVATE INTERESTS**: FUELED BY INVESTMENT AND CONTROLLED BY RULES AND REGULATIONS.

IN ORDER TO PREVENT UNDESIRABLE DEVELOPMENTS, PLANNERS AND POLITICIANS TRY TO IMAGINE WHAT SHOULD AND WHAT SHOULDN'T HAPPEN...

BRA

§!!

どいてくれ~!

...AND DESIGN THE **RULES TO ENSURE THE DESIRED DEVELOPMENTS — OR PREVENT THE UNWANTED.**

BUT AS LIFE EVOLVES, **THE CITY** (AND ITS REGULATIONS) **HAS TO EVOLVE WITH IT** TO MAKE SURE THAT IT **FITS TO THE WAY WE WANT TO LIVE,** AND NOT MAKE US LIVE THE WAY THE CITY FORCES US TO.

THE **TØJHUS SITE** IN **ISLANDS BRYGGE** IN **CENTRAL COPENHAGEN** IS A NEW DEVELOPMENT OF OPEN PERIMETER BLOCKS FOR LIVING AND GLASS BOXES FOR WORKING IN A REFLECTING POOL.

?

THE ONLY RELIEF FROM THE RELATIVELY ANONYMOUS NEW BUILDINGS ARE **THREE OLD WAREHOUSES** WHOSE DEEP PLANS AND LOFTY LAYOUTS HAVE PROVEN IDEAL FOR A HOST OF RECORDING STUDIOS AND GALLERIES.

THE OWNERS CALLED US TO SEE IF THE PARKING LOT NEXT TO THE WAREHOUSES COULD BE **A TESTBED OF SOMETHING OTHER THAN RESIDENTIAL SLABS** AND OFFICE PERIMETER BLOCKS.

[TH]E MASTER PLAN CALLED FOR A **5-STOREY** [FU]LL CONVENTIONAL BLOCK LEAVING [SP]ACE FOR A NEW SQUARE. THE CLIENT [WA]NTED **DOUBLE DENSITY** AND APARTMENTS [SO] HIGH THAT THEY COULD **VIEW THE SEA !**

SO WE DECIDED TO TAKE **A CLOSE LOOK AT THE BUILDING CODE OF COPENHAGEN.** AMONG OTHER THINGS [TH]E BUILDING CODE DEFINES AN EQUATION FOR [H]OW TALL A BUILDING CAN BE, PROPORTIONATE TO ITS PROXIMITY TO THE NEAREST NEIGHBOURS.

nabobygning

variabel afstand

THE FORMULA IS: **MAXIMUM HEIGH[T] = 3 M + 80% OF THE DISTANCE TO THE NEIGHBOUR.** THE FARTHER AWAY, THE HIGHER YOU CAN BUILD.

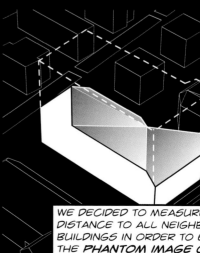

WE DECIDED TO MEASURE THE DISTANCE TO ALL NEIGHBOURING BUILDINGS IN ORDER TO ESTABLIS[H] THE **PHANTOM IMAGE OF THE MAXIMUM BUILDING ENVELOPE[.]**

TO OUR SURPRISE *A WAREHOUSE-LIKE VOLUME APPEARED,* ADDING A FOURTH WAREHOUSE TO THE EXISTING THREE.

BY *REJECTING THE DEFAULT TYPOLOGIES* AND EXPLORING THE ABSTRACT WORLD OF BUREAUCRATIC CODES, WE UNCOVERED A MATHEMATICAL CONSTRUCT...

I CAN SEE MY HOUSE FROM HERE!

...THAT, ALTHOUGH OF ABSTRACT ORIGIN, WAS *MORE SIMILAR TO THE NEIGHBOURING BUILDINGS* THAN THE CONVENTIONAL OUTLINES OF THE MASTER PLAN.

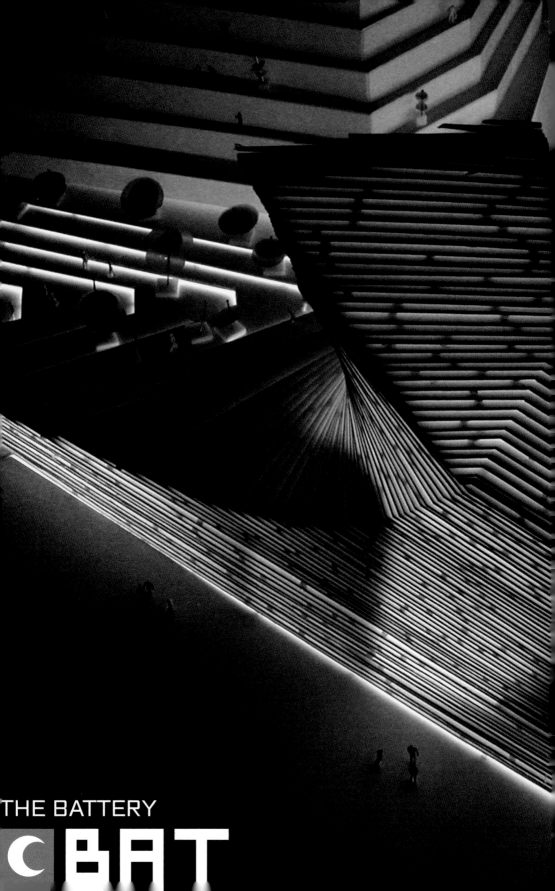

THE BATTERY

◐ BAT

MORGENAVISEN

Jyllands-Poste

Danmarks internationale

OF THE PROPHET MOHAMMED AND **TRIGGERED AN OUTRAGE** IN MOST OF THE ISLAMIC WORLD.

FLAGS WERE BURNED ALONG WITH **EMBASSIES** AND IMAGES OF THE **DANISH PRIME MINISTER.**

THE **STREET IN FRONT OF OUR OFFICE** (IN THE NEIGHBORHOOD MOST HEAVILY POPULATED WITH MUSLIMS) WAS TURNED IN TO A **BATTLEFIELD** BY ANGRY AND FRUSTRATED IMMIGRANT KIDS BREAKING WINDOWS AND BURNING CARS.

COPENHAGEN WAS FLOODED WITH FOREIGN AND ISLAMIC MEDIA DOCUMENTING **THE MONUMENTAL FAILURE OF THE INTEGRATION OF MUSLIM IMMIGRANTS INTO DANISH SOCIETY.**

COULD YOU KEEP IT DOWN A BIT ? WE'RE TRYING TO WORK IN HERE !

AT THE SAME TIME, BY CHANCE (OR WAS IT FATE ?), **WE WERE FINISHING UP OUR FIRST SKETCHES** FOR WHAT **COULD BE A FIRST ATTEMPT AT A SUCCESSFUL INTEGRATION OF ISLAM** IN DENMARK. BUT THE STORY HAD ALREADY BEGUN DECADES EARLIER...

IN 1992 THE COPENHAGEN CITY COUNCIL DECIDED THAT THE **OLD ARMY SHOOTING RANGE** IN THE MIDDLE OF THE CITY SHOULD BE CONVERTED INTO AN **EXTENSION OF COPENHAGEN UNIVERSITY.**

IT SHOULD BE A **LOW DENSITY CAMPUS OF 3-STOREY BUILDINGS**, SINCE LOW DENSITY WAS SEEN AS A GUARANTEE OF LIGHT AND FRESH AIR.

UNIVERSITY

AS A SYMBOL OF CULTURAL INTEGRATION IT **ALSO HAD TO CONTAIN A MOSQUE...**

SHORTLY AFTER A NEW SUBWAY WAS BUILT, AN URBAN NEIGHBORHOOD EMERGED AROUND IT AND THE **UNIVERSITY EXPANDED IN THE OPPOSITE DIRECTION.**

IN THE MEANTIME, EXPERTS FOUND THAT URBAN LIFE REQUIRES URBAN DENSITY. **THE NEW NEIGHBORHOOD WAS MADE HIGHER AND DENSER** IN ORDER TO ENSURE PEOPLE IN THE STREETS AND CUSTOMERS IN THE CAFÉS.

WE'VE GONE OVER BUDGET **AGAIN** ?!! **SACRE BLEU** !!

THE RULES HOWEVER REMAINED THE SAME: 3 FLOORS AND A MOSQUE. BUT THE **ISLAMIC COMMUNITY COULDN'T AGREE ON WHAT KIND OF MOSQUE...**

...AND THE **PRIVATE DEVELOPERS DIDN'T KNOW WHAT TO DO** WITH A SITE RESERVED FOR ISLAMIC ARCHITECTURE. SO THE SITE REMAINED EMPTY. UNTIL...

...ONE DAY A CLIENT CALLED US AND ASKED US TO DO A SUPER DENSE DEVELOPMENT, **4 TIMES DENSER THAN CURRENT STANDARDS.**

THE MASSIVE DEVELOPMENT OF HOUSING AND OFFICE WOULD CREATE THE NEED FOR RETAIL, CULTURE AND LEISURE TO OCCUPY THE GROUND FLOOR WITH **AN ABUNDANCE OF URBAN LIFE.**

AND THE **REVENUE WOULD POTENTIALLY BECOME SO GREAT** THAT IT WOULD BE POSSIBLE TO **SPONSOR THE MOSQUE** AS PART OF THE PROJECT. IT WAS CLEAR THAT WE WOULD HAVE TO BUILD **HIGHER AND DENSER** THAN YOU TRADITIONALLY DO IN COPENHAGEN.

AND IT WAS CLEAR THAT THE PROJECT WAS GOING TO BE **ALL ABOUT INTEGRATION !** THE FUNCTIONAL INTEGRATION OF **ALL ASPECTS OF URBAN LIFE IN ONE COMMUNITY:**

APARTMENTS

CHILD CARE

SPORTS FACILITIES

OFFICES

SHOPP

CULTURAL INSTITUTIONS...

...AND A **MOSQUE**.

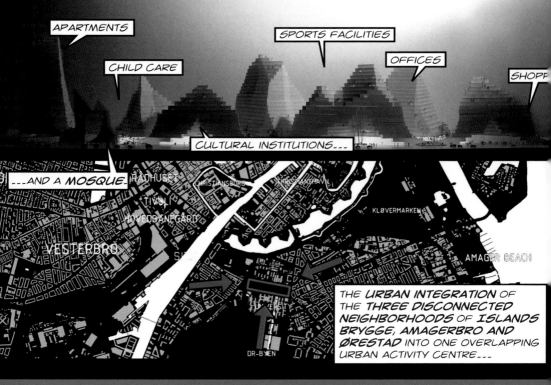

THE **URBAN INTEGRATION** OF THE **THREE DISCONNECTED NEIGHBORHOODS OF ISLANDS BRYGGE, AMAGERBRO AND ØRESTAD** INTO ONE OVERLAPPING URBAN ACTIVITY CENTRE...

AND FINALLY, THE CULTURAL INTEGRATION OF **ISLAMIC AND DANISH CULTURE,** BY INCORPORATING **THE FIRST MOSQUE EVER BUILT IN DENMARK** INTO THE CENTER OF THE COMPLEX.

IF YOU STUDY **COPENHAGEN'S COAT OF ARMS,** YOU GAIN AN INTERESTING INSIGHT INTO THE CITY'S HERALDIC IDENTITY.

 +  =

THREE TOWERS STAND SIDE BY SIDE **WITH THEIR FEET IN WATER,** THE SPIRES OF THE TOWERS CROWNED BY **TWO DAVID STARS** AND **A CRESCENT MOON** – THE IMAGE OF A MODERN **MULTICULTURAL METROPOLIS** WITH HARBOURFRONTS POPULATED BY PEOPLE OF ALL RELIGIONS.

IMAGINE IF THIS PROJECT COULD GIVE NEW ENERGY TO THIS **ALCHEMICAL FORMULA** FOR CITY LIFE, THAT LAYS HIDDEN IN COPENHAGEN'S COAT OF ARMS: **TOWERS + WATER + DIVERSITY = A LIVING COPENHAGEN !**

SO WE ONCE AGAIN DECIDED TO PUSH **TOWARDS** THE LIMIT OF THE CODE.

REVISITING *THE FORMULA WE EXPLORED AT* TØJHUSET*...

...WE MEASURED THE **DISTANCE TO ALL NEIGHBOURS** TO SEE WHAT PHANTOM IMAGE MIGHT APPEAR.

...A **MOUNTAIN RIDGE** OF A VOLUME EMERGED.

* *SEE "BUREAUCRATIC BEAUTY"*

142

FOLLOWING THE MASTER PLAN OF THE SURROUNDING LOTS, WE *CARVED PASSAGES* ACROSS THE SITE *TO CONNECT THE NEIGHBOURS*, TRANSFORMING THE RIDGE INTO *INDIVIDUAL PEAKS*.

THE TOWERS LEFT STANDING WERE TOO DEEP FOR HUMAN OCCUPATION SO *WE CARVED OUT CAVES* FOR PUBLIC PROGRAMS DEEP INSIDE.

ON THE GROUND WE *CONNECTED THE PEAKS* TO CREATE A *CONTINUOUS PUBLIC INTERIOR*, AND OPENED THE CAVES FOR *DAYLIGHT AND VIEWS*.

THE RESULTING ARCHITECTURE IS AN *ARTIFICIAL LANDSCAPE* OF *URBAN PEAKS AND PARK-LIKE CANYONS, PUBLIC CAVES* AND *RESIDENTIAL RICE FIELDS*.

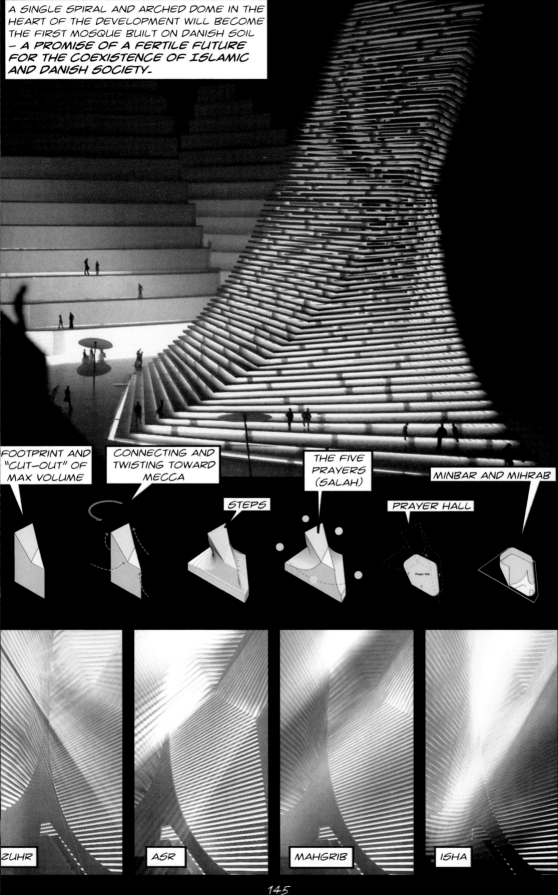

A SINGLE SPIRAL AND ARCHED DOME IN THE HEART OF THE DEVELOPMENT WILL BECOME THE FIRST MOSQUE BUILT ON DANISH SOIL — A PROMISE OF A FERTILE FUTURE FOR THE COEXISTENCE OF ISLAMIC AND DANISH SOCIETY.

FOOTPRINT AND "CUT-OUT" OF MAX VOLUME

CONNECTING AND TWISTING TOWARD MECCA

STEPS

THE FIVE PRAYERS (SALAH)

PRAYER HALL

Prayer Hall

MINBAR AND MIHRAB

ZUHR

ASR

MAHGRIB

ISHA

145

AN *ARCHITECTURE OF SYNERGY*, THAT INTEGRATES THE *TERRACED LANDSCAPES OF ASIA'S RICE FIELDS...*

...*BASRA'S MINARET...*

...THE *FOREST OF COLUMNS IN CORDOBA'S MOSQUE...*

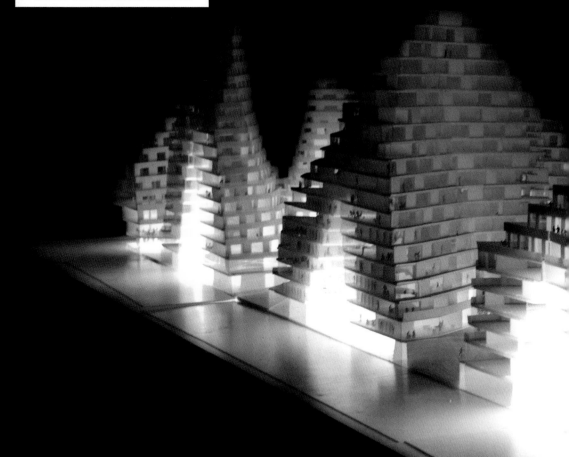

AND THE *IMPRESSIVE VAULTS OF EUROPE'S GOTHIC CATHEDRALS.*

THE TOWER OF BABEL COLLAPSED BECAUSE OF CONFUSION BETWEEN THE DIFFERENT LANGUAGES.
آداب عرض ہے
HELLO!
THE NEW PEAKS OF THE BATTERY ARE BUILT UPON A MULTICULTURAL COCKTAIL OF RELIGION, CULTURAL ACTIVITY AND ARCHITECTURE.

VILNIUS WORLD TRADE CENTER 1

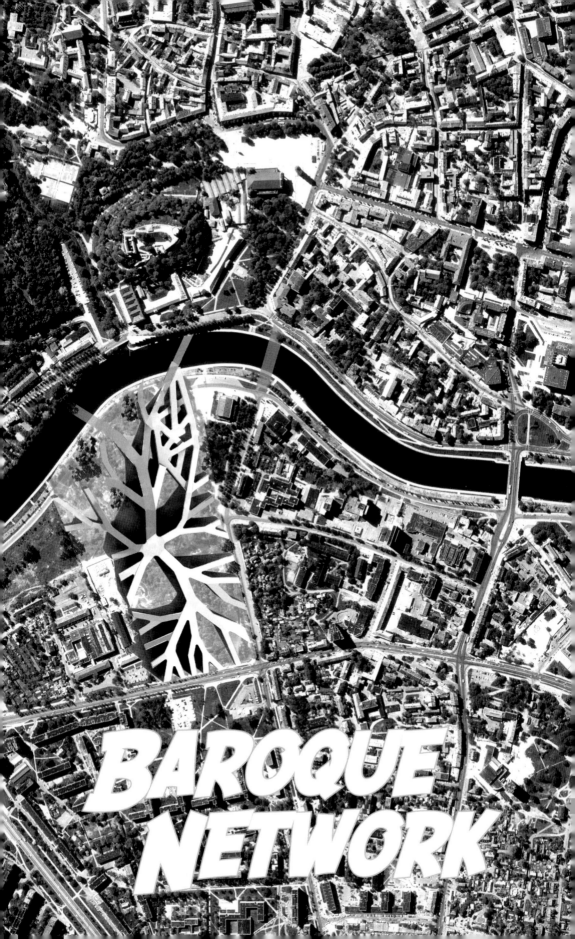

BAROQUE
NETWORK

VILNIUS IS THE **GEOGRAPHICAL CENTER** OF EUROPE.

EUROPOS CENTRAS

ITS DOWNTOWN IS A **UNESCO WORLD HERITAGE BAROQUE CITY** THAT HAS EMERGED ON THE FOOT OF A SMALL HILL AT THE CONFLUENCE OF THE NERIS AND VILNIA RIVERS.

RIGHT ACROSS FROM THE **BAROQUE CITY,** ON THE OTHER SIDE OF THE RIVER, **WE WERE ASKED TO DESIGN A NEW VILNIUS WORLD TRADE CENTER.**

INCORPORATING OFFICES, SHOPS, CONFERENCE FACILITIES, THEATRES, HOTELS, APARTMENTS, A MUSEUM, A HOSPITAL AND TWO BANKS, IT WAS **MORE LIKE DESIGNING A CITY THAN A BUILDING.**

CENTRE

BAROQUE CITY

HOW DO YOU DESIGN *A SINGLE* BUILDING FOR A SPRAWL OF PROGRAMS ?

WHEN ASKED TO DESIGN 300.000 M²
OF MIXED PROGRAM IN ONE GO, YOU
ENTER THE TWILIGHT ZONE **BETWEEN
ARCHITECTURE AND URBANISM.**

URBANISM, THE ART
AND SCIENCE OF CREATING
A LIVING CITY, IS MOST
SUCCESSFUL WHEN IT
HAPPENS **SLOWLY...**

... WHILE **PROPERTY
DEVELOPMENT** IS MOST
PROFITABLE WHEN IT
HAPPENS **FAST** !

HOW COULD WE INTEGRATE
SUCH A **LARGE PROGRAM**
INTO A **HISTORICALLY
FRAGILE CONTEXT** ?

WE LOOKED AT ALL THE EXISTING
WORLD TRADE CENTRES IN
THE WORLD: A PARADE OF
SKYSCRAPERS SPAWNED BY
THE (LATE) TWIN TOWERS OF
DOWNTOWN MANHATTAN.

BAROQUE VS MODERNISM

NEXT TO THE BAROQUE CITY
CENTRE, **SKYSCRAPERS
WERE NOT AN OPTION.**

THE INVESTORS AND THE CITY
WANTED **A "BILBAO"** (THEY
ARE CURRENTLY CONTRACTING
ZAHA HADID, EVIDENTLY THE
GEHRY OF OUR TIME, TO DESIGN
THE VILNIUS GUGGENHEIM).

ORGANIC VS ORTHOGONAL

WE WERE CAUGHT BETWEEN THE **DESIR
FOR A MASTERPIECE** AND THE **NEED
FOR A MASTER PLAN** ! PERHAPS THIS
COULD BE OUR RECIPE – DESIGNING A
BUILDING LIKE WE WOULD PLAN A CITY. S
WE LOOKED AT THE NEIGHBORHOOD ON
THE OTHER SIDE OF THE RIVER.

WE FOUND A **DIAGRAM OF A TREE** ACCOMPANIED BY THE WORDS OF THE LITHUANIAN POET TOMAS VENCLOVA: "THE UNIQUE AND DIVERSE OLD TOWN OF VILNIUS IS ONE OF THE LARGEST IN CENTRAL AND EASTERN EUROPE; EVEN THE NEWER PARTS OF THE CITY HAVE INHERITED ITS IRREGULAR, ORGANIC PLANNING PRINCIPLE."

THE HISTORICAL CITY CENTRE HAD **EVOLVED THROUGH CENTURIES** OF CONSTANT **MODIFICATIONS AND MUTATIONS**, GENERATING A BOTH INTUITIVE AND SURPRISING SPATIAL STRUCTURE.

WE TRIED **MAPPING DOWNTO VILNIUS** ONTO THE SITE.

BUT THAT WOULD CREATE A SERIES OF **SEPARATE BUILDINGS CUT OFF FRC EACH OTHER** BY STREETS AND SQUARE IF WE WANTED TO CREATE A WORLD TRADE CENTER, A NETWORK OF SEPARA FUNCTIONS **FUSED TOGETHER** TO FOR A WHOLE, WE NEEDED TO **INVERT THE PATTERN:** TURNING THE STREETS INTO BUILDINGS, AND THE BLOCKS INTO PARK.

THE RESULT WAS A **NETWORK STRUCTURE** – LIKE A **GIANT ROOT ZONE** REACHING OUT, CREATING **CONNECTIONS TO ALL THE NEIGHBOURING STREETS.** THE COURTYARDS AND GARDENS WOULD PENETRATE ALL THE WAY FROM THE PERIMETER TO THE CENTRE, LIKE **CANYONS CARVING INTO THE HIGHLANDS.**

THE COMPLEX FUNCTIONAL DIAGRAM OF INTERNAL AND EXTERNAL ADJACENCIES COULD SUDDENLY BE SOLVED BY SIMPLY **ADDING ONE PROGRAM TO ANOTHER** OR BIFURCATING BRANCHES TO MERGE MULTIPLE PROGRAMS INTO ONE ENTITY.

WE SIMPLY STARTED WITH THE WORLD TRADE CENTRE CONFERENCE CENTRE AT THE... WELL... CENTRE, AND FROM THERE WE GREW THE ADJACENT FUNCTIONS IN VARIOUS DIRECTIONS.

LIKE THE ROOTS OF A TREE REACHING FOR WATER, VARIOUS PROGRAMS WERE **REACHING TOWARDS** THE **DOWNTOWN**, THE **RIVER** OR THE **PARK**.

THE **MUSEUM WENT TOWARDS THE WATER**, WHILE THE **BANK REACHED FOR THE ARTERY ROADS**.

BY ADJUSTING THE HEIGHTS TO **MATCH THE SURROUNDINGS**, AND ADDING DENSITY TOWARDS THE EPICENTRE OF THE NETWORK, WE GRADUALLY CREATED THE **SILHOUETTE OF A SECOND HILL** ON THE OPPOSITE SIDE.

MORE **LANDSCAPE** THAN **BUILDING**, MORE **URBANISM** THAN **ARCHITECTURE**.

WHEN COMPARED TO THE OTHER WORLD TRADE CENTRES OF THE WORLD, OURS DEFINITELY **STOOD OUT**.

WE COULD BOAST TO BE THE **ARCHITECTS OF THE SHORTEST WORLD TRADE CENTER IN THE WORLD** !

SEEN FROM THE AIR, THE **EXPRESSIVE ARCHITECTURE** SUDDENLY **BLENDED IN**, LIKE A **PATCH OF THE BAROQUE CITY'S ORGANIC PATTERN** TURNED **INSIDE OUT** – A NETWORK OF STREETS TURNED INTO A NETWORK OF BUILDINGS.

THE **ORGANIZATION DIAGRAM AS THE ARCHITECTURAL EXPRESSION** !

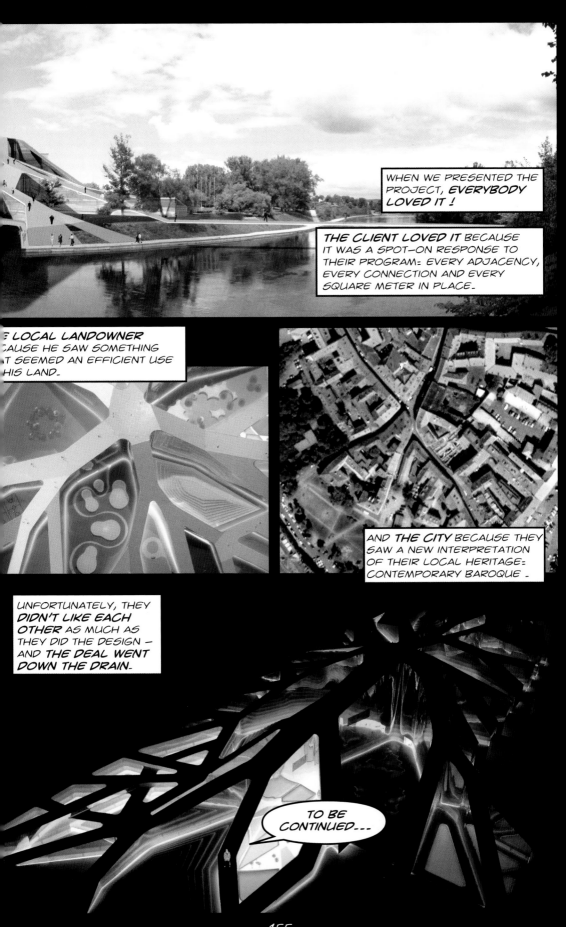

WHEN WE PRESENTED THE PROJECT, *EVERYBODY LOVED IT !*

THE CLIENT LOVED IT BECAUSE IT WAS A SPOT—ON RESPONSE TO THEIR PROGRAM= EVERY ADJACENCY, EVERY CONNECTION AND EVERY SQUARE METER IN PLACE.

E LOCAL LANDOWNER CAUSE HE SAW SOMETHING T SEEMED AN EFFICIENT USE HIS LAND.

AND *THE CITY* BECAUSE THEY SAW A NEW INTERPRETATION OF THEIR LOCAL HERITAGE= CONTEMPORARY BAROQUE.

UNFORTUNATELY, THEY *DIDN'T LIKE EACH OTHER* AS MUCH AS THEY DID THE DESIGN — AND *THE DEAL WENT DOWN THE DRAIN.*

TO BE CONTINUED---

BAROQUE CITY
UPSIDE DOWN

VILNIUS WORLD TRADE CENTER 2

WTC2

HALF A YEAR AFTER THE RISE AND FALL OF OUR FIRST VILNIUS WORLD TRADE CENTER, WE WERE CALLED UP BY THE CLIENT AGAIN.

THEY HAD FOUND **A NEW SITE** THAT COULD FIT THE PROGRAM.

THE TIME WAS SHORT BUT SINCE THEY HAD LOVED OUR FIRST SCHEME, THEY REALLY **WANTED US TO REPEAT IT ON THE NEW SITE.**

NEW SITE

WE WERE NOSTALGIC ABOUT OUR FLING WITH CONTEMPORARY BAROQUE AND PRAYED THE NEW SITE WOULD BE AN EASY FIT...

APPARENTLY, THERE IS NO GOD...

THE NEW SITE WAS SEVERED BY **A HIGHWAY DOWN THE MIDDLE.** THE PROGRAM WOULDN'T FIT IN A LOW STRUCTURE BECAUSE THE HIGHWAY OCCUPIED ALMOST HALF THE LAND, **MAKING A UNIFIED NETWORK IMPOSSIBLE !**

WE DIDN'T HAVE TIME TO COME UP WITH SOMETHING INTERESTING FROM SCRATCH !

IN A POTENT COCKTAIL OF LAZINESS, OPPORTUNISM AND SHEER PANIC, **WE TURNED THE ENTIRE PROJECT UPSIDE DOWN.**

158

BY TRANSFORMING THE SINGLE PEAK INTO THREE FEET, WE COULD CREATE A STABLE STRUCTURE MORE LIKE THE CANOPY THAN THE ROOTS OF A TREE. THE ELEVATED STRUCTURE WOULD LEAVE THE **GROUND OPEN** FOR **PARKING** AND **PARKS**.

THE ROOF WOULD FORM *A BIG NETWORK-LIKE PARK* SURROUNDED BY THE WTC'S PUBLIC PROGRAMS, LOBBIES AND RESTAURANTS.

BY *REACHING OVER THE HIGHWAY,* WE COULD CLAIM THE LAND (OR AT LEAST THE AIR) OF THE SITE LOST TO TRAFFIC.

FROM WITHIN THE STRUCTURE, YOU WOULD HAVE *VIEWS TO THE PASSING CARS BENEATH* OR THE SKY ABOVE. THE EXPANDED CANOPY WOULD FURTHER INCREASE THE PROPORTION OF ATTRACTIVE REAL ESTATE.

FROM URBAN PATTERN INSIDE-OUT, TO UPSIDE-DOWN, THE VILNIUS WORLD TRADE CENTER WILL FORM THE GATE FROM THE AIRPORT TO THE CITY CENTER.

ALTHOUGH EVOLVING ONE MUTATION FURTHER AWAY FROM ITS FOUNDING FATHERS, IT STILL UNDENIABLY CARRIES *THE CHARACTERISTICS OF ITS ORIGINAL DNA.*

THE 7 PEAKS OF AZERBAIJAN

ZIRA ZERO ISLAND

ZIR

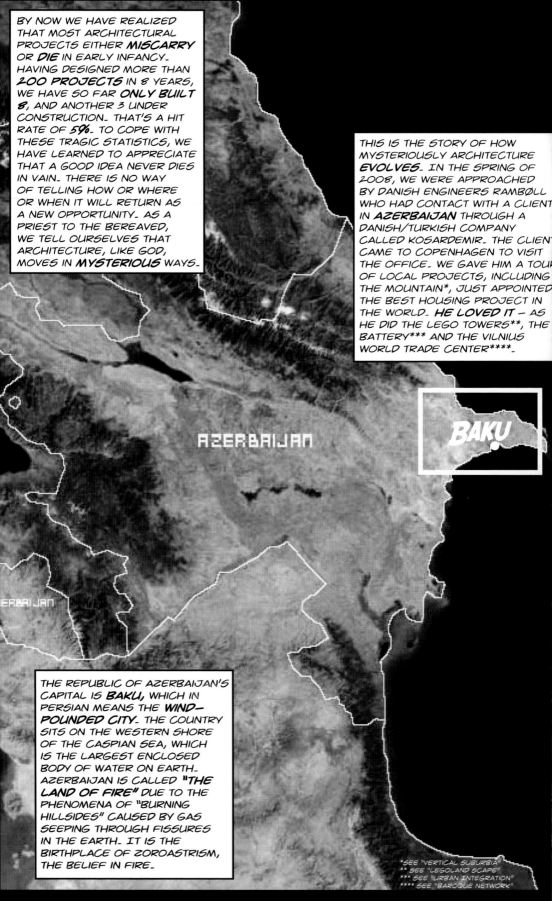

BY NOW WE HAVE REALIZED THAT MOST ARCHITECTURAL PROJECTS EITHER **MISCARRY** OR **DIE** IN EARLY INFANCY. HAVING DESIGNED MORE THAN **200 PROJECTS** IN 8 YEARS, WE HAVE SO FAR **ONLY BUILT 8**, AND ANOTHER 3 UNDER CONSTRUCTION. THAT'S A HIT RATE OF **5%**. TO COPE WITH THESE TRAGIC STATISTICS, WE HAVE LEARNED TO APPRECIATE THAT A GOOD IDEA NEVER DIES IN VAIN. THERE IS NO WAY OF TELLING HOW OR WHERE OR WHEN IT WILL RETURN AS A NEW OPPORTUNITY. AS A PRIEST TO THE BEREAVED, WE TELL OURSELVES THAT ARCHITECTURE, LIKE GOD, MOVES IN **MYSTERIOUS** WAYS.

THIS IS THE STORY OF HOW MYSTERIOUSLY ARCHITECTURE **EVOLVES**. IN THE SPRING OF 2008, WE WERE APPROACHED BY DANISH ENGINEERS RAMBØLL WHO HAD CONTACT WITH A CLIENT IN **AZERBAIJAN** THROUGH A DANISH/TURKISH COMPANY CALLED KOSARDEMIR. THE CLIENT CAME TO COPENHAGEN TO VISIT THE OFFICE. WE GAVE HIM A TOUR OF LOCAL PROJECTS, INCLUDING THE MOUNTAIN*, JUST APPOINTED THE BEST HOUSING PROJECT IN THE WORLD. **HE LOVED IT** – AS HE DID THE LEGO TOWERS**, THE BATTERY*** AND THE VILNIUS WORLD TRADE CENTER****.

AZERBAIJAN

BAKU

ERBAIJAN

THE REPUBLIC OF AZERBAIJAN'S CAPITAL IS **BAKU,** WHICH IN PERSIAN MEANS THE **WIND-POUNDED CITY**. THE COUNTRY SITS ON THE WESTERN SHORE OF THE CASPIAN SEA, WHICH IS THE LARGEST ENCLOSED BODY OF WATER ON EARTH. AZERBAIJAN IS CALLED **"THE LAND OF FIRE"** DUE TO THE PHENOMENA OF "BURNING HILLSIDES" CAUSED BY GAS SEEPING THROUGH FISSURES IN THE EARTH. IT IS THE BIRTHPLACE OF ZOROASTRISM, THE BELIEF IN FIRE.

*SEE "VERTICAL SUBURBIA"
** SEE "LEGOLAND SCAPE"
*** SEE "URBAN INTEGRATION"
**** SEE "BAROQUE NETWORK"

HE TOLD US THAT THE **CAUCASUS** ARE THE ALPS OF CENTRAL ASIA. SPECIFICALLY, THE **7 PEAKS** ARE DEEPLY ROOTED IN THE HEARTS OF THE AZERI PEOPLE. AS A YOUNG POST—SOVIET DEMOCRACY IN THE MIDDLE OF REDEFINING ITS NATIONAL IDENTITY, THEIR **DRAMATIC LANDSCAPE** IS A BIG POINT OF REFERENCE.

HE ALSO TOLD US ABOUT THE **ISLAND OF ZIRA**. BAKU IS ORGANIZED LIKE THE AZERBAIJANI FLAG: 3 STRIPES OF BLUE, RED AND GREEN (RGB) AND IN THE MIDDLE A CRESCENT AND A STAR. BAKU IS A CRESCENT BAY OVERLOOKING AN ISLAND, ZIRA, AT THE ENTRANCE OF THE BAY.

BECAUSE OF ITS **CENTRAL POSITION**, ZIRA HAD BEEN A NAVAL BASE, BUT IT WAS THEN ABANDONED. AND THE PRESIDENT HAD NEVER ALLOWED DEVELOPMENT ON IT, BECAUSE A FAILURE WOULD POTENTIALLY RUIN THE **CASPIAN VIEW** FOR THE ENTIRE CITY.

AZERBAIJAN

ZIRA ISLAND

HE ASKED US TO CREATE A **NEW CITY** FOR CULTURE AND LEISURE THAT WOULD MAKE THE **7 PEAKS OF AZERBAIJAN** MANIFEST FROM A DISTANCE.

WE SAID WE WOULD DO IT ON ONE CONDITION: IF WE COULD
MAKE IT A ZERO-EMISSION ISLAND — *ZIRA ZERO ISLAND*.

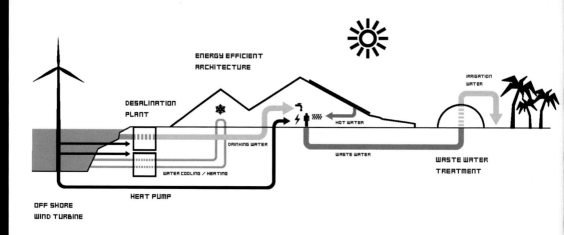

SINCE THE ISLAND HAD **NO EXISTING INFRASTRUCTURE**, WE WOULD HAVE TO PROVIDE
ALL RESOURCES: ENERGY, HEAT AND WATER. WITH ABUNDANT SUN, WIND AND SALTWATE
WE WOULD BE ABLE NOT ONLY TO CREATE THE **IMAGE** OF MOUNTAINS, BUT RATHER
AN ENTIRE **ECOSYSTEM** OF PEAKS AND VALLEYS, CREEKS AND PONDS, SHADE AND
SHELTER. THE MOUNTAIN AS A **METAPHOR** AS WELL AS A **MODEL** FOR A NEW TOWN.

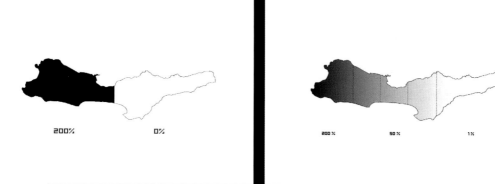

THE ISLAND ITSELF IS **HALF FLAT, HALF HILLY**. WE CONCENTRATE THE URBAN
DEVELOPMENT ON THE FLAT PART CREATING THE **ARTIFICIAL TOPOGRAPHY** WHE
NONE EXISTS — WHILE LEAVING THE **NATURAL LANDSCAPE** INTACT.

THE URBAN HALF IS DISTRIBUTED AMONGST **7 MOUNTAINS**
CONNECTED BY **PARKS AND PROMENADES**.

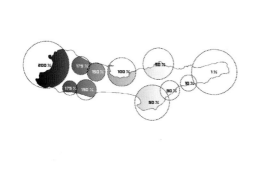
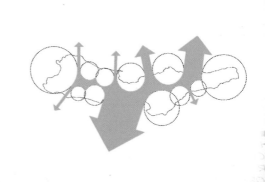

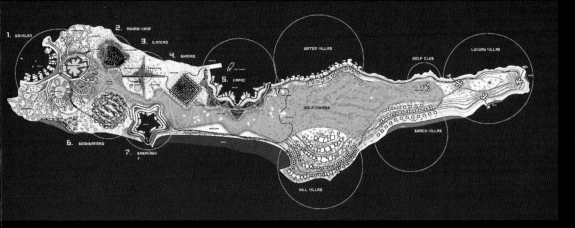

THE LANDSCAPING OF THE ISLAND IS DERIVED FROM **WIND SIMULATIONS** OF THE **MICROCLIMATES** CREATED BY THE MOUNTAINS. SWIRLY PATTERNS CREATED BY THE WIND MOVING ITS WAY THROUGH THE SEVEN PEAKS INFORM THE PLANTING OF TREES AND THE DESIGN OF PUBLIC SPACES. WHERE THE **WINDS AND TURBULENCE** ARE STRONGEST, THE TREES BECOME **DENSER**, CREATING LOWER WIND SPEEDS AND A **COMFORTABLE** OUTDOOR LEISURE CLIMATE.

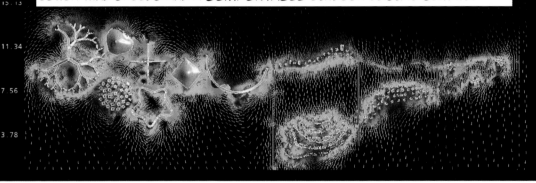

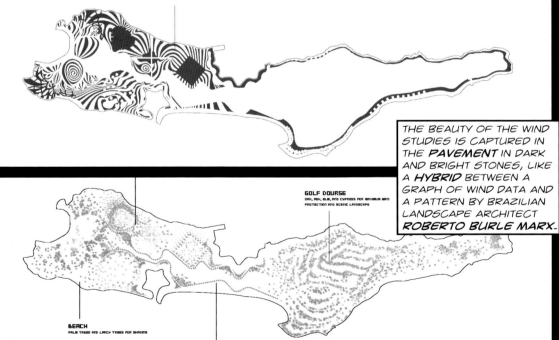

THE BEAUTY OF THE WIND STUDIES IS CAPTURED IN THE **PAVEMENT** IN DARK AND BRIGHT STONES, LIKE A **HYBRID** BETWEEN A GRAPH OF WIND DATA AND A PATTERN BY BRAZILIAN LANDSCAPE ARCHITECT **ROBERTO BURLE MARX.**

HE 7 MOUNTAINS ARE EACH AN **ARCHITECTURAL TRANSLATION** OF A SPECIFIC OUNTAIN INTO BUILT FORM. RATHER THAN WORKING WITH VARIATIONS OF A **CUBE** R VARIOUS **RECTANGLES** (LIKE MOST ARCHITECTS), WE STARTED WITH ANOTHER, ORE **COMPLEX** GIVEN SHAPE THIS TIME.

= ZERO ISLAND

1M

1M

⚡ 850 KW

x **20.000**

= 17.000.000

KWH/YEAR

SUN – THE BUILDINGS OF THE ISLAND ARE HEATED AND COOLED BY **HEAT PUMPS** CONNECTED TO THE SURROUNDING CASPIAN SEA. **SOLAR HEAT PANELS** INTEGRATED IN THE ARCHITECTURE CREATE A STEADY SUPPLY OF HOT WATER, WHILE **PHOTOVOLTAICS** ON STRATEGICALLY LOCATED FACADES AND ROOFTOPS POWER DAYTIME FUNCTIONS SUCH AS SWIMMING POOLS AND AQUA PARKS.

WATER – WASTEWATER AND STORMWATER ARE COLLECTED AND LED TO A WASTE WATER TREATMENT PLANT, WHERE IT IS THEN CLEANED PROCESSED AND **RECYCLED** FOR IRRIGATION. THE SOLID PARTS OF THE WASTE WATER ARE PROCESSED, **COMPOSTED** AND FINALLY TURNED INTO TOPSOIL, **FERTILIZING** THE ISLAND. THE CONSTANT IRRIGATION AND FERTILIZATION OF THE ISLAND SUPPORTS THE **LUSH GREEN** CONDITION OF A TROPICAL ISLAND, WITH A MINIMAL ECOLOGICAL FOOTPRINT.

12.000.000 M3
NEEDED

=

= Ø 90

4

WIND – ZIRA ZERO ISLAND BENEFITS FROM THE FACT THAT BAKU IS **"THE CITY OF WIND"**. BY HARVESTING THE WIND ENERGY THROUGH AN OFFSHORE **WIND FARM**, THE ISLAND WILL HAVE ITS OWN CO_2–NEUTRAL POWER SUPPLY. ALSO, LOCATING THE WIND TURBINES ON THE SEA, TRANSFORMS THE **EXISTING** OFFSHORE OIL PLATFORMS AND FOUNDATIONS IN BAKU INTO A MORE SUSTAINABLE FUTURE OF **WIND TURBINE PLATFORMS**.

90 M

x **16** = 140.000.00

KWH/YEAR

⚡ 3 MW

THE FIRST MOUNTAIN, **SAVALAN**, IS CONCEIVED AS A **NETWORK** OF DIFFERENT PROGRAMS FROM THE HOTEL AT THE CENTER, **BRANCHING** OUT INTO APARTMENTS AND ROW HOUSES AND FINALLY **INVERTING** INTO A STREET GRID WITH SHOPS, BARS AND CAFES.

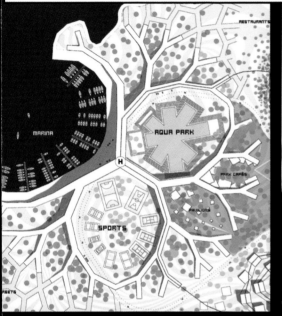

SAVALAN

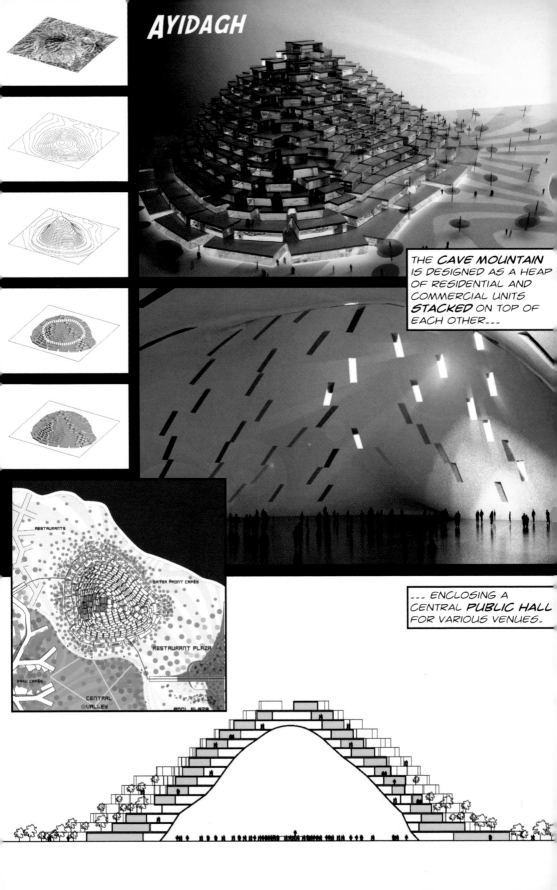

AYIDAGH

THE *CAVE MOUNTAIN* IS DESIGNED AS A HEAP OF RESIDENTIAL AND COMMERCIAL UNITS *STACKED* ON TOP OF EACH OTHER...

... ENCLOSING A CENTRAL *PUBLIC HALL* FOR VARIOUS VENUES.

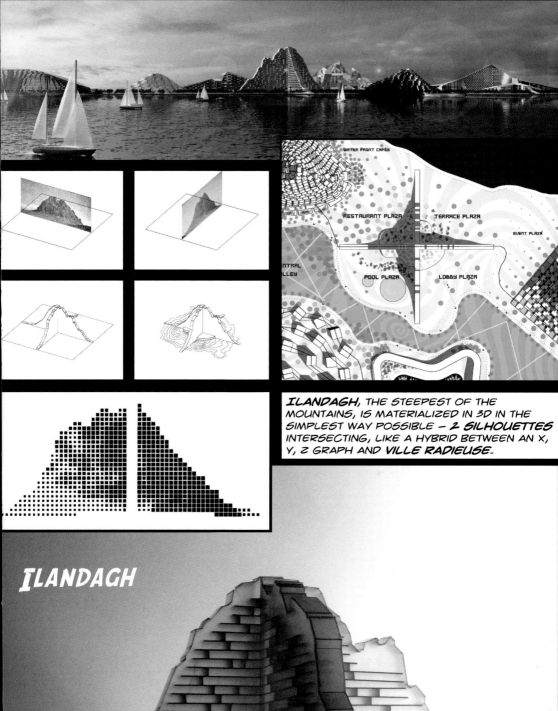

ILANDAGH, THE STEEPEST OF THE MOUNTAINS, IS MATERIALIZED IN 3D IN THE SIMPLEST WAY POSSIBLE — *2 SILHOUETTES* INTERSECTING, LIKE A HYBRID BETWEEN AN X, Y, Z GRAPH AND *VILLE RADIEUSE.*

WATER FRONT CAFÉS

RESTAURANT PLAZA   TERRACE PLAZA

EVENT PLAZA

CENTRAL VALLEY

POOL PLAZA   LOBBY PLAZA

ILANDAGH

THE **KING'S MOUNTAIN** IS A SOFT SILHOUETTE **PERFORATED** BY SQUARE COURTYARDS. FROM GOOGLE EARTH THE MOUNTAIN APPEARS LIKE A **GIANT CHESS BOARD**, AN HOMAGE TO **KASPAROV**, NATIVE SON OF BAKU.

SHAHDAGH

THE **WEDDING CROWN MOUNTAIN** IS WRAPPED AROUND THE **EXISTING PORT.** USING THE STRUCTURAL PRINCIPLES OF URUGUAYAN ENGINEER **ELADIO DIESTE,** THE THIN SLAB ACHIEVES **STABILITY** BY FORMING A SINE CURVE AT GROUND LEVEL. THE RESULTING DEFORMATIONS CREATE **HILLSIDE TERRACES** AND **COVERED CAVES** ON BOTH SIDES OF THE MOUNTAIN.

KAPAZ

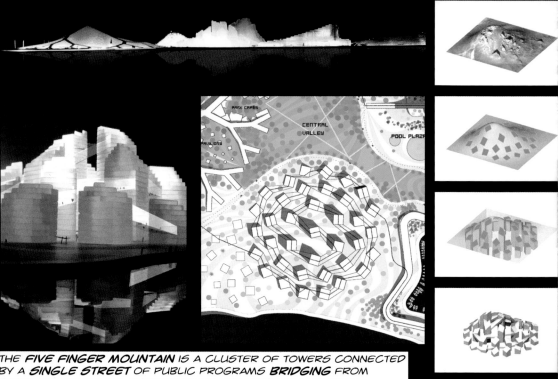

THE **FIVE FINGER MOUNTAIN** IS A CLUSTER OF TOWERS CONNECTED BY A **SINGLE STREET** OF PUBLIC PROGRAMS **BRIDGING** FROM TOWER TO TOWER ALL THE WAY FROM THE BASE TO THE PEAK.

BESHBARMAQ

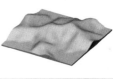

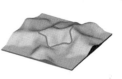

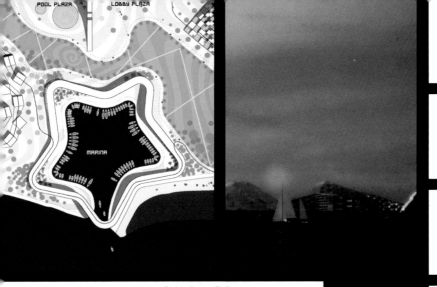

POOL PLAZA   LOBBY PLAZA

MARINA

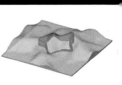

AND FINALLY, THE **WATERSHED RIDGE** IS CONCEIVED AS A **GIANT COURTYARD** WRAPPED AROUND A CENTRAL **MARINA**. THE PERIMETER BLOCK INCREASES AND DECREASES ITS HEIGHT AND **LIFTS OFF THE GROUND** TO ALLOW VISITORS TO ENTER THE MARINA FROM LAND AS WELL AS FROM THE SEA.

BABADAGH

L MOUNTAINS ARE ONNECTED WITH A ENTRAL **HIKING** ATH, MAKING IT OSSIBLE TO **CLIMB** HE **7 PEAKS** IN A NGLE DAY.

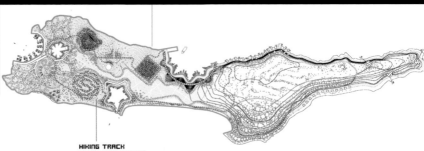

HIKING TRACK
PUBLIC PATH LEADING TO ALL SEVEN PEAKS

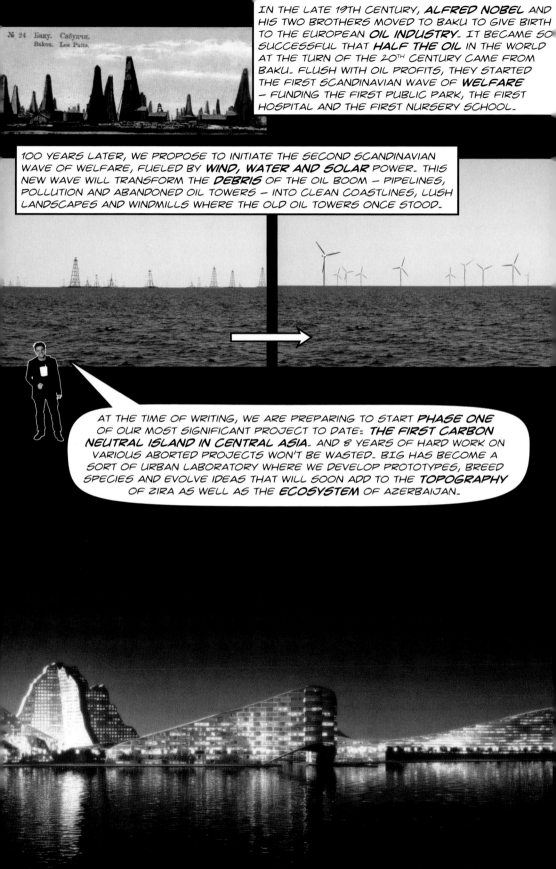

IN THE LATE 19TH CENTURY, **ALFRED NOBEL** AND HIS TWO BROTHERS MOVED TO BAKU TO GIVE BIRTH TO THE EUROPEAN **OIL INDUSTRY**. IT BECAME SO SUCCESSFUL THAT **HALF THE OIL** IN THE WORLD AT THE TURN OF THE 20TH CENTURY CAME FROM BAKU. FLUSH WITH OIL PROFITS, THEY STARTED THE FIRST SCANDINAVIAN WAVE OF **WELFARE** — FUNDING THE FIRST PUBLIC PARK, THE FIRST HOSPITAL AND THE FIRST NURSERY SCHOOL.

100 YEARS LATER, WE PROPOSE TO INITIATE THE SECOND SCANDINAVIAN WAVE OF WELFARE, FUELED BY **WIND, WATER AND SOLAR** POWER. THIS NEW WAVE WILL TRANSFORM THE **DEBRIS** OF THE OIL BOOM — PIPELINES, POLLUTION AND ABANDONED OIL TOWERS — INTO CLEAN COASTLINES, LUSH LANDSCAPES AND WINDMILLS WHERE THE OLD OIL TOWERS ONCE STOOD.

AT THE TIME OF WRITING, WE ARE PREPARING TO START **PHASE ONE** OF OUR MOST SIGNIFICANT PROJECT TO DATE: **THE FIRST CARBON NEUTRAL ISLAND IN CENTRAL ASIA**. AND 8 YEARS OF HARD WORK ON VARIOUS ABORTED PROJECTS WON'T BE WASTED. BIG HAS BECOME A SORT OF URBAN LABORATORY WHERE WE DEVELOP PROTOTYPES, BREED SPECIES AND EVOLVE IDEAS THAT WILL SOON ADD TO THE **TOPOGRAPHY** OF ZIRA AS WELL AS THE **ECOSYSTEM** OF AZERBAIJAN.

NOT TO MENTION THE FUTURE POSTCARDS FROM BAKU.

SUPERHARBOUR
★HAU

THE BIG PICTURE

Not so long ago, and not so far away... a group of architects decided to use their collective creativity and competence. Not on small decorative details - but on big questions -

WHY DO WE SPEND OUR **BEST PLACES** ON THE MOST **NOISY** AND **DUSTY** ACTIVITIES ?

WHY ARE WE PUSHED TO THE **PERIPHERY,** WHEN WE WANT TO LIVE TOGETHER IN THE **CENTRES ?**

DO 5 MILLION PEOPLE NEED MORE THAN ONE HARBOUR---

AND **COULD ONE PORT BE THE GATE TO---**

---300 MILLION PEOPLE ?

COULD DENMARK CREATE A **BALTIC SUPERHARBOUR ?**

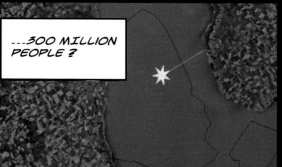

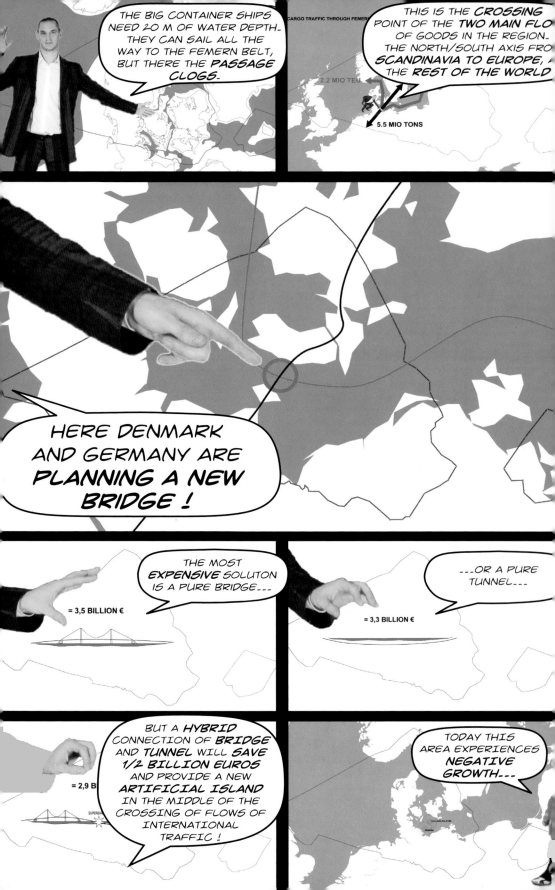

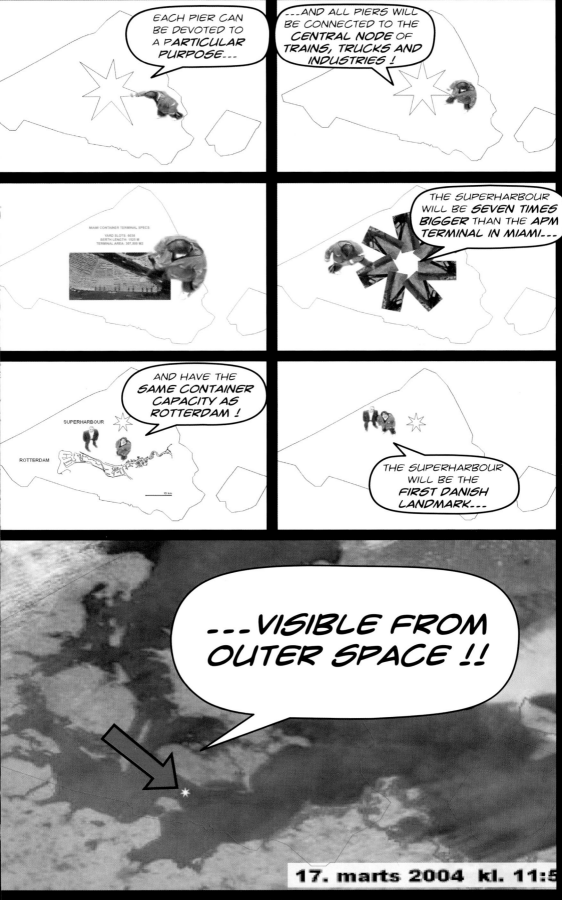

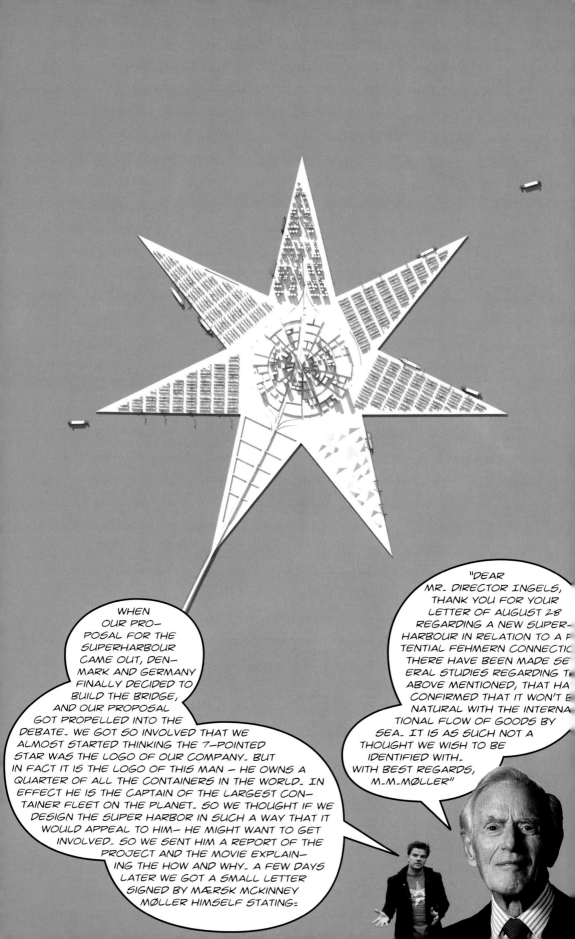

URBAN TYPOGRAPHY

THE **TRANSFORMATION OF HARBOUR CITIES** FROM INDUSTRY TO CULTURE, LEISURE AND LIVING THAT WE IDENTIFIED AND ATTEMPTED TO ACCELERATE WITH THE **SUPERHARBOUR** WOULD TURN OUT TO BE LIKE A PREMATURE JOB DESCRIPTION FOR OUR FOLLOWING YEARS.

EVEN THOUGH WE DIDN'T GET TO REALIZE THE SUPERHARBOUR, THE FIRST JOB WE DID GET TO REALIZE — THE HARBOUR BATH — WAS A DIRECT RESULT OF THE **DEINDUSTRIALIZATION OF THE URBAN WATERFRONTS.**

SHORTLY AFTER THAT, WE WERE INVITED TO PLAN THE **GRADUAL INTRODUCTION OF URBAN PROGRAMS IN AND AROUND VEJLE HARBOR.** SET AT THE END OF VEJLE FJORD, THE HARBOR HAS PREVENTED THE URBAN LIFE OF VEJLE FROM EVER REACHING THE SEA.

A HIGHWAY CROSSES THE FJORD ON A 60 METER ELEVATED BRIDGE, MAKING THE HARBOR **THE CITY'S NAMETAG FOR 4 MILLION ANNUAL PASSENGERS.**

VEJLE

PART OF THE TASK CAME TO INCLUDE CREATING AN **OUTLINE FOR A NEW RESIDENTIAL PROJECT** ON THE TIP OF THE HARBOUR: A THIN SLICE OF LAND WEDGED BETWEEN A HIGH SCHOOL, A FOOTBALL FIELD AND THE SEA.

A PROJECT WITH SUFFICIENT DENSITY AND NORMAL HEIGHT (4 FLOORS) WOULD HAVE TO BE **A LONG SLAB**, COMPLETELY **BLOCKING BOTH VIEW AND ACCESS**. IF WE INSTEAD BUILT HALF AS WIDE AND TWICE AS TALL, WE WOULD CREATE A DOTTED LINE OF **5 LITTLE TOWERS**.

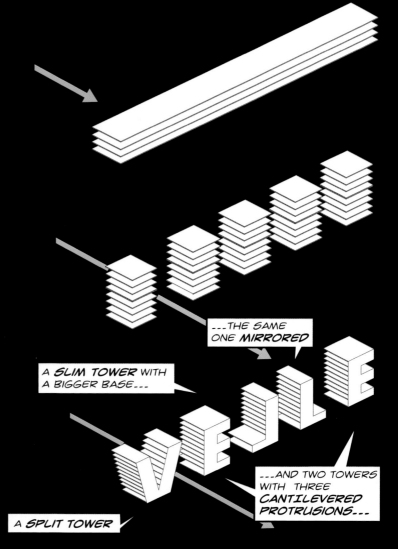

ALTHOUGH PERFECT IN THEORY, **THE RESULT WAS DEPRESSINGLY BORING** – THE EPITOME OF AN UNINSPIRED SUBURBAN RESIDENTIAL PROJECT. WAS THIS GENERIC MODERNISM THE RIGHT WAY TO **GREET THE 4 MILLION ANNUAL PASSERSBY ?**

HOW COULD WE ADD **LOCAL SPECIFICITY ?**

---THE SAME ONE **MIRRORED**

A **SLIM TOWER** WITH A BIGGER BASE...

---AND TWO TOWERS WITH THREE **CANTILEVERED PROTRUSIONS**...

BY GENTLY MANIPULATING **THE FIVE TOWERS INTO THREE TYPOLOGIES**...

A **SPLIT TOWER**

---WE TRANSFORMED THEM INTO A **GIANT TOWN SIGN** – LITERALLY ! TO OUR SURPRISE IT WORKED. **WE LOVED IT.**

IDENTITY DESIGNERS AND BRAND CONSULTANTS THOUGHT WE HAD INVENTED A NEW BRANCH OF THEIR FIELD. **URBAN TYPOGRAPHY !**

W TOWERS

SPLIT PERSONALITY

NICKNAMED THE CITY OF A **HUNDRED SPIRES**, PRAGUE'S PANORAMA OF HISTORICAL TOWERS IS A **SACRED TREASURE** TO ITS ARCHITECTS.

THE PRAGUE CASTLE'S COMPOSITE SILHOUETTE OF MULTIPLE SPIRES HOLDS THE RECIPE OF WHAT COULD BE A WELCOME ADDITION TO THE LOCAL SKYLINE — A **BUNDLE OF SLIM TOWERS** RATHER **THAN A BIG FAT SLAB.**

WHEN ASKED TO DO A **MIXED-USE TOWER** IN ~~CENSORED~~ — A FORMER-FACTORY-TURNED-URBAN-NEIGHBORHOOD — WE WERE FACED WITH THE DILEMMA OF HOW TO DO A PROJECT WITH A **PROFITABLE FOOTPRINT** THAT WOULD COMPLY WITH **THE PROPORTIONS OF THE PRAGUE PANORAMA.**

THE BRIEF CONSISTED OF **RETAIL** ON THE BOTTOM FLOORS, **OFFICES** ABOVE AND **CONDOS** AT THE TOP: THREE PROGRAMS OF **COMPLETELY DIFFERENT** IDEAL PROPORTIONS.

SO WE DECIDED TO MAKE A **BIG EFFICIENT SLAB...**

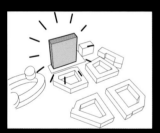

...CREATING A **NOISE BARRIER** THAT PROTECTS THE CITY FROM THE NOISY TRAFFIC. SHAPED BY THE SITE, IT WAS A SQUARE SLAB 80 METERS WIDE AND TALL AND 20 METERS DEEP.

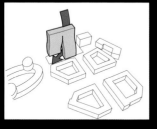

TO OPEN THE SITE TO THE SUBWAY, WE **TWISTED THE SLAB OPEN,** LEAVING A SLIT FOR A BRIDGE TO PASS THROUGH FROM STATION TO STREET. THE TWO HALVES WERE 800 M² EACH, PERFECT FOR OFFICES.

THE SPLIT SLAB WAS **ROTATED TO REFIT THE SITE**, AT THE SAME TIME OPTIMIZING THE ORIENTATION OF THE APARTMENT PROGRAMS TOWARDS EAST AND WEST, FOR BETTER **VIEWS** AND **SUNLIGHT.**

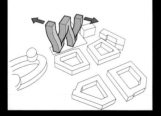

AS A LAST MANIPULATION, THE SLAB WAS CUT OPEN WITH **TWO INCISIONS** TO CREATE A PERFECT 400 M² FLOOR PLAN FOR CORNER APARTMENTS IN THE UPPER PART OF THE BUILDING.

THE RESULT IS
A BUILDING THAT
GRADUALLY
TRANSFORMS FROM
ONE TYPOLOGY TO
THE OTHER, FROM THE
GROUND FLOOR TO
THE PENTHOUSE,
ASSUMING IDEAL
LAYOUTS FOR VARIOUS
PROGRAMS: RETAIL,
OFFICE AND HOUSING.

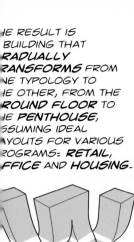

IN THE MIDDLE,
ALL FLOOR PLANS
INTERSECT, CREATING A
600 M² COMMON FLOOR
FOR COMMUNAL
FACILITIES, CANTEEN
AND CONFERENCE
ROOMS.

THE RESULTING
BUILDING IS A FORM OF
SPLIT PERSONALITY
ARCHITECTURE: BOTH
A SUPER-EFFICIENT
SOVIET SLAB AND
CZECH CLUSTER OF
TOWERS.

FROM EAST/WEST,
A WALL OF
PROGRAM.

FROM NORTH/SOUTH,
A CHANDELIER OF
SPIRES.

AS A BONUS, THE TOWER FORMS
A GIANT W FOR ~~CENSORED~~, AN
ACCIDENTAL REALIZATION OF
OUR ABORTED ATTEMPT AT
URBAN TYPOGRAPHY.

TWISTED MINDS

IN THE BEGINNING OF THE MILLENNIUM, WE DID A MASTER PLAN IN AN ARRANGED MARRIAGE WITH THE DUTCH LANDSCAPE ARCHITECT GURU, ADRIAN GEUZE OF **WEST 8**.

THE SCHEME BECAME A SCANDINAVIAN REMAKE OF THEIR GREAT **BORNEO SPORENBURG MASTER PLAN**, COMBINING DENSE ROWHOUSES WITH SO-CALLED SILO TOWERS.

DURING THE HECTIC HOURS OF DEADLINE AND LAST MINUTE DECISIONS, WE TOSSED TWO SLABS INTO THE MODEL, ECHOING THE NEIGHBORING **WAREHOUSE TYPOLOGIES**.

TO MAKE THEM "SPECIAL", WE **TWISTED** THEM INTO TWO **FANS** OF STACKED FLOORS.

WE WON THE COMPETITION, AND SINCE WE WERE **ARCHITECTS**, AND WEST 8 **URBANISTS**, THEY WENT AHEAD TO DETAIL THE **MASTER PLAN**, WHILE WE WERE ASKED TO DETAIL THE **FAN BUILDINGS** FOR THE FIRST PHASE. THE CLIENTS SEEMED TO BE FANS OF THE FAN BUILDINGS, SO NOW WE HAD TO FIGURE OUT HOW (AND WHY) TO DO THEM.

DENMARK IS THE CULTURE OF **CONSENSUS** AND **EQUALITY**.

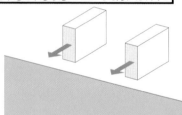

SO THE HARBOR FRONT IS DOMINATED BY BUILDINGS **PERPENDICULAR** TO THE WATER — ENSURING THAT NO ONE MONOPOLISES THE VIEW, GIVING EVERYBODY AN **EQUALLY GOOD** (OR BAD ?) **VIEW OF THE WATER**.

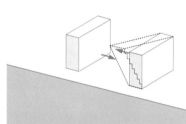

HONORING THE TRADITION, WE PROPOSED TO **TWIST** THE PERPENDICULAR SLABS TO ORIENT THE APARTMENTS TOWARDS THE SOUTHWEST, FOCUSING THEIR VIEWS MORE DIRECTLY ON THE **WATER**.

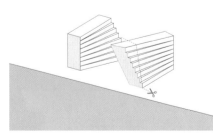

WE THEN **TRIMMED THE RIGHT FAN** BUILDING TO FURTHER IMPROVE THE **VIEW** OF THE LEFT ONE.

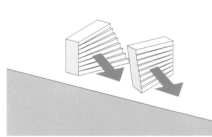

THE RESULT WAS , WITH SOUTHWEST-FACING TERRACES OVERLOOKING THE WATER, AND LEANING TO THE NORTH.

THE TWIST CREATED AN OBVIOUS CHALLENGE: **HOW TO BUILD A SLAB LEANING 26 METERS TO ONE SIDE, WITHOUT IT TUMBLING OVER ?**

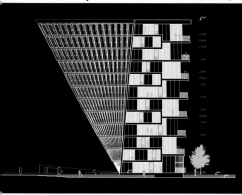

AFTER RUNNING THROUGH VARIOUS INCREASINGLY STRUCTURALLY AND/OR ECONOMICALLY UNREALISTIC OPTIONS, WE FOUND THE SOLUTION IN THE MOST UNEXPECTED PLACE: **THE KIDS' ROOM.**

THE DANISH DESIGN CLASSIC, THE **TRIP TRAP CHAIR,** WAS LIKE A STRUCTURAL MODEL OF OUR DESIGN.

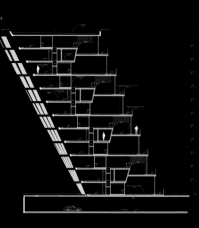

THE TWO BUILDINGS WERE SITTING ON A **SUNKEN PLINTH OF PARKING.** THE PARTITION WALLS BETWEEN THE APARTMENTS WOULD BE COMBINED TO FORM **TILTING COLUMNS REACHING ALL THE WAY TO THE PARKING BASEMENT.**

LIKE THE BIG FOOT OF THE TRIP TRAP CHAIR, THE PARKING WOULD **PREVENT THE BUILDING FROM TUMBLING OVER.**

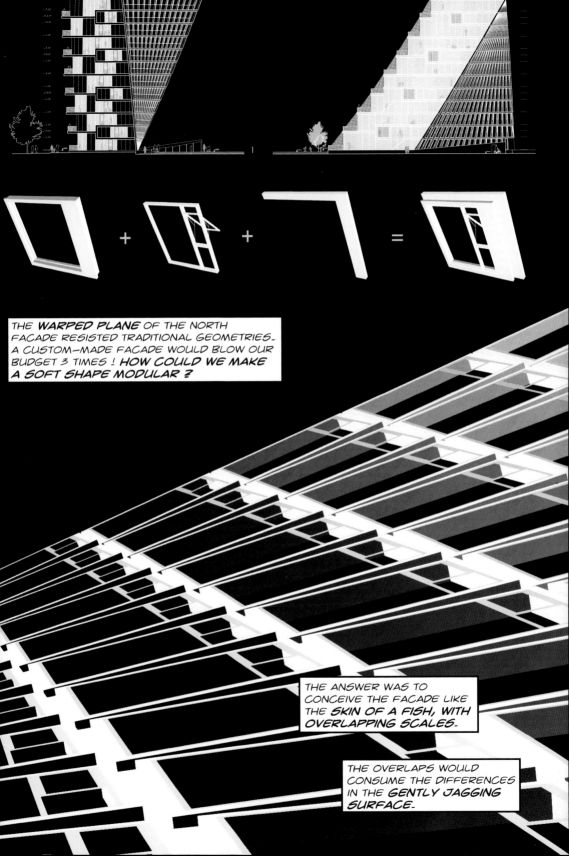

THE **WARPED PLANE** OF THE NORTH FACADE RESISTED TRADITIONAL GEOMETRIES. A CUSTOM—MADE FACADE WOULD BLOW OUR BUDGET 3 TIMES ! **HOW COULD WE MAKE A SOFT SHAPE MODULAR ?**

THE ANSWER WAS TO CONCEIVE THE FACADE LIKE THE **SKIN OF A FISH, WITH OVERLAPPING SCALES.**

THE OVERLAPS WOULD CONSUME THE DIFFERENCES IN THE **GENTLY JAGGING SURFACE.**

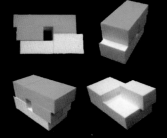

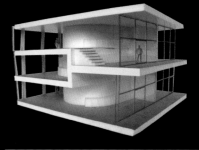

FINALLY, THE FANNING SLAB ONLY ALLOWED FOR **ELEVATOR ACCESS IN ONE END.** THE ELEVATOR WOULD BE THE **PIVOTING POINT** OF A SERIES OF CENTRAL CORRIDORS REACHING OUT TO THE **TILTED END** OF THE BUILDING.

SINCE ALL APARTMENTS NEEDED SOUTH SUN AND A VIEW, WE CONCEIVED A SECT AS A FURTHER **EVOLUTION OF** **LE CORBUSIER'S UNITÉ D'HABITATIO**

* SEE "URBAN TETRIS"

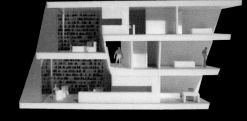

THE GENEROUS FLOORS ON THE SUNNY SIDE CONTAIN THE **PUBLIC SPACES, KITCHEN** AND **LIVING,** OVERLOOKING A GENEROUS TERRACE.

THE NORTHEAST IS DEVOTED TO **INTIMATE BEDROOMS.** THE UNITS WRAP AROUND THE CENTRAL CORRIDOR, GIVING ALL RESIDENTS A **SPLIT-LEVEL CONDO** OF TWO OR THREE LEVELS.

...O THE SOUTHWEST, AN ...-STOREY BUILDING....

...12 FLOORS TO THE NORTH EAST.

CADAVRE EXQUIS

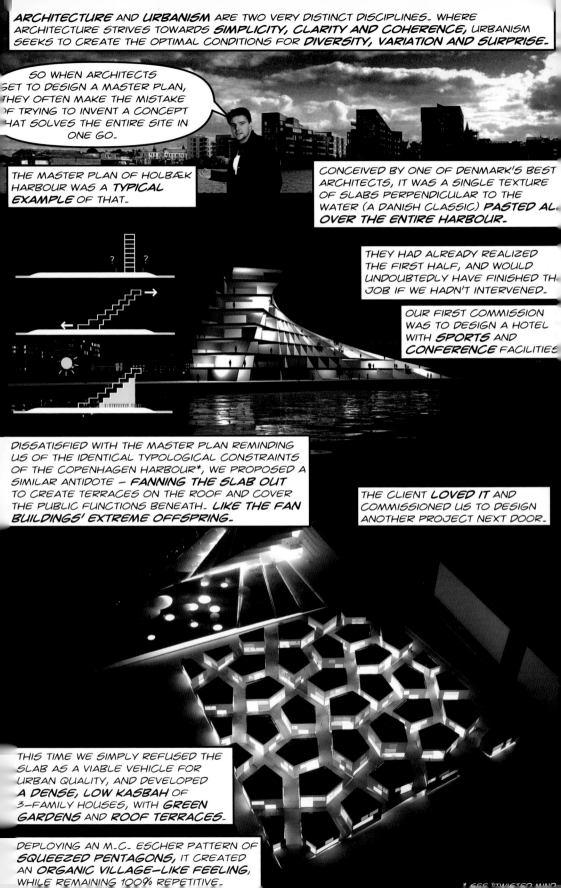

ARCHITECTURE AND URBANISM ARE TWO VERY DISTINCT DISCIPLINES. WHERE ARCHITECTURE STRIVES TOWARDS SIMPLICITY, CLARITY AND COHERENCE, URBANISM SEEKS TO CREATE THE OPTIMAL CONDITIONS FOR DIVERSITY, VARIATION AND SURPRISE.

SO WHEN ARCHITECTS GET TO DESIGN A MASTER PLAN, THEY OFTEN MAKE THE MISTAKE OF TRYING TO INVENT A CONCEPT THAT SOLVES THE ENTIRE SITE IN ONE GO.

THE MASTER PLAN OF HOLBÆK HARBOUR WAS A TYPICAL EXAMPLE OF THAT.

CONCEIVED BY ONE OF DENMARK'S BEST ARCHITECTS, IT WAS A SINGLE TEXTURE OF SLABS PERPENDICULAR TO THE WATER (A DANISH CLASSIC) PASTED ALL OVER THE ENTIRE HARBOUR.

THEY HAD ALREADY REALIZED THE FIRST HALF, AND WOULD UNDOUBTEDLY HAVE FINISHED THE JOB IF WE HADN'T INTERVENED.

OUR FIRST COMMISSION WAS TO DESIGN A HOTEL WITH SPORTS AND CONFERENCE FACILITIES.

DISSATISFIED WITH THE MASTER PLAN REMINDING US OF THE IDENTICAL TYPOLOGICAL CONSTRAINTS OF THE COPENHAGEN HARBOUR*, WE PROPOSED A SIMILAR ANTIDOTE – FANNING THE SLAB OUT TO CREATE TERRACES ON THE ROOF AND COVER THE PUBLIC FUNCTIONS BENEATH. LIKE THE FAN BUILDINGS' EXTREME OFFSPRING.

THE CLIENT LOVED IT AND COMMISSIONED US TO DESIGN ANOTHER PROJECT NEXT DOOR.

THIS TIME WE SIMPLY REFUSED THE SLAB AS A VIABLE VEHICLE FOR URBAN QUALITY, AND DEVELOPED A DENSE, LOW KASBAH OF 3-FAMILY HOUSES, WITH GREEN GARDENS AND ROOF TERRACES.

DEPLOYING AN M.C. ESCHER PATTERN OF SQUEEZED PENTAGONS, IT CREATED AN ORGANIC VILLAGE-LIKE FEELING, WHILE REMAINING 100% REPETITIVE.

* SEE "TWISTED MIND"

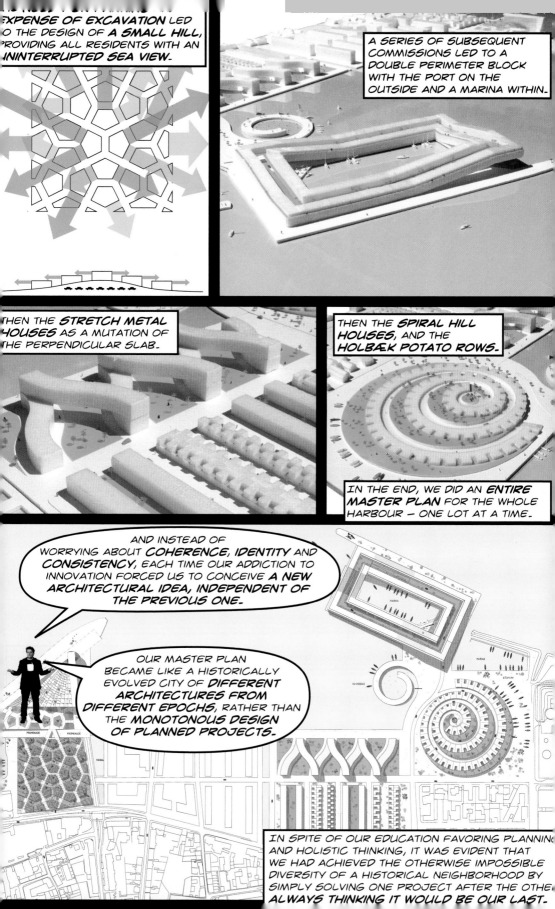

SWEPT UNDER THE CARPET

MARITIME YOUTH HOUSE

IN 2002, WE WERE INVITED TO A COMPETITION TO DESIGN A SO-CALLED **MARITIME YOUTH HOUSE** AT SUNDBY SAILING CLUB ON THE ISLAND OF AMAGER IN COPENHAGEN.

IT WAS PART JUNIOR SAILING CLUB, PART SOCIAL PROJECT, MEANT TO **TEACH THE LOCAL KIDS TO RIG SAILS AND TIE KNOTS** RATHER THAN **STEAL CARS OR PAINT GRAFFITI.**

THE SITE WAS **BEAUTIFUL**: WATER ON TWO SIDES WITH A VIEW TO A NEW LANDFILL AND MARINA...

...THE MIDDLEGROUND WINDMILLS AND SWEDEN BEYOND.

WHEN STANDING THERE IT WAS **HARD TO UNDERSTAND** WHY AMAGER IS NICKNAMED "THE SHIT ISLAND".

BUT ONCE WE READ THE GEOTECHNICAL REPORT, WE UNDERSTOOD WHERE THAT NAME CAME FROM. **THE SITE WAS VERY POLLUTED.**

A THIRD OF THE BUILDING BUDGET WAS RESERVED FOR DIGGING UP THE TOPSOIL AND DRIVING IT FOR 5 MINUTES AROUND THE CORNER TO THE LANDFILL NEXT DOOR, PAYING A DEPOSIT TAX OF **3–4 MILLION DKK.**

IT SEEMED **SURREAL** TO SPEND THAT AMOUNT OF MONEY TO MOVE THE PROBLEM 800 METERS AWAY.

SO WE HAD OUR ENGINEERS STUDY THE SOIL SAMPLES.

THEY FOUND THAT THE POLLUTANTS WERE HEAVY METALS THAT **WOULDN'T VAPORIZE OR INTERACT** WITH THE SURROUNDINGS.

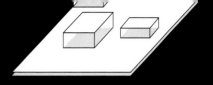

DIGGING UP THE TOPSOIL AND COVERING IT WITH CLEAN DIRT WOULD BE EQUIVALENT TO *PUTTING A LID ON THE GROUND.*

SO WE ASKED OURSELVES: WHY DON'T WE *COVER THE ENTIRE SITE* WITH A *BIG WOODEN DECK*?

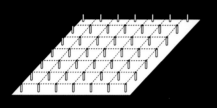

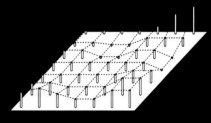

THE GIANT TERRACE WOULD ALLOW US TO *LEAVE THE POLLUTION* WHERE IT IS, RATHER THAN PUSHING THE PROBLEM AROUND, AND SAVE US THE DEPOSIT TAX TO SPEND ON PUBLIC SPACE RATHER THAN ON CLEANING UP POLLUTION.

WHEN HAMMERING PILES INTO THE GROUND WE COULD *STICK SOME OF THEM DEEPER,* CREATING A BEACH...

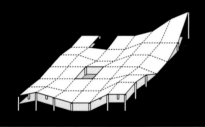

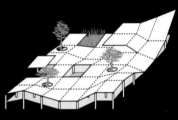

... SOME STICKING UP HIGHER, CREATING SHELTER FOR BOATSHEDS AND CLUBHOUSES. WITHOUT ACTUALLY DESIGNING ANYTHING, WE TOLD THE CLIENTS THAT THEY COULD CONSIDER THE WOODEN DECK A SORT OF *SOCIAL CARPET...*

... THAT THEY COULD *PUSH AND PULL TO ACCOMMODATE ALL THE ACTIVITIES* THEY COULD THINK OF. THIS ELASTIC CONCEPT WOULD BE ABLE TO INCORPORATE ANY DEMAND OR DESIRE.

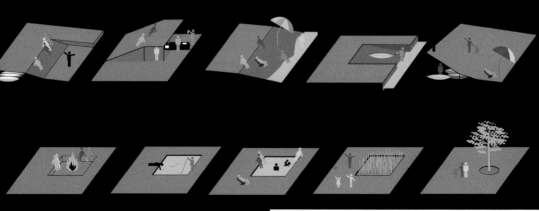

TELLING YOUR CLIENTS THAT *THEY CAN GET ANYTHING THEY WANT* TURNED OUT TO BE A SUCCESSFUL STRATEGY AND *WE WON* THE COMPETITION WITHOUT AN ACTUAL DESIGN.

IN COPENHAGEN, *ALL BUILDINGS* NEED TO LEAVE *8 METERS OF SPACE* FOR A PUBLIC PROMENADE ALONG THE WATER.

BECAUSE THE CITY SAW THE ROOF AS PUBLIC SPACE *WE COULD PUSH OUR BUILDING ALL THE WAY TO THE WATER'S EDGE.*

STEEP ENOUGH TO **SLIDE** ON WITH A NORMAL PAIR OF JEANS

THE UNDULATING LANDSCAPE HAS AN **INSTANTLY ENERGIZING IMPACT** ON KIDS, MAKING THEM RUN AROUND !

THE MARITIME YOUTH HOUSE IS A TYPICAL EXAMPLE OF OUR STRATEGY FOR **TURNING ANALYSIS INTO A** CREATIVE PROCESS

THE DRIVING IDEA IS **TURNING A PROBLEM** (THE POLLUTION) **INTO A POTENTIAL** (THE PUBLIC SPACE).

AS A RESULT, WE HAVE INFLATED THE AMBITION OF THE PROJECT *FROM A SMALL CLUBHOUSE...*

...TO A GENEROUS PUBLIC SPACE...

... WHERE NOT ONLY THE SAILORS, SOCIAL WORKERS AND KIDS HANG OUT — BUT A PLACE WHERE THE LOCALS COME TO WALK THEIR DOG, OR KISS THEIR GIRLFRIEND.

THIS ADDITIONAL GENEROSITY IS THE RESULT OF REFUSING TO MOVE THE PROBLEM, BUT RATHER *TO SWEEP IT UNDER THE* (WOODEN) *CARPET.*

DANISH MARITIME MUSEUM

TO BE
AND NOT TO BE

WHEN WE WENT TO SEE THE SITE AT THE BEGINNING OF THE COMPETITION, WE WERE QUITE *DISAPPOINTED.* OUR JOB WAS TO BUILD *A MUSEUM IN A BASEMENT.*

AN EXTREMELY *WET BASEMENT* — CONTRARY TO ITS NAME, *THE DRY DOCK WAS FULL OF WATER !*

ADDITIONALLY, BECAUSE OF THE PROXIMITY TO *HAMLET'S HOME,* WE WEREN'T EVEN ALLOWED TO STICK AN INCH ABOVE GROUND — *A SEASIDE SITE WITHOUT A SEA VIEW !*

THE PROGRAM OF THE MUSEUM WAS ALMOST *TWO TIMES* THE FOOTPRINT OF THE DOCK, FORCING US TO BUILD *ON TWO LEVELS.* THE MUSEUM WOULD BE A *CONCEALED CLAUSTROPHOBIC BASEMENT WITH NO VIEW.*

WE FOUND IT *DIFFICULT* TO FIND THE ENTHUSIASM TO START THE PROJECT.

THEN, WE SAW A PHOTO OF THE *EMPTY DOCK.* IT WAS A *MAJESTIC STRUCTURE,* 150 METERS LONG AND 25 METERS WIDE, IN THE SHAPE OF A HULL.

IT WOULD BE A *PITY* TO DROWN THIS *INDUSTRIAL CATHEDRAL* IN MUSEUM PROGRAM. OR EVEN *TO BURY IT UNDER FAUX FORTIFICATIONS.*

STUDYING THE TECHNICAL REPORTS, WE DISCOVERED THAT NOT ONLY WAS THE DRY DOCK FULL OF WATER, IT WAS **DEPENDENT** ON THE WATER TO KEEP IT FROM **COLLAPSING** !

IF EMPTIED, THE PRESSURE FROM THE SURROUNDING SOIL WOULD MAKE THE WALLS **CAVE IN.**

IN ORDER TO KEEP IT STANDING, WE WOULD HAVE TO BUILD A **NEW DOCK** INSIDE THE DOCK TO **TAKE THE PRESSURE.**

OR PLACE **PILES** FOR A NEW DOCK WALL AROUND THE DOCK.

WHAT IF WE WOULD CREATE TH NEW OUTER WALL AT SUCH A DISTANCE THAT WE COULD ACCOMMODATE THE MARITIME MUSEUM IN THE **SPACE BETWEEN THE OLD AND THE NEW DOCK WALLS** ?

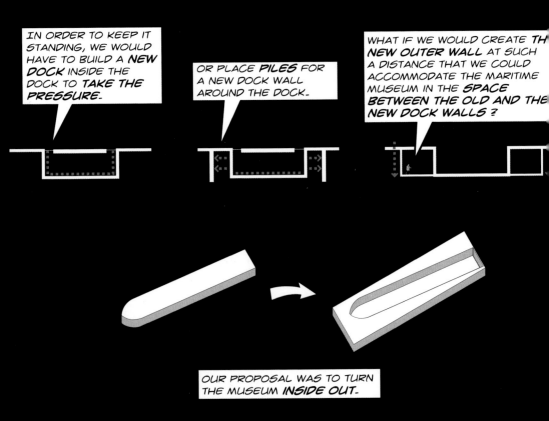

OUR PROPOSAL WAS TO TURN THE MUSEUM **INSIDE OUT.**

ALL WE WOULD HAVE TO DO WAS TO DESIGN **THREE BRIDGES** ACROSS THE DOCK.

AND A LAST BRIDGE DESCENDING INTO THE DC RICOCHETING OFF THE W. AND **LEADING PEOPLE INTO THE MUSEUM.**

ONE BRIDGE TO **STOP THE WATER FROM COMING IN** AND COMPLETE THE **WATERFRONT PROMENADE.**

ANOTHER BRIDGE TO CONNECT THE **DOCKLANDS** TO THE **CASTLE.**

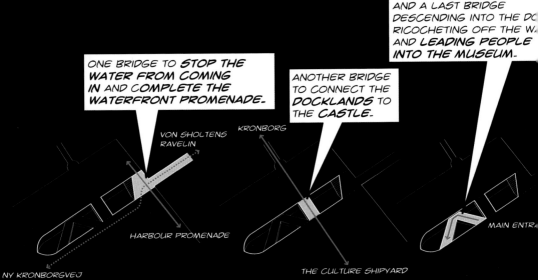

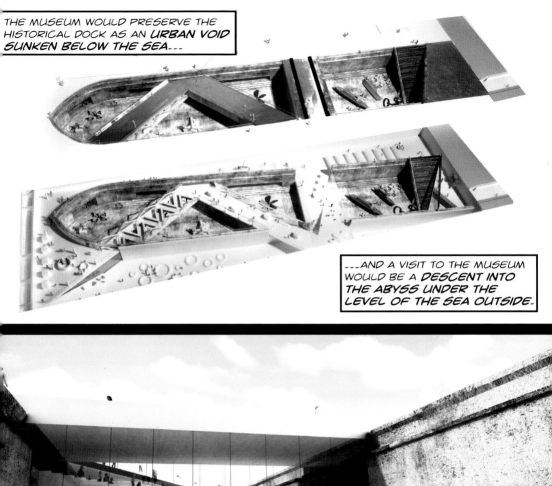

THE MUSEUM WOULD PRESERVE THE HISTORICAL DOCK AS AN **URBAN VOID** *SUNKEN BELOW THE SEA...*

...AND A VISIT TO THE MUSEUM WOULD BE A **DESCENT INTO** *THE ABYSS UNDER THE LEVEL OF THE SEA OUTSIDE.*

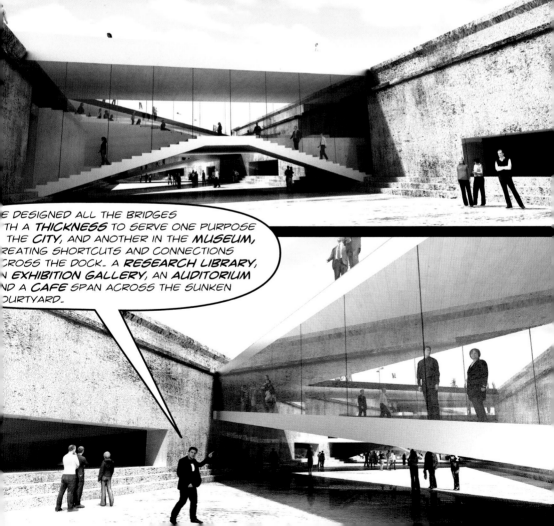

E DESIGNED ALL THE BRIDGES TH A **THICKNESS** TO SERVE ONE PURPOSE THE **CITY**, AND ANOTHER IN THE **MUSEUM**, REATING SHORTCUTS AND CONNECTIONS CROSS THE DOCK. A **RESEARCH LIBRARY**, N **EXHIBITION GALLERY**, AN **AUDITORIUM** ND A **CAFE** SPAN ACROSS THE SUNKEN OURTYARD.

DUE TO A DANISH LAW THAT DEMANDS THAT ALL WORKSPACES HAVE **DAYLIGHT** AND **VIEWS**, THE STAFF OFFICES WERE SCHEDULED TO BE LOCATED IN SOME ADJACENT BUILDINGS, FORCING ALL THE EMPLOYEES TO **MIGRATE** TO AND FROM THE MUSEUM ON A DAILY BASIS. THE NEW MUSEUM WOULD BE LIKE A **BODY** WITHOUT A **HEAD**.

NO LIGHT, NO VIEW... THAT'S ILLEGAL !

WHAT A LONG WALK !

JUST RIGHT !

WITH THE DRY DOCK TRANSFORMED INTO A **COURTYARD**, WE WERE FREE TO RETURN THE STAFF TO THE MUSEUM.

THE MUSEUM EXPERIENCE WOULD SIMPLY BE A **CONTINUOUS DESCENT** FROM THE **TOP** OF THE PIER TO THE **BOTTOM** OF THE DOCK.

BUT HOW TO CREATE AN **ENTIRE MUSEUM** ON A CONTINUOUS SLOPE? STEPS, RAMPS ?

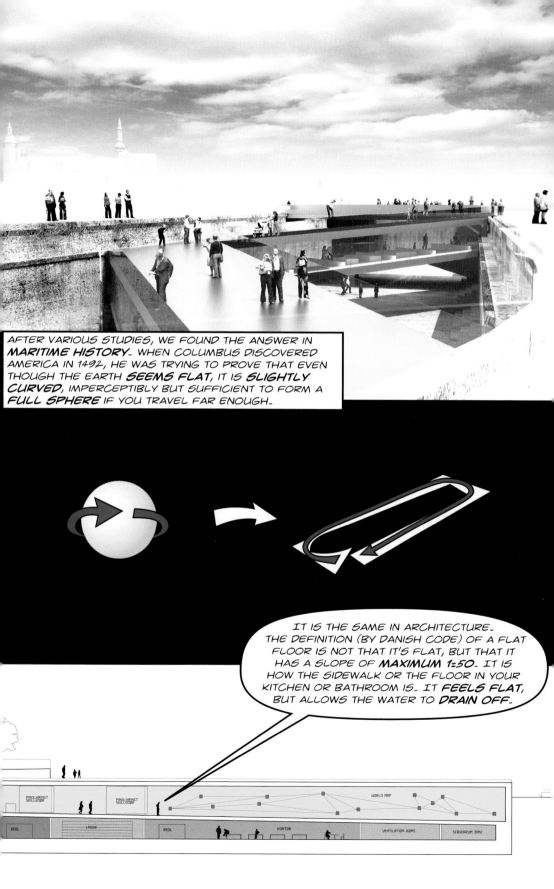

AFTER VARIOUS STUDIES, WE FOUND THE ANSWER IN
MARITIME HISTORY. WHEN COLUMBUS DISCOVERED
AMERICA IN 1492, HE WAS TRYING TO PROVE THAT EVEN
THOUGH THE EARTH **SEEMS FLAT,** IT IS **SLIGHTLY
CURVED,** IMPERCEPTIBLY BUT SUFFICIENT TO FORM A
FULL SPHERE IF YOU TRAVEL FAR ENOUGH.

IT IS THE SAME IN ARCHITECTURE.
THE DEFINITION (BY DANISH CODE) OF A FLAT
FLOOR IS NOT THAT IT'S FLAT, BUT THAT IT
HAS A SLOPE OF **MAXIMUM 1:50.** IT IS
HOW THE SIDEWALK OR THE FLOOR IN YOUR
KITCHEN OR BATHROOM IS. IT **FEELS FLAT,**
BUT ALLOWS THE WATER TO **DRAIN OFF.**

BUT GRADUALLY, THE CEILING HEIGHTS WOULD GET HIGHER AND HIGHER UNTIL...

...YOU WERE STANDING AT THE **BOTTOM** OF THE DOCK.

WHEN WE SUBMITTED THE PROJECT FOR THE COMPETITION, WE WERE QUITE SURE **THERE WAS NO WAY WE COULD EVER WIN**. ONE OF THE FIRST CONDITIONS OF THE BRIEF WAS THAT YOU HAD TO BUILT **WITHIN** THE DOCK — AND WE BUILT **AROUND** IT.

TO OUR PLEASANT SURPRISE, THE JURY SAW BEYOND THAT AND **CHOSE OUR PROJECT** IN SPITE OF THE BRIEF.

BUT THEN SOMETHING STRANGE HAPPENED. THE DANISH ARCHITECTS ASSOCIATION — OUR OWN UNION — SUED THE CLIENT FOR HAVING CHOSEN A PROJECT THAT BROKE ONE OF THE CONDITIONS OF THE BRIEF. THEY DIDN'T DISPUTE THAT OUR PROJECT WAS THE BEST SOLUTION, MERELY THAT THE CLIENT WASN'T **ALLOWED** TO CHOOSE IT.

IT MADE US **SERIOUSLY** RECONSIDER OUR MEMBERSHIP. THE ARGUMENT WAS THAT IF ALL THE OTHER COMPETITORS HAD KNOWN THAT IT WAS OK TO DO WHAT WE DID, THEY COULD HAVE **DONE THE SAME**, AND PERHAPS EVEN BETTER.

STUCK IN MARITIME METAPHORS, IT REMINDED US OF THE STORY OF THE **COLUMBUS EGG**: WHEN COLUMBUS RETURNED FROM HIS DISCOVERY OF AMERICA, HIS FELLOW EXPLORERS STARTED QUESTIONING HIS FEAT.

"**ANYONE** COULD HAVE FOUND AMERICA IF THEY WOULD HAVE JUST SAILED LONG ENOUGH", THEY SAID. IN RESPONSE, COLUMBUS TOOK AN EGG AND ASKED THE GENTLEMEN TO PLACE IT ON THE TABLE IN AN **UPRIGHT POSITION**. THINKING IT EASY, THEY STARTED TRYING TO BALANCE THE EGG.

AFTER A ROUND OF FAILED ATTEMPTS, THEY CONCLUDED **IT COULDN'T BE DONE**. COLUMBUS TOOK THE EGG AND HIT IT HARD ON THE TABLE, MAKING THE BOTTOM CRACK FLAT SO IT COULD **STAND**.

D'OH !

HEY, THAT'S **CHEATING** ! YOU DIDN'T SAY WE COULD CRACK THE SHELL. IF YOU DO THAT IT'S **EASY**.

THAT'S RIGHT. IT'S IMPOSSIBLE UNTIL SOMEONE SHOWS YOU **HOW**.

TO OUR LUCK, OUR CLIENTS WERE BY NOW SO SMITTEN BY OUR PROJECT THAT THEY **CANCELLED THE COMPETITION** AND CHOSE US AS THEIR ARCHITECTS ANYWAY. THE MUSEUM WILL STAND (OR RATHER SINK) AS A NEW FORM OF **PUBLIC SPACE** SUNKEN EIGHT METERS BELOW THE SEA AS AN **URBAN VOID** IN THE HELSINGØR DOCKLANDS.

THE STRATEGY OF THE **VOID** ALSO BECAME THE ANSWER TO THE **INHERENT DILEMMA** OF THE COMPETITION.

THE UNESCO AUTHORITIES DEMANDED THAT THE MUSEUM SHOULD BE **COMPLETELY INVISIBLE**...

WHILE THE MUSEUM WANTED A **MASTERPIECE** TO ATTRACT MAXIMUM ATTENTION...

BY TURNING THE MUSEUM INTO A **VOID**, WE COULD COMBINE THE NEED FOR **DISCRETION** WITH THE DESIRE FOR **ATTENTION** !

TO BE **AND** NOT TO BE !!

 HELSINGØR PSYCHIATRIC HOSPITAL

COLOR THERAPY

NOT SO FAR FROM HAMLET'S KRONBORG LIES **HELSINGØR HOSPITAL** ON A BEAUTIFUL GREEN MEADOW NEXT TO A LITTLE POND. IN 2002, THEY ANNOUNCED A **COMPETITION TO DESIGN A PSYCHIATRIC HOSPITAL** NEXT TO THE POND.

WE KNEW THAT THE HOSPITAL WOULD LIKELY HOST PATIENTS WITH **DEPRESSION** OR **PARANOIA**, BUT AFTER HAVING READ THE BRIEF, WE WERE CERTAIN THAT **THE STAFF WAS DEFINITELY SCHIZOPHRENIC!** THE BRIEF WAS **ONE LONG CONTRADICTION IN TERMS, EVERY PARAGRAPH A PARADOX:**

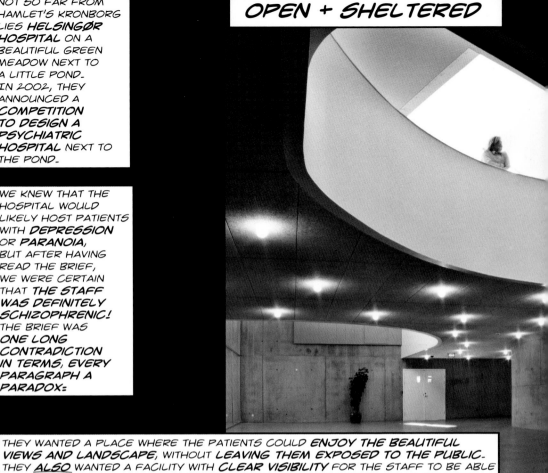

THEY WANTED A PLACE WHERE THE PATIENTS COULD *ENJOY THE BEAUTIFUL VIEWS AND LANDSCAPE*, WITHOUT *LEAVING THEM EXPOSED TO THE PUBLIC*. THEY <u>*ALSO*</u> WANTED A FACILITY WITH *CLEAR VISIBILITY* FOR THE STAFF TO BE ABLE TO MONITOR EVERYBODY *WITHOUT CREATING A BIG BROTHER ATMOSPHERE.*

CENTRALIZED + DECENTRALIZED

IT HAD TO OPERATE LIKE A HOSPITAL, **EFFICIENT** AND **RATIONAL** AS ONE SINGLE ENTITY, BUT <u>**AT THE SAME TIME**</u> LEAVE **AUTONOMY** TO ALL THE DEPARTMENTS, GIVING IT AN **INTIMATE SCALE** AND A **SAFE SENSE OF HOME.**

FREEDOM + CONTROL

THEY WANTED TO PROVIDE A **SENSE OF FREEDOM** WITHOUT INHIBITING THEIR PATIENTS' RANGE OF CHOICES, AND **AT THE SAME TIME** HAVE **TOTAL CONTROL OF WHO WOULD BE WHERE AND WHEN.**

PRIVATE + PUBLIC

THEY WANTED LOTS OF **COMMUNAL SPACES** BECAUSE SOCIAL INTERACTION IS A MAJOR TOOL IN THE REHABILITATION OF THE PATIENTS — AND **AT THE SAME TIME** THEY REQUIRED **TOTAL PRIVACY** AND SECLUSION TO PROTECT THE PATIENTS IN THEIR DAILY LIVES

WE TRIED TO CALL VARIOUS **PSYCHIATRISTS** AND **DOCTORS**, LOOKING FOR STRAIGHT ANSWERS AND FIRM GUIDELINES, BUT WE ALWAYS ENDED UP WITH **PARADOXICAL COMBINATIONS OF BOTH/AND**

ONCE AGAIN THE MOTTO OF HAMLET CAME TO MIND: OUR JOB WAS TO DESIGN SOMETHING THAT **HAD TO BE AND NOT TO BE — A HOSPITAL.**

OUR IDEA WAS TO START BY ORGANIZING **A SINGLE DORMITORY DEPARTMENT** WHERE THE **DAILY LIFE** OF THE PATIENTS HAPPENS.

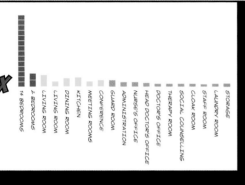

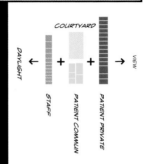

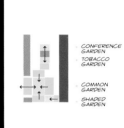

A LAST PARADOX WAS THAT THE SITE WAS **HALF THE SIZE OF THE PROGRAM** SO IT WOULD **HAVE TO BE ON TWO LEVELS,** BUT **AT THE SAME TIME,** THEY SPECIFIED THAT ALL ROOMS NEEDED **DIRECT ACCESS TO THE OUTSIDE** !?

TO RESOLVE IT, WE LET THE **LANDSCAPE OVERFLOW THE DORMITORIES,** MAKING THE COURTYARDS APPEAR AS **CUTOUTS IN THE TURF.**

LEVEL 0

LEVEL 1

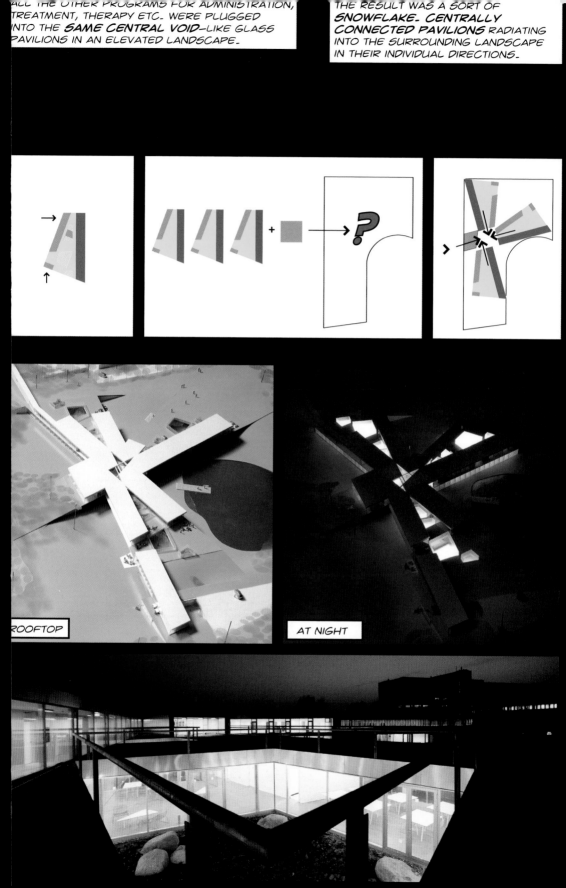

ALL THE OTHER PROGRAMS FOR ADMINISTRATION, TREATMENT, THERAPY ETC. WERE PLUGGED INTO THE **SAME CENTRAL VOID**—LIKE GLASS PAVILIONS IN AN ELEVATED LANDSCAPE.

THE RESULT WAS A SORT OF **SNOWFLAKE. CENTRALLY CONNECTED PAVILIONS** RADIATING INTO THE SURROUNDING LANDSCAPE IN THEIR INDIVIDUAL DIRECTIONS.

ROOFTOP

AT NIGHT

WE IMAGINED A SANDWICH OF **PATIENTS** ON ONE SIDE AND **STAFF** ON THE OTHER SIDE WITH ALL THE **COMMUNAL SPACES** WEDGED IN BETWEEN.

PATIENTS...

---COURTYARD---

TO INJECT **DAYLIGHT** AND **AIR**, WE INSERTED A HANDFUL OF **COURTYARDS.**

COMMUNAL SPACES...

...STAFF.

WHEN WE WON THE COMPETITION, THE DOCTORS AND NURSES COMPLIMENTED US ON OUR DIAGNOSIS OF **ARCHITECTURAL SCHIZOPHRENIA**. WE WERE THE FIRST ONES WHO EVER UNDERSTOOD THEM AND THEIR **DAILY DILEMMAS**.

ONCE THE PSYCHIATRIC HOSPITAL STARTED TO MATERIALIZE, WE ATTEMPTED TO STAY CLEAR OF THE CLASSIC HOSPITAL INTERIORS — SYSTEM CEILINGS, WHITE PAINTED WALLS AND GREY LINOLEUM FLOORS, BY STICKING TO A VERY **SOBER PALETTE OF MATERIALS:** GLASS, ALUMINUM, CONCRETE AND WOOD INTERRUPTED BY THE LUSH VEGETATION IN ALL THE COURTYARDS.

AS THE BUDGET STARTED RUNNING OUT, WE REPLACED LANDSCAPING WITH SIMPLY THROWING ALL THE **BOULDERS** DUG OUT FROM THE SITE BACK INTO THE COURTYARDS AS **SCANDINAVIAN "OBJETS TROUVÉS".**

IN THE END, OUR WOODEN FLOORS WERE **TOO EXPENSIVE,** AND WE HAD TO CHANGE THEM TO **SOMETHING CHEAPER** — PAINT.

WE WANTED TO RETAIN THE **WARMTH** AND **HAPPINESS** OF THE **WOOD** AND PROPOSED A SERIES OF **WARM COLOURS:** YELLOW, ORANGE, PINK AND RED.

OUTRAGE ! A PANEL OF **15 PSYCHIATRIC DOCTORS** AND **NURSES** SENT US STRAIGHT BACK TO THE COLOR PALETTE: THIS WAS A PSYCHIATRIC HOSPITAL. DIDN'T WE KNOW THE IMPACT OF COLORS ON THE HUMAN MIND ?

WE TRIED AGAIN WITH MORE **SEDATE COLORS.** THIS TIME A **SPRING TIME PALETTE:** GREEN, LIGHT GREEN, YELLOW, TURQUOISE.

AGAIN, WE WERE MET BY A **WALL OF PHOBIAS...**

THIS YELLOW IS TOO **BRIGHT...**

...AND TOO **WARM...**

...AND TOO **DARK...**

...AND TOO **COLD.**

DAMN ! WE'RE HEADING STRAIGHT FOR **GREY LINOLEUM...**

WE ASKED OURSELVES: IF WE AS ARCHITECTS RECOMMEND SOME COLORS, THEN WE HAVE NO AUTHORITY, AND IF WE TRY TO CLAIM EXPERTISE, WE WILL BE DISREGARDED AS **ARROGANT TASTE JUDGES WITH NO RESPECT FOR PEOPLE'S OPINIONS.**

THAT WOULDN'T WORK.

WHO COULD HELP US THAT WOULD CLAIM **NATURAL AUTHORITY** WITHOUT APPEARING **ARROGANT** ?

EURÊKA !

AN **ARTIST** WE THOUGHT ! OR EVEN BETTER: **A DEAD ARTIST !**

SO WE LOOKED AT VARIOUS PAINTINGS BY **DEAD ARTISTS** AND ENDED UP WITH **A HANDFUL OF VAN GOGH'S SUNFLOWERS !** HE WAS DEAD, AND EVEN BETTER **HE HAD BEEN CLINICALLY INSANE !**

WE PRINTED SOME PAINTINGS AND PIPETTED THE RANGE OF **SPRING COLOURS** WE WANTED FROM PLACES IN THE BACKGROUND.

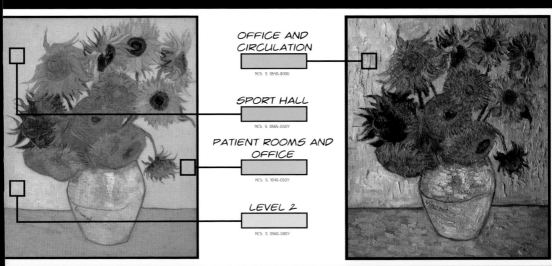

OFFICE AND CIRCULATION

NCS: S 0540-B30G

SPORT HALL

NCS: S 0565-G50Y

PATIENT ROOMS AND OFFICE

NCS: S 1040-G50Y

LEVEL 2

NCS: S 0560-G80Y

THE GOOD THING ABOUT IMPRESSIONISTS IS THAT THEY USE PRACTICALLY **ALL COLOURS** IN THEIR COMPOSITE TECHNIQUE !

SO THE **SPRINGTIME COLORS** WERE FINALLY APPROVED...

--- THE YELLOW...

...THE GREEN...

SJAKKET YOUTH CLUB

SJA

RE-SQUAT

IN THE EXACT OPPOSITE SIDE OF TOWN OF THE MARITIME YOUTH HOUSE IN SOUTHEAST COPENHAGEN IS THE **TOUGHEST HOOD** IN TOWN, APPROPRIATELY CALLED **NORTHWEST**.

IT IS (OR WAS) ALSO THE PLACE OF **"JAGTVEJEN 69"**, THE YOUTH HOUSE CALLED **"UNGEREN"**, A **LEGALLY SQUATTED** SAFE HAVEN FOR **AUTONOMOUS KIDS**.

EVERYTHING WAS IN HARMONY UNTIL THE PROPERTY WAS **DEEMED A LIABILITY** AND **SOLD** BY THE CITY TO A RIGHT-WING CHRISTIAN CULT CALLED "THE FATHERHOUSE".

WHEN THE KIDS **REFUSED** TO MOVE, AND THE NEW OWNERS **INSISTED**, OUR 'HOOD' TURNED INTO A **BATTLEFIELD BETWEEN KIDS AND COPS**.

BEFORE

RIGHT NEXT TO BIG HQ AND THE FORMER "YOUTH HOUSE" IS THE AREA IN COPENHAGEN WITH THE **LARGEST** AND **MOST DIVERSE IMMIGRANT POPULATION.** MORE THAN **60 DIFFERENT NATIONALITIES** RESIDE IN A SMALL AREA (AN ETHNIC COMPOSITION **SIMILAR** TO THAT OF THE **BIG WORKFORCE !)**

AFTER

SOME OF THE LOCAL KIDS, 2ND GENERATION IMMIGRANTS, GROW UP IN THE CONFUSION BETWEEN THEIR **ISLAMIC PATRIARCHAL FAMILY STRUCTURE** AND THE **SOFT MATRIARCHAL SCHOOL SYSTEM.** SOME OF THEM FALL OUT OF THE SYSTEM AND **ROAM THE STREETS.**

DURING THE SECOND **CARTOON CRISIS,** THESE KIDS WENT **BERSERK, BURNING CARS** AND **TRASH CANS** LIKE THEY HAD SEEN THEIR FELLOW **FRUSTRATED TEENS** DO MONTHS BEFORE.

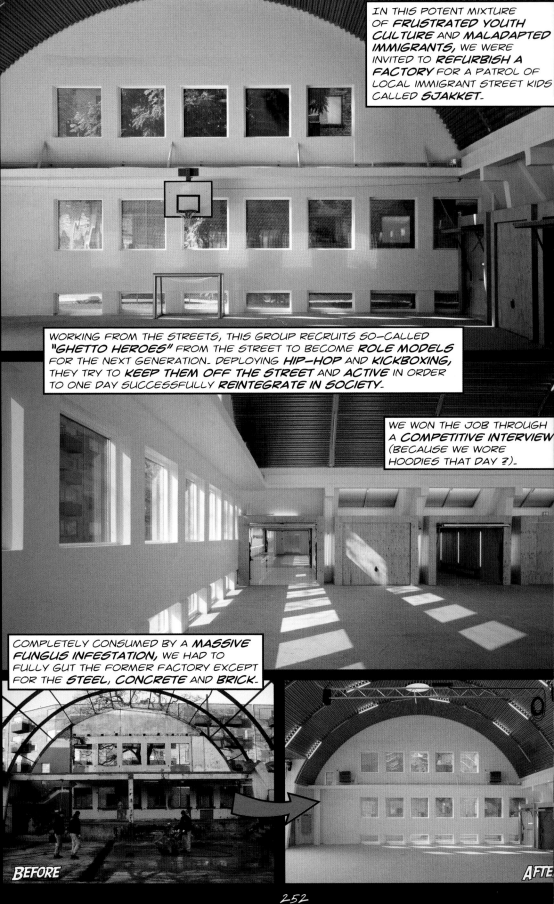

IN THIS POTENT MIXTURE OF **FRUSTRATED YOUTH CULTURE** AND **MALADAPTED IMMIGRANTS**, WE WERE INVITED TO **REFURBISH A FACTORY** FOR A PATROL OF LOCAL IMMIGRANT STREET KIDS CALLED **SJAKKET**.

WORKING FROM THE STREETS, THIS GROUP RECRUITS SO-CALLED **"GHETTO HEROES"** FROM THE STREET TO BECOME **ROLE MODELS** FOR THE NEXT GENERATION. DEPLOYING **HIP-HOP** AND **KICKBOXING**, THEY TRY TO **KEEP THEM OFF THE STREET** AND **ACTIVE** IN ORDER TO ONE DAY SUCCESSFULLY **REINTEGRATE IN SOCIETY**.

WE WON THE JOB THROUGH A **COMPETITIVE INTERVIEW** (BECAUSE WE WORE HOODIES THAT DAY ?).

COMPLETELY CONSUMED BY A **MASSIVE FUNGUS INFESTATION**, WE HAD TO FULLY GUT THE FORMER FACTORY EXCEPT FOR THE **STEEL, CONCRETE** AND **BRICK**.

BEFORE

AFTE

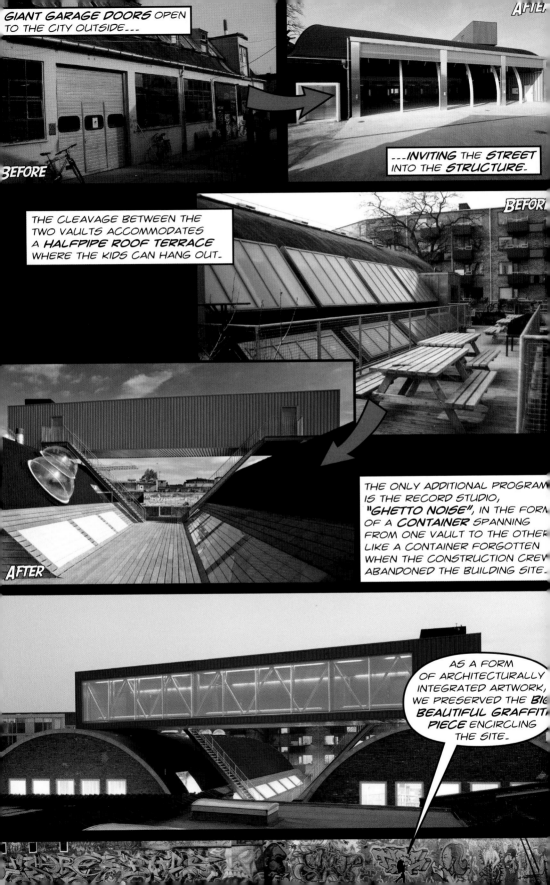

AT THE TIME OF WRITING, WE JUST WON THE COMPETITION TO CREATE A **NEW PUBLIC SPACE** WEDGING THROUGH A **1,5 KM STRIP** OF THIS URBAN AREA. AS AN HOMAGE TO THE **ETHNIC DIVERSITY** OF THE AREA, WE PROPOSED MAKE IT A **GLOBAL GALLERY OF URBAN FURNITURE.**

RATHER THAN CUSTOM-DESIGNING BENCHES, TRASH CANS AND LAMPPOSTS, WE HAVE ASKED ALL THE NEIGHBORS TO SUGGEST THINGS FROM THEIR MORE THAN **60 DIFFERENT NATIVE COUNTRIES** THAT THEY MISS AND THINK WOULD **IMPROVE THE DANISH URBAN SPACE.**

THE RESULT (WE HOPE) WILL BE A FORM OF **MODERN ROMANTIC GARDEN** THAT, BY SAMPLING THE BEST OF ALL THE RESIDENT CULTURES, WILL REFLECT THE **TRUE DIVERSITY** OF THE AREA...

...AND REVEAL THE **TRUE COLORS** OF **CONTEMPORARY** COPENHAGEN.

WATER CULTURE HOUSE

ODA

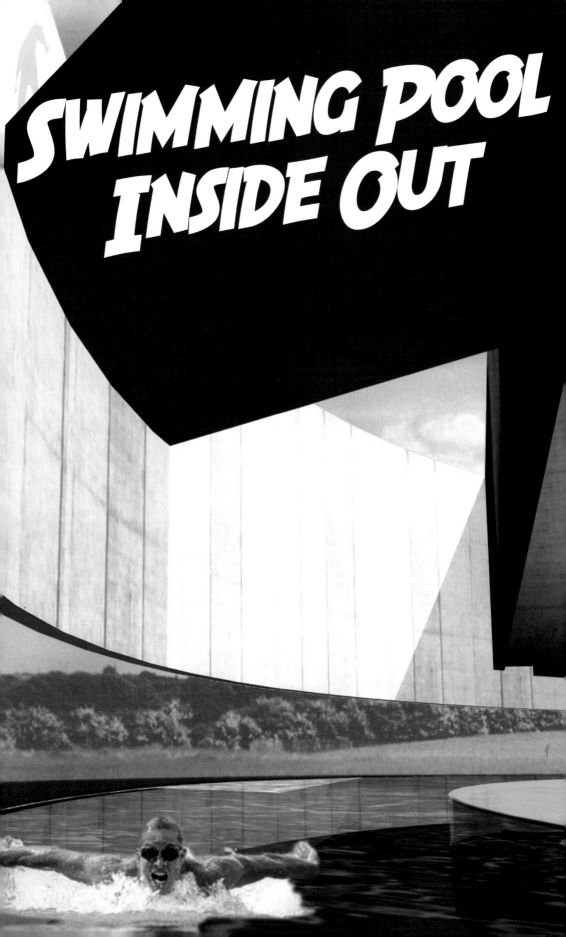

SWIMMING POOL INSIDE OUT

IN 2001, WE DID A COMPETITION FOR AN AQUA CENTER IN THE CITY OF **AALBORG** IN NORTHERN DENMARK.

OUR IDEA WAS TO TURN THE TRADITIONAL SWIMMING POOL **INSIDE OUT**. SO RATHER THAN DESIGNING A **HOUSE** AND PUTTING SOME **POOLS INSIDE** OF IT...

---WE STARTED BY ORGANIZING ALL THE **WATER** FIRST — AND THEN SUBORDINATED THE **LAND AREAS** AFTERWARDS.

THERE WERE **4 POOLS**:

...A **SWIMMING** POOL...

...A **RELAXING** POOL...

...A **PLAYING** POOL...

...AND A **DIVING** POOL...

FOR THE SWIMMING POOL, WE THOUGHT RATHER THAN DOING SOME **COMPACT** POOL WITH SHORT DIMENSIONS...

---WE WOULD STRETCH IT OUT TO BECOM[E] A **150 METER LONG CANAL**.

WE THEN **PLUGGED** THE OTHER POOLS ONTO THE CANAL, LIKE **LAGOONS** ALONG A **CREEK**. SO RATHER THAN HAVING TO GO **ASHORE** WHEN CHANGING FROM ONE POOL TO THE OTHER, WE COULD CREATE A **CONTINUOUS WATERSCAPE** OF POOLS ALLOWING VISITORS TO SWIM FROM ONE ACTIVITY TO THE OTHER.

FINALLY, WE **CONNECTED** THE ENDS OF THE CANAL, BENDING IT LIKE A RUNNING TRACK IN A STADIUM...

---TRANSFORMING THE **WATERSCAPE** OF POOLS INTO A **BIG LAKE** WITH AN **ISLAND** IN THE MIDDLE.

THE ISLAND HAS **DIFFERENT PENINSULAS** FOR **DIFFERENT ACTIVITIES** AND A LIFEGUARD SPOT IN A **PANOPTICON POSITION** IN THE CENTER OF THE CIRCLE.

TO CELEBRATE THE FACT THAT PEOPLE COULD **SWIM AROUND THE COUNTRYSIDE**, RATHER THAN **GOING BACK AND FORTH INSIDE A SWIMMING HALL**, WE CHOSE TO FLOAT THE FACADE THREE METERS ABOVE THE GROUND TO LIBERATE THE 360 PANORAMA OF THE **HILLY LANDSCAPE OF AALBORG**.

NORMALLY, A SWIMMING POOL WOULD BE SURROUNDED BY A **LAYER OF FAT: ARRIVAL HALL, DRESSING ROOMS, SAUNAS** AND **SPAS**, BLOCKING MOST OF THE RELATIONSHIP TO THE OUTSIDE.

IN THIS CASE, WE ORGANISED ALL THESE FUNCTIONS AS **PROGRAMMATIC BEAMS** SPANNING ACROSS THE CEILING. ALL OF THESE BEAMS WOULD REST ON **COLUMNS** STANDING ON THE ISLAND, AND REACH OUT AND CARRY THE FACADE.

THERE WAS **ONE BIG BEAM** FOR THE **THERMAL BATHS, TWO** FOR **DRESSING ROOMS**, ONE FOR WOMEN AND ONE FOR MEN, AND FINALLY, A **RESTAURANT** AND **LOBBY** CONNECTING TO THE EXISTING BUILDINGS NEXT DOOR.

AT NIGHT, THE POOL WOULD HOVER LIKE A **UFO** ABOVE THE LANDSCAPE, WITH PEOPLE SWIMMING BENEATH IT.

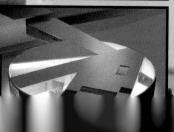

AROUND THE ISLAND, PEOPLE WOULD SWIM WITH THE **LAGOONS** ON ONE SIDE...

...AND THE **LANDSCAPE** OF THE OTHER.

VISITORS WOULD ARRIVE FROM THE **RESTAURANT BRIDGE,** ENTER THE **ROOF,** GET INTO THEIR **SWIMSUITS**...

...DESCEND TO THE **ISLAND**...

...AND **JUMP IN THE LAKE.**

WE WON THE COMPETITION AND STARTED TO DEVELOP THE VARIOUS SPACES, THE **DIVING POOL,** THE **PLAYING POOL,** AND THE **THERMAL BATHS.**

FIRST BUILDING EVER !

THEN IT WAS TIME FOR **MUNICIPAL ELECTIONS** IN AALBORG. AFTER THE ELECTIONS, THE NEW MUNICIPAL GOVERNMENT DECIDED **TO CUT THE PROJECT OUT OF THE PUBLIC BUDGET AND CANCELED THE POOL !**

WE WERE SHOCKED ! BUT AFTER A BRIEF PERIOD OF GRIEF, WE DECIDED TO RESPOND BY CUTTING AALBORG OUT OF OUR PROJECT, AND GO LOOKING FOR A **NEW HOST TOWN.**

SOON WE HAD A MEETING WITH THE MAYOR OF **RANDERS**: A YOUNG DYNAMIC MAYOR WITH AN **AFFINITY FOR SWIMMING** AND AN **EYE FOR ARCHITECTURE.**

UNFORTUNATELY, THEY FOUND **FUNGUS** IN TWO OF THEIR PUBLIC SCHOOLS SHORTLY AFTER, AND THE BILL OF 100 MILLION DKK WAS ENOUGH TO **KILL OUR PROJECT ONCE AGAIN.**

AT THIS TIME, A FRIEND OF MINE JUST GRADUATED AS A **GAME DESIGNER** FROM THE IT UNIVERSITY.

WE THOUGHT: **IF WE CAN'T SWIM** IN IT, AT LEAST WE MIGHT GET **TO KILL EACH OTHER** IN OUR WATERCULTURE HOUSE !

SO WE TURNED IT INTO A **COUNTERSTRIKE** LEVEL !

WHEN WORKING ON IT, CHRISTIAN TOLD US THAT IN GAME DESIGN, YOU DON'T DISTINGUISH BETWEEN **MINIMALISM, CONSTRUCTIVISM** OR **MODERNISM.** YOU TALK ABOUT GAMEPLAY: THE IDEA THAT YOU ATTEMPT TO CREATE **MAXIMUM FUN** WITH **MINIMAL MEANS.**

WE LIKED THE IDEA, AND THOUGHT PERHAPS THAT WAS THE **BEST WAY** TO DESCRIBE OUR APPROACH TO ARCHITECTURE — TO CREATE **MAXIMUM EFFECT** WITH **MINIMAL MEANS.** SO WE SPENT THE BETTER HALF OF 5 MONTHS PLAYING FIERCELY WITHIN OUR VIRTUAL SWIMMING POOL. CONCLUSION ? **SUPER GOOD GAMEPLAY !**

OVER THE NEXT 4 YEARS, I TRAVELED ALL OVER DENMARK MEETING MAYORS OF VARIOUS CITIES, UNTIL FINALLY IN THE SPRING OF 2006, WE HAD TOUCHDOWN IN **ODENSE** — THE HOMETOWN OF HANS CHRISTIAN ANDERSEN !

WE STARTED A STRANGE PROCESS OF **RETROFITTING** OUR OLD CONCEPT ONTO THE NEW SITE. WE WEREN'T REALLY ALTERING EITHER **PROGRAM** NOR **SPACES**, BUT ACTUALLY ONLY THE **VIEW**: FROM THE **GREEN FIELDS OF AALBORG**...

...TO **THE PORT OF ODENSE**, AND FRANKLY THE BUILDING SITS **MUCH NICER** IN ITS FOSTER SITE THAN IT DID IN ITS ORIGINAL PLACE OF BIRTH.

ON OPENING DAY, THIS MIGHT BE THE SIGN AT THE ENTRANCE:

~~AALBORG~~
~~ANDERS~~
~~ILLEROD~~
~~ALLERUR~~
~~ALBY~~
~~REDERIKSSUND~~
DENSE
ATERCULTURE HOUSE

BINGO !

T THE TIME OF WRITING, YEARS AFTER THE FIRST IASCO, AFTER THE ALBORG ELECTIONS, WE UST HAD A CASE OF ISTORY REPEATING.

UNICIPAL ELECTIONS...
EW MAYOR...**CANCELED** ROJECT.

DENSE

SO RIGHT NOW, OUR **BEST SHOT** IS THAT THIS MIGHT BE THE VIEW FROM THE CIRCULAR POOL 3 YEARS FROM NOW...

STAVANGER CONCERT HALL

STA

PUBLIC PROSCENIUM

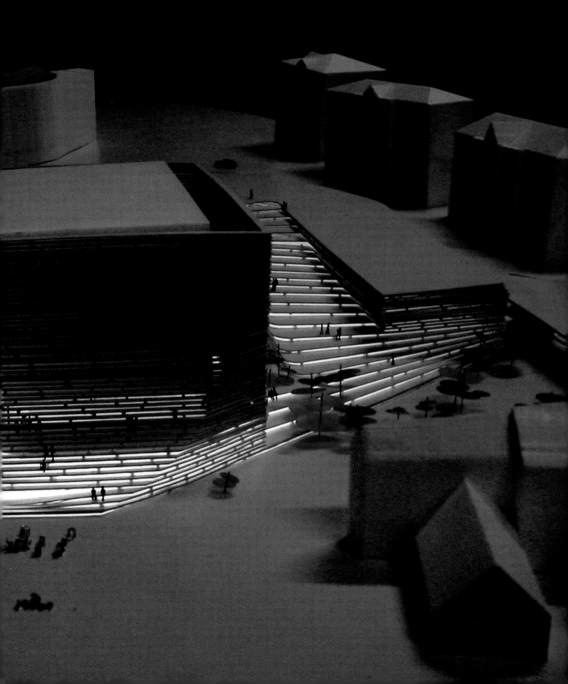

EUROPE OF REGIONS, THE DEMAND FOR REGIONAL CAPITALS TO BECOME CATALYSTS OF DEVELOPMENT AND GROWTH IS INTENSIFIED.

IN THE INTER-REGIONAL COMPETITION TO ATTRACT SKILLS AND QUALIFICATIONS, **THE BILBAO EFFECT** HAS BECOME A POWERFUL WEAPON FOR GLOBAL MEDIA ATTENTION.

STAVANGER IS A REGIONAL TOWN TURNED OIL CAPITAL OF NORWAY.

THE CITYSCAPE OF **WHITE WOODEN HOUSES** IS DWARFED BY FLUORESCENT ORANGE OIL TANKERS.

THE OIL BOOM HAS **INCREASED THE QUALITY OF LIFE** SO DRASTICALLY ON ALL LEVELS THAT EVEN STATOIL'S CANTEEN COOK HAS WON **LA TOQUE D'OR.**

WHEN THE STOMACH IS FULL, THE NEXT STEP IS THE MIND, AND WITH **PLANS FOR A NEW CONCERT HOUSE** STAVANGER SOUGHT TO POSITION ITSELF AS **A NEW FINANCIAL AND CULTURAL NODE** IN NORTHERN EUROPE.

UTZON'S SYDNEY OPERA AND **GEHRY'S GUGGENHEIM** HAVE BOTH SHOWED THE POTENTIAL IMPACT OF A **CULTURAL INSTITUTION MATERIALIZED AS ARCHITECTURAL MASTERPIECE !**

AND CONCERT HOUSES SEEM TO BE THE WEAPON OF CHOICE, AS **PORTO, COPENHAGEN,** AND **OSLO** HAVE ALL RECENTLY MADE THE INVESTMENT.

BUT TRADITIONALLY THESE CULTURAL INSTITUTIONS **ONLY SERVE A FRAGMENT OF THE POPULATION** – MOST PEOPLE ONLY EVER SEE THE BUILDING FROM THE OUTSIDE – MERELY THE FEW GET TO KNOW THE FEELING INSIDE.

WE ASKED OURSELVES:

WHAT IF WE COULD CREATE A CONCERT HOUSE THAT WOULD BE **AS ACTIVE AND ACCESSIBLE ON THE OUTSIDE AS ON THE INSIDE ?**

THE SITE WAS THE PARKING LOT OF AN ABANDONED FERRY TERMINAL, **A FLAT PIECE OF PIER** BLOWN OUT OF THE BEDROCK, WITH THE WOODEN HOUSES OF HISTORICAL STAVANGER RIGHT ABOVE.

A BUILDING THE SIZE OF THE CONCERT HALL WOULD BECOME **A BIG OBJECT BLOCKING THE VIEW AND CONNECTION** FROM THE CITY TO THE SEA.

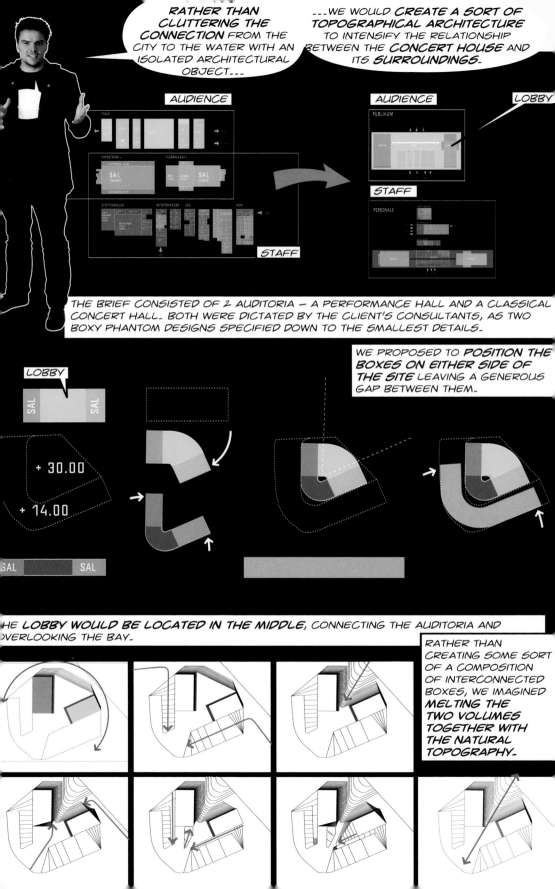

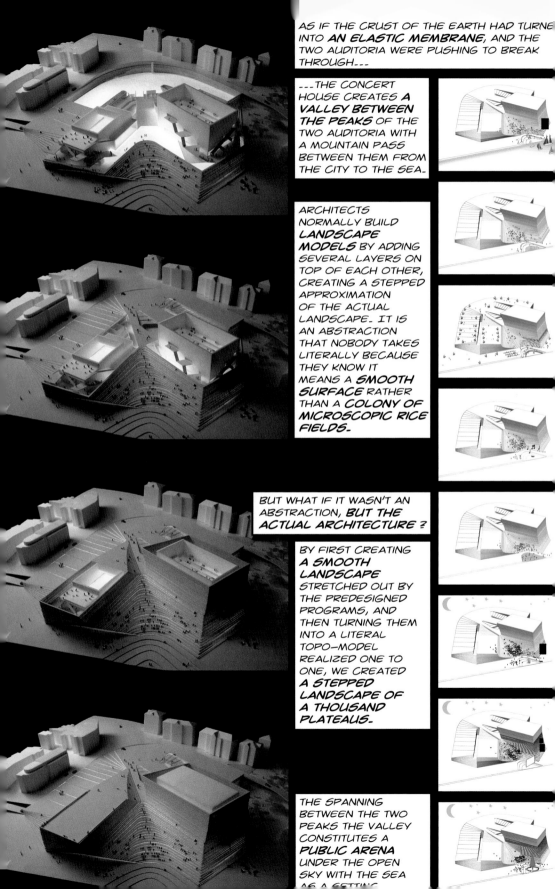

AS IF THE CRUST OF THE EARTH HAD TURNE
INTO **AN ELASTIC MEMBRANE,** AND THE
TWO AUDITORIA WERE PUSHING TO BREAK
THROUGH---

---THE CONCERT
HOUSE CREATES **A
VALLEY BETWEEN
THE PEAKS** OF THE
TWO AUDITORIA WITH
A MOUNTAIN PASS
BETWEEN THEM FROM
THE CITY TO THE SEA.

ARCHITECTS
NORMALLY BUILD
**LANDSCAPE
MODELS** BY ADDING
SEVERAL LAYERS ON
TOP OF EACH OTHER,
CREATING A STEPPED
APPROXIMATION
OF THE ACTUAL
LANDSCAPE. IT IS
AN ABSTRACTION
THAT NOBODY TAKES
LITERALLY BECAUSE
THEY KNOW IT
MEANS A **SMOOTH
SURFACE** RATHER
THAN A **COLONY OF
MICROSCOPIC RICE
FIELDS.**

BUT WHAT IF IT WASN'T AN
ABSTRACTION, **BUT THE
ACTUAL ARCHITECTURE ?**

BY FIRST CREATING
**A SMOOTH
LANDSCAPE**
STRETCHED OUT BY
THE PREDESIGNED
PROGRAMS, AND
THEN TURNING THEM
INTO A LITERAL
TOPO—MODEL
REALIZED ONE TO
ONE, WE CREATED
**A STEPPED
LANDSCAPE OF
A THOUSAND
PLATEAUS.**

THE SPANNING
BETWEEN THE TWO
PEAKS THE VALLEY
CONSTITUTES A
PUBLIC ARENA
UNDER THE OPEN
SKY WITH THE SEA
AS A SETTING

RATHER THAN BEING AN *ICONIC OBJECT* FOR THE POSTCARD, OR AN *ELITIST INSTITUTION FOR THE FEW* — THE STAVANGER CONCERT HOUSE WOULD BE A *PUBLIC LANDSCAPE*.

PART TOPOGRAPHY, PART ARCHITECTURE — AS ACTIVE, ACCOMMODATING AND *ACCESSIBLE* ON THE OUTSIDE...

...AS ON THE INSIDE.

FAMOUS FOR ITS **NATURAL LANDSCAPE** AND RICH FROM ITS NATURAL RESOURCES, STAVANGER'S CONCERT HALL WOULD BE AN ARCHITECTURAL **INTERPRETATION OF ITS NATURAL TOPOGRAPH**

ONCE SUBMITTED, ALL THE COMPETITION ENTRIES WERE EXHIBITED IN THE FERRY TERMINAL. A LOCAL COMPOSER ANNOUNCED "A THOUSAN PLATEAUS" HIS FAVORITE. **FROZEN MUSIC**, HE CALLED IT.

AT NIGHT, ILLUMINATED FROM WITHIN AND POPULATED PEOPLE, THE STRIATED FACADE APPEARS LIKE **SHEE OF MUSIC**, AND THE MOVEMENT OF THE PUBLIC LIKE **EVER-CHANGING SOCIAL SYMPHONY.**

THE PEOPLE OF STAVANGER WERE GIVEN THE POSSIBILITY TO VOTE ON THEIR CONCERT HOUSE OF CHOICE. THE JURY'S AND THE PUBLIC'S VOTE WERE ANNOUNCED TWO DAYS IN A ROW — THE PUBLIC FIRST ! **WE WON THE PUBLIC VOTE,** AND CERTAIN THAT THE JURY COULDN'T OVERHEAR THE VOICE OF THE PEOPLE, **WE WENT OUT TO CELEBRATE.**

THE DAY AFTER, HUNG OVER, THE PARTY WAS **OVER.**

WE DIDN'T GET A THING. **THE JURY HAD CHOSEN A PROJECT CALLED I—BOX** BY AN OFFICE CALLED MED—PLAN — SHORT FOR MEDICAL PLANNING. THEY WERE **USED TO DESIGNING HOSPITALS...**

...AND THE STAVANGER CONCERT HALL **LOOKED LIKE ONE.**

HALF A YEAR LATER, OUR DESIGN FOR STAVANGER WON **THE GOLDEN LION** AT THE VENICE BIENNALE FOR THE **BEST CONCERT HALL OUT OF 60 SHORTLISTED ENTRIES.**

A NORWEGIAN ARCHITECTURAL CRITIC NOTICED, MAKING THE HEADLINE IN THE DAILY PAPER: **"THE PEOPLE CHOSE THE ARCHITECTURE OF THE FUTURE !"**

OUR MISSION HAD BEEN TO **GIVE PUBLIC ACCESS TO A HIGH—BROW INSTITUTION** — ALTHOUGH UNBUILT, THE IDEA HAD **TRIGGERED AN ARCHITECTURE ACCESSIBLE TO THE PUBLIC.**

LANDSBANKI

БНI

NATIONAL ~~BANK~~ STAGE OF ICELAND

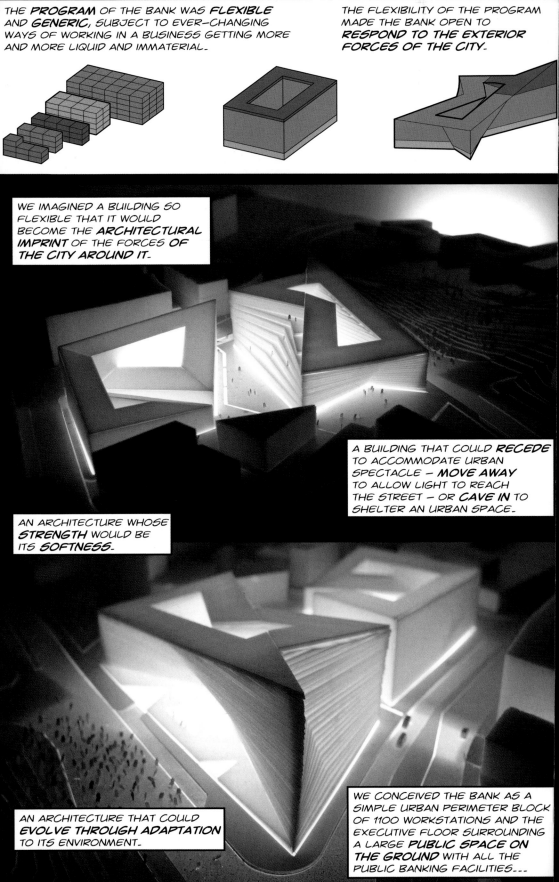

THE **PROGRAM** OF THE BANK WAS **FLEXIBLE** AND **GENERIC**, SUBJECT TO EVER-CHANGING WAYS OF WORKING IN A BUSINESS GETTING MORE AND MORE LIQUID AND IMMATERIAL.

THE FLEXIBILITY OF THE PROGRAM MADE THE BANK OPEN TO **RESPOND TO THE EXTERIOR FORCES OF THE CITY.**

WE IMAGINED A BUILDING SO FLEXIBLE THAT IT WOULD BECOME THE **ARCHITECTURAL IMPRINT** OF THE FORCES **OF THE CITY AROUND IT.**

A BUILDING THAT COULD **RECEDE** TO ACCOMMODATE URBAN SPECTACLE – **MOVE AWAY** TO ALLOW LIGHT TO REACH THE STREET – OR **CAVE IN** TO SHELTER AN URBAN SPACE.

AN ARCHITECTURE WHOSE **STRENGTH** WOULD BE ITS **SOFTNESS.**

AN ARCHITECTURE THAT COULD **EVOLVE THROUGH ADAPTATION** TO ITS ENVIRONMENT.

WE CONCEIVED THE BANK AS A SIMPLE URBAN PERIMETER BLOCK OF 1100 WORKSTATIONS AND THE EXECUTIVE FLOOR SURROUNDING A LARGE **PUBLIC SPACE ON THE GROUND** WITH ALL THE PUBLIC BANKING FACILITIES...

...INCLUDING *CAFE AND ART GALLERIES* FOR LANDSBANKINN'S EXTENSIVE ART COLLECTION.

THE BLOCK WAS BORDERED BY TWO RADICALLY DIFFERENT *CONTEXTS* AND *URBAN SCALES.*

ON ONE SIDE THE OPEN SPACES OF *PARK AND SEA...*

...AND ON THE OTHER SIDE, THE INTIMATE SCALE OF THE *HISTORIC DOWNTOWN.*

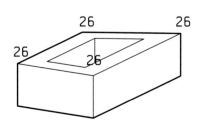

RATHER THAN BLINDLY FOLLOWING THE LOCAL PLAN, WE PROPOSED TO **TILT THE ROOF** OF THE URBAN BLOCK ...

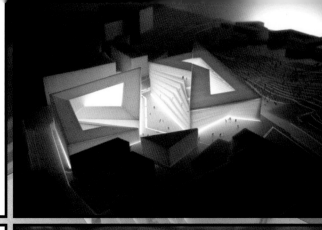

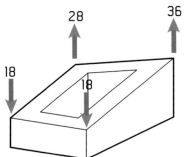

... TO CREATE A DIFFERENTIATED VOLUME *RESPONDING SPECIFICALLY TO THE IMMEDIATE SURROUNDINGS.*

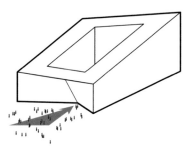

TOWARDS LÆKJARTORG THE ENTIRE FACADE WOULD **CAVE IN**, CREATING A COVERED EXTENSION OF THE SQUARE, ALLOWING CITIZENS TO LINGER UNDER THE **SHELTER** OF THE BANK.

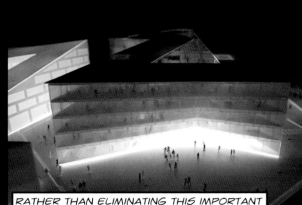

RATHER THAN ELIMINATING THIS IMPORTANT TRADITION OF THE SITE, THE NATIONAL BANK WOULD BECOME THE FRAMEWORK FOR THIS URBAN SPECTACLE. ONCE A YEAR THE BANK WOULD TRANSFORM INTO **THE NATIONAL STAGE OF ICELAND.**

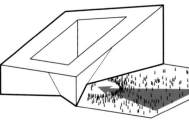

TOWARDS ARNARHÖLL THE FACADE WOULD **CAVE IN** TO CREATE AN **URBAN STAGE** EXACTLY WHERE THE **NATIONAL DAY CELEBRATIONS** TAKE PLACE.

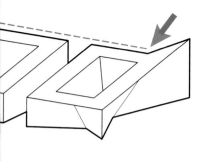

THE NORTH FACADE WAS PULLED
BACK TO **ALIGN WITH THE URBAN
WATERFRONT** ALONG GEIERSGATA.

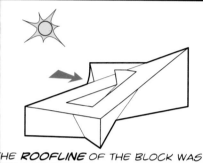

THE **ROOFLINE** OF THE BLOCK WAS
PULLED BACK AWAY FROM THE
CULTURAL PATH, TRANSFORMING
IT FROM A NARROW CRACK TO A
WELL–ILLUMINATED CANYON.

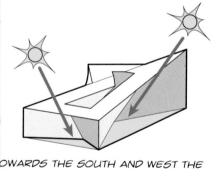

TOWARDS THE SOUTH AND WEST THE
FACADE IS PULLED BACK TO CREATE
A **SUNLIT CAVES** WHILE **MINIMIZING
DIRECT SUNLIGHT** ON THE FACADES.

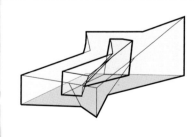

FINALLY THE TWO RECEDING FACADES
FORM AN **URBAN ARCHWAY** OVER
THE CENTRAL COURTYARD, TURNING IT
INTO AN URBAN VOID ILLUMINATED BY
A ZIGZAG–SHAPED SKYLIGHT, LIKE A
CRACK IN A GLACIER.

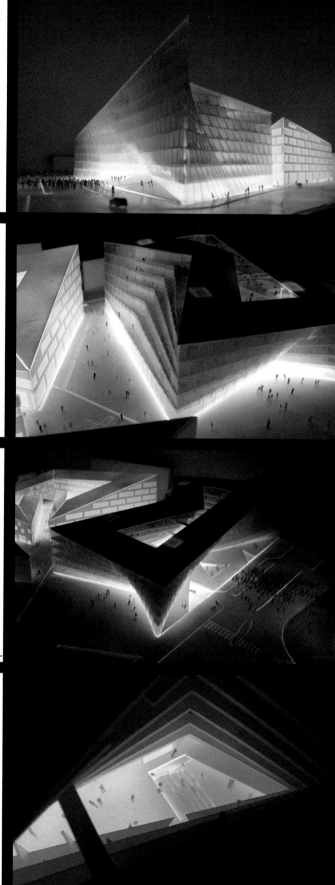

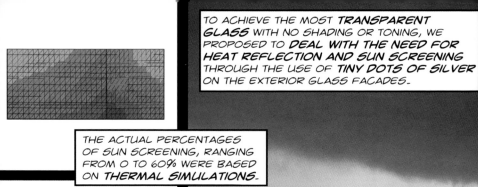

TO ACHIEVE THE MOST **TRANSPARENT GLASS** WITH NO SHADING OR TONING, WE PROPOSED TO **DEAL WITH THE NEED FOR HEAT REFLECTION AND SUN SCREENING** THROUGH THE USE OF **TINY DOTS OF SILVER** ON THE EXTERIOR GLASS FACADES.

THE ACTUAL PERCENTAGES OF SUN SCREENING, RANGING FROM 0 TO 60% WERE BASED ON **THERMAL SIMULATIONS.**

THIS IS LANDSBANKI SEEN FROM THE CITY.

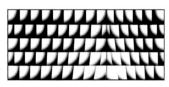

THIS IS THE BANK DIRECTOR'S OFFICE.

THE SILVER DOTS WOULD CONSTITUTE AN **IMPERCEPTIBLE RASTER RESPONDING TO THE REQUIREMENTS OF THE SUN SHADING:** DENSE TOWARDS THE SOUTH, NOTHING TOWARDS THE NORTH, ETC.

AND THIS IS HIM.

THE RASTER WOULD GIVE THE GLASS A CERTAIN MATERIAL QUALITY.

THE INTERIOR SPACE WOULD BE DISTORTED LIKE A **NEGATIVE IMPRINT OF THE URBAN BLOCK** OUTSIDE, **REVEALING** THE WORK INSIDE AS WELL AS **REFLECTING** VARIOUS ACTIVITIES BELOW OR THE SKY ABOVE.

ON THE INTERIOR GLASS TOWARDS THE CENTRAL VOID, A RASTER OF GOLDEN DOTS OF VARYING DENSITY WOULD **VARY THE PRIVACY** AS WELL AS **REFLECT DAYLIGHT ALL THE WAY TO THE BOTTOM OF THE VOID.**

HAVING SPENT THE SUMMER HOLIDAYS AND WORK WEEKENDS IN ICELAND DURING THE 2 STAGE COMPETITION, WE HAD GRADUALLY FALLEN IN LOVE WITH THE **MIDNIGHT SUN**, THE **HOT SPRINGS** AND THE **WHALE MEAT** (AND EVEN GOTTEN USED TO THE FART-LIKE SULPHUR SMELL OF THEIR HOT SHOWERS !)_

WHEN WE **LEARNED THAT WE HAD WON THE COMPETITION** IN JUNE 2008, WE WERE ECSTATIC AT THE PERSPECTIVE OF GETTING TO COMPLETE THE HEART OF THEIR CAPITAL !

IN A CLOUD OF CHAMPAGNE CORKS I PROPOSED **A TOAST FOR OUR LATEST ACHIEVEMENT,** PREDICTING THAT THIS TIME **ONLY TWO THINGS COULD ENDANGER THE COMPLETION** THE BANK:

SLUSSEN

SOCIAL INFRASTRUCTURE

STOCKHOLM, **THE VENICE OF SCANDINAVIA,**
IS BUILT ON A HANDFUL OF **ROCKY ISLANDS**
WHERE THE ARCHIPELAGO MEETS THE BIG LAKES.

GAMLA
STAN

SÖDERMALM

WHERE SALT AND FRESH WATER FLOW TOGETHER LIES **SLUSSEN** (THE LOCK),
AT THE **ONLY NATURAL FORD** BETWEEN THE NORTHERN AND SOUTHERN
EMBANKMENTS, CONNECTING **SÖDERMALM** (THE SOUTHSIDE) TO **GAMLA STAN**
(THE ISLAND OF OLD TOWN), HOME OF THE SWEDISH ROYAL FAMILY*.

SLUSSEN HAS HISTORICALLY BEEN THE **CRADLE OF STOCKHOLM** AND ONE
OF THE MAIN REASONS THAT THE SWEDISH CAPITAL GREW FROM THIS SPOT.
OVER TIME, IT HAS EVOLVED THROUGH A **SERIES OF INCARNATIONS...**

1634

1750

1850

...UNTIL ITS CURRENT DESIGN,
THE **CLOVERLEAF** FROM

1935

WHEN IT WAS BUILT, IT WAS SEEN AS A
STATE—OF—THE—ART ANSWER TO THE BIG
QUESTION OF THE TIME: HOW TO INTEGRATE THE
AUTOMOBILE IN THE **HISTORICAL CITIES** ?

THE MODERNIST PLANNING FOCUS ON THE
INFRASTRUCTURE FOR CAR TRAFFIC HAS ENCASED
GAMLA STAN AND SÖDERMALM IN A **BROAD BELT OF
ASPHALT** BLOCKING MOST OF THE WATERFRONT BEHIND
A **BARRIER OF CARS.** SLUSSEN IS THE **EPITOME** OF
THE **PRIORITIZATION** OF **CAR TRAFFIC** AT THE EXPENSE
OF **ALL OTHER FORMS OF URBAN MOVEMENT.**

70 YEARS LATER, THE CONCRETE IS CRUMBLING — IN SOME PLACES, THE COLUMNS ARE ACTUALLY HANGING FROM THE CEILING. BECAUSE OF THE COMPLEXITY OF THE TASK AND THE CONTROVERSY OF THE SITE, STOCKHOLM HAS BEEN **PARALYZED** FOR YEARS WITHOUT BEING ABLE TO ACT... UNTIL NOW.

WHEN WE GOT INVITED TO AN **INTERNATIONAL COMPETITION** FOR THE REFURBISHMENT OF THE AREA, WE WENT THERE TO TAKE A LOOK.

WHAT WE FOUND WAS **STRANGELY INTRIGUING.**

A DYNAMIC **THREE-DIMENSIONAL** URBAN SPACE ON **MULTIPLE LEVELS** SHAPED BY THE **FLOW** OF **CARS, TRAINS** AND **BUSES.**

THE CONTINUOUS MOVEMENT AND TURNING RADII OF CARS INTRODUCED A **SOFT CURVILINEAR MORPHOLOGY** IN THE OTHERWISE **RECTANGULAR** SCANDINAVIAN TOWNSCAPE.

COULD WE TRANSFORM THIS UNIQUE THREE-DIMENSIONAL FORM OF URBAN SPACE TO ACCOMMODATE — **NOT CARS...**

...BUT **PEOPLE ?**

WE PROPOSE TO **TURN SLUSSEN INSIDE OUT...**

...BY **WRAPPING** ALL THE **VEHICULAR INFRASTRUCTURE** IN MULTIPLE LAYERS OF PUBLIC PROGRAMS AND URBAN SPACES.

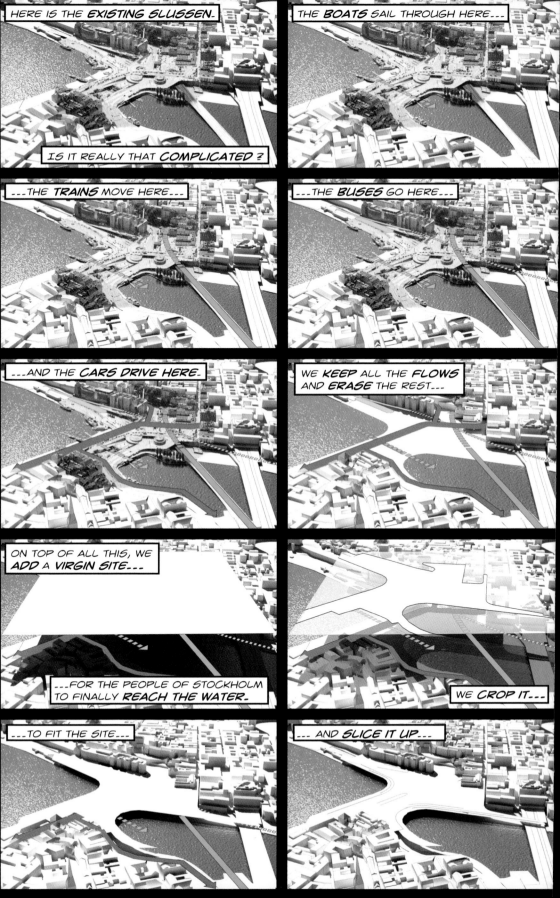

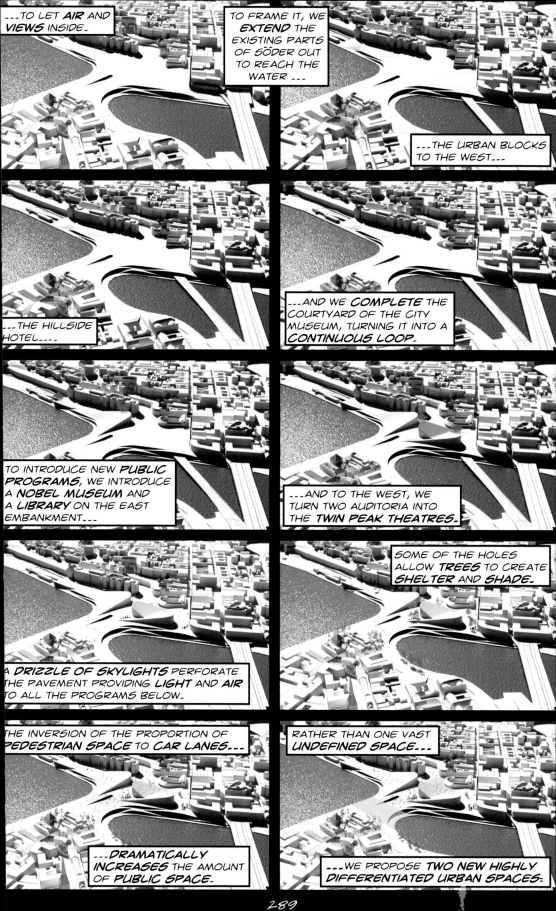

OUR PROPOSAL IS A **NEW GENERATION** EVOLVED FROM **THE EXISTING SLUSSEN.** RATHER THAN BEING AN INFRASTRUCTURAL NODE FOR CAR TRAFFIC, WE TURN SLUSSEN INTO AN **URBAN INFRASTRUCTURE FOR PUBLIC LIFE.**

IT WILL BE SHAPED BY THE **FLOW OF PEOPLE** RATHER THAN FLOW OF **CARS.**

CARS, BUSES AND TRAINS WILL BE ORGANIZED TO SUPPORT THE *FREE FLOW OF PUBLIC LIFE* FROM THE *CITY* TO THE *WATER.*

ITS SLOPES AND CURVES WILL SEEK TO CREATE *PLACES* FOR PEOPLE TO *MOVE, REST* AND *ENJOY* LIVING NEXT TO THE WATER...

...FROM THE ROOF OF *GONDOLEN*...

...TO THE LEVEL OF THE *QUAY.*

ONE OF THE NEW URBAN SPACES IS *SHELTERED* AND *WELL-DEFINED* AT THE *HEART* OF ALL THE *OLD* AND *NEW* PROGRAMS...

THE HOUSING BRIDGE

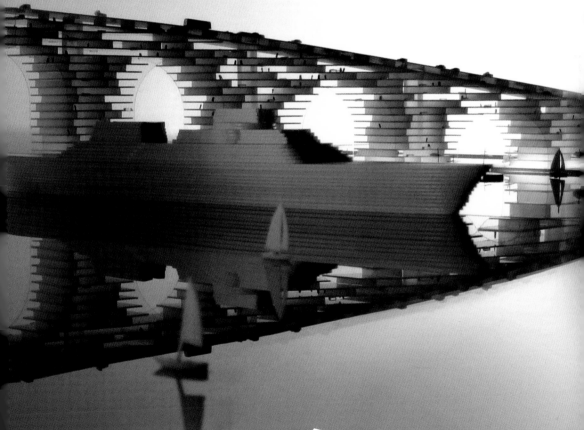

DOMUS PONTUS

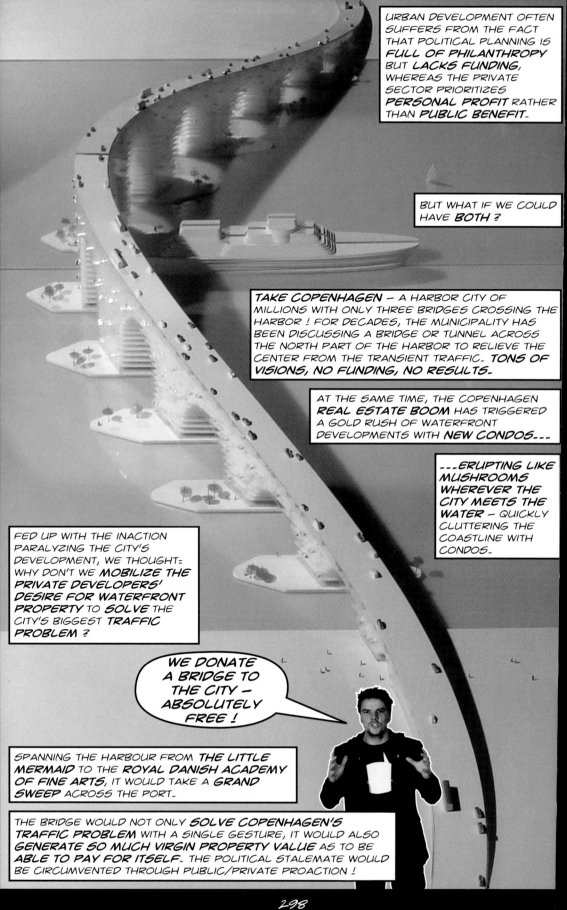

URBAN DEVELOPMENT OFTEN SUFFERS FROM THE FACT THAT POLITICAL PLANNING IS *FULL OF PHILANTHROPY* BUT *LACKS FUNDING*, WHEREAS THE PRIVATE SECTOR PRIORITIZES *PERSONAL PROFIT* RATHER THAN *PUBLIC BENEFIT*.

BUT WHAT IF WE COULD HAVE *BOTH* ?

TAKE COPENHAGEN – A HARBOR CITY OF MILLIONS WITH ONLY THREE BRIDGES CROSSING THE HARBOR ! FOR DECADES, THE MUNICIPALITY HAS BEEN DISCUSSING A BRIDGE OR TUNNEL ACROSS THE NORTH PART OF THE HARBOR TO RELIEVE THE CENTER FROM THE TRANSIENT TRAFFIC. *TONS OF VISIONS, NO FUNDING, NO RESULTS.*

AT THE SAME TIME, THE COPENHAGEN *REAL ESTATE BOOM* HAS TRIGGERED A GOLD RUSH OF WATERFRONT DEVELOPMENTS WITH *NEW CONDOS...*

...ERUPTING LIKE MUSHROOMS WHEREVER THE CITY MEETS THE WATER – QUICKLY CLUTTERING THE COASTLINE WITH CONDOS.

FED UP WITH THE INACTION PARALYZING THE CITY'S DEVELOPMENT, WE THOUGHT: WHY DON'T WE *MOBILIZE THE PRIVATE DEVELOPERS' DESIRE FOR WATERFRONT PROPERTY* TO *SOLVE* THE CITY'S BIGGEST *TRAFFIC PROBLEM* ?

WE DONATE A BRIDGE TO THE CITY — ABSOLUTELY FREE !

SPANNING THE HARBOUR FROM *THE LITTLE MERMAID* TO THE *ROYAL DANISH ACADEMY OF FINE ARTS*, IT WOULD TAKE A *GRAND SWEEP* ACROSS THE PORT.

THE BRIDGE WOULD NOT ONLY *SOLVE COPENHAGEN'S TRAFFIC PROBLEM* WITH A SINGLE GESTURE, IT WOULD ALSO *GENERATE SO MUCH VIRGIN PROPERTY VALUE AS TO BE ABLE TO PAY FOR ITSELF.* THE POLITICAL STALEMATE WOULD BE CIRCUMVENTED THROUGH PUBLIC/PRIVATE PROACTION !

THE TOP OF THE BRIDGE WOULD BE FOR VEHICULAR TRAFFIC, CARS, BIKES AND PEDESTRIANS, ALLOWING CROSSING PASSENGERS **SPECTACULAR VIEWS OF THE COPENHAGEN SKYLINE**, ACROSS THE PORT AND ALL THE WAY TO SWEDEN. AND RIGHT BELOW THE STREET, A LAYER OF PARKING.

THE REST OF THE BRIDGE WOULD BE A **ONE KM LONG SLAB OF HOUSING AND OFFICES** VARYING FROM ONE TO FIFTEEN FLOORS.

ON LAND, **PUBLIC-ORIENTED FACILITIES** WOULD ADDRESS THE ADJACENT CITY. ON THE WATER, **OFFICES** WOULD OCCUPY THE BIGGER FLOOR PLATES BELOW THE **PARKING**, AND THEN **HOUSING** FURTHER DOWN TOWARDS THE WATER.

WELCOME TO MY DESERTED ISLAND !

NORMALLY, THE **PENTHOUSE** WOULD BE THE MOST ATTRACTIVE. IN THE BRIDGE, IT WOULD BE THE **GROUND FLOOR** WHERE THE RESIDENTS WOULD HAVE ACCESS TO THEIR OWN LITTLE ISLAND IN THE MIDDLE OF THE PORT.

THE BRIDGE WOULD BECOME **FOR COPENHAGEN WHAT PONTE VECCHIO IS TO FLORENCE.**

PEOPLE WOULD ARRIVE AT THE TOP, PARK THEIR BIKE OR CAR, AND TAKE THE ELEVATOR DOWN TO THEIR APARTMENT, WHERE THEY COULD ENJOY A COFFEE ON THEIR BALCONY WHILE WAVING TO THE **JAPANESE CRUISE PASSENGERS SAILING BY.**

LIKE A **ROMAN VIADUCT**, THE BRIDGE WOULD BE A WALL OF PROGRAM WITH GIANT ARCHWAYS OF VARYING SIZES FOR THE SHIPS TO PASS. MORE THAN ONE KM LONG FROM START TO FINISH, IT WOULD REACH THE HEIGHT OF 60 METERS HALFWAY, ALLOWING EVEN THE BIG CRUISE SHIPS TO GO THROUGH.

WE PRESENTED THE PROJECT TO THE DIRECTOR OF THE HARBOR, WHICH RESULTED IN **GREAT INTEREST BUT NO RESULTS.** ENCOURAGED BY A CLIENT, WE FILED AN APPLICATION FOR A **GLOBAL PATENT**, THINKING THAT BECAUSE OF PONTE VECCHIO OR THE RIALTO AN **INHABITED BRIDGE** WOULD HARDLY WARRANT NOVELTY STATUS. **TO OUR SURPRISE,** THE PATENT OFFICE REPLIED THAT WATER-BASED INHABITATION CONSTITUTING THE LOADBEARING STRUCTURE WAS A FIRST OFF, AND **OUR FIRST PATENTED BIG IDEA WAS IN THE BAG !**

4 YEARS LATER, THE HARBOR ANNOUNCED AN INVITED COMPETITION TO DESIGN A BUILDING IN THE NORTH HARBOR BRIDGING ACROSS THE WATER TO CONNECT THE TRAIN STATION TO THE MARBLE PIER. WON BY STEVEN HOLL WITH A DESIGN OF TWO TOWERS HOLDING THE CABLES FOR A BRIDGE BETWEEN THEM — HALF TWIN TOWERS, HALF BROOKLYN BRIDGE — THEY WILL FORM **THE NEW LANDMARK** FOR COPENHAGEN BY SEA.

THE CLOVER BLOCK
KLM

AS **ARCHITECTS** OUR ROLE IS OFTEN REDUCED TO THE **BEAUTIFICATION OF PREDETERMINED PROGRAMS**. A CLIENT CALLS US UP ON THE PHONE, AFTER HAVING DETERMINED ALL ISSUES OF A PROJECT, AND ASKS US TO *'MAKE IT NICE'*.

ARCHITECTS ONLY GET INVOLVED WHEN **THE DECISION TO BUILD HAS BEEN MADE**, WHEN **THE SITE HAS BEEN FOUND** AND WHEN **THE SIZE AND CONTENT OF THE PROGRAM HAVE BEEN DECIDED**. THUS ARCHITECTS, AND THEREFORE ARCHITECTURE, RARELY HAVE ANY DECISIVE INFLUENCE ON HOW THE PHYSICAL STRUCTURES OF SOCIETY EVOLVE. **THE ROLE OF ARCHITECTURE IS OFTEN REDUCED TO COSMETICS.**

ARCHITECTURE IS HUMAN SOCIETY'S PHYSICAL MANIFESTATION ON THE CRUST OF THE EARTH — **AN ARTIFICIAL PART OF THE PLANET'S GEOGRAPHY.** IT IS WHERE WE ALL LIVE. ARCHITECTURE IS **"THE STUFF THAT SURROUNDS US"**. AND AS ARCHITECTS CONSTANTLY WORKING IN AND WITH THE CITY, YOU WOULD THINK THAT WE WOULD BE AT THE FRONTIER OF ENVISIONING OUR URBAN FUTURE. HOWEVER WHILE WE SIT AT HOME WAITING FOR THE PHONE TO RING OR SOMEONE TO ANNOUNCE A COMPETITION, **THE FUTURE IS BEING DECIDED BY THOSE WITH POWER: THE POLITICIANS OR THOSE WITH MONEY: THE DEVELOPERS.**

AT **BIG**, WE HAVE LARGELY FOLLOWED THE SAME PATHS AS OUR COLLEAGUES THROUGH GENERATIONS, ATTEMPTING TO **INJECT UNEXPECTED INNOVATIONS INTO COMMISSIONS, DISCOVER UNEXPLORED POSSIBILITIES IN COMPETITION BRIEFS.** BUT NO MATTER HOW CLEVER WE ATTEMPT TO BE, **WE ALWAYS RESPOND TO SOMEONE ELSE'S QUESTIONS.**

OR THAT'S HOW IT WAS UNTIL THE **FALL OF 2005**, WHEN COPENHAGEN WAS HAVING **MUNICIPAL ELECTIONS.** ONE MAJOR ISSUE WAS THAT **THE REAL ESTATE PRICES HAD SKYROCKETED, PROPELLING POOR PEOPLE OUT OF TOWN.** THE SITUATION WAS SO BAD THAT NORMAL INCOME PEOPLE SUCH AS NURSES AND COPS COULD NOT AFFORD TO LIVE IN TOWN. THE CITY HOSPITAL HAD MORE THAN 50 VACANT POSITIONS FOR NURSES, LEAVING PATIENTS WITHOUT CARE.

THE SOCIAL DEMOCRATIC MAYOR RITT BJERREGAARD GOT ELECTED ON A **PROMISE** TO SOLVE THE SITUATION **BY MAKING 5000 HOMES FOR 5000 KR/MONTH IN 5 YEARS----**

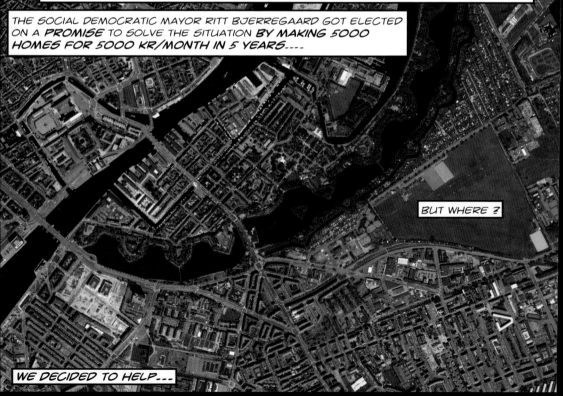

BUT WHERE ?

WE DECIDED TO HELP...

COPENHAGEN'S **OLD AIRFIELD** FROM 1920 HAS BEEN CONVERTED INTO A **SPORTS FIELD** FOR THE **COMMUNITY LIFE OF THE UNIONS** AND **LOCAL GROUPS OF CITIZENS.**

A **WINDSWEPT OASIS** IN THE CENTRE OF THE CITY...

...SURROUNDED BY **P-PATCH GARDENS** OR **INDUSTRY** AND POPULATED BY **FOOTBALLERS** COMPLAINING ABOUT THE **BUMPY FIELDS** AND THE **LACK OF SHELTER.**

WITH THE **FUTURE BRIDGE CONNECTION**, THE **METRO** AND THE NEWLY OPENED **AMAGER BEACH PARK**, THE LOCATION IS **IDEAL FOR HABITATION.** BUT YOU WOULD HAVE TO BE A TOTAL IDIOT TO SUGGEST REMOVING ONE OF THE CORNERSTONES OF **AMAGER'S OPEN AIR** AND **SPORTS LIFE.**

PROPOSING TO BUILD ON IT WOULD BE **POLITICAL SUICIDE !**

BUT WHAT IF WE DIDN'T HAVE TO **CHOOSE BETWEEN** FOOTBALL **OR** HOUSING ?

IF WE COULD BUY A **NARROW STRIP OF LAND 30 METERS WIDE** ALONG THE EDGE...

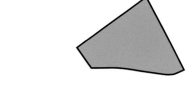

WHAT IF WE COULD **HAVE** BOTH ? FOOTBALL **AND** HOUSING ?

...WE WOULD GET A 3 KM LONG BUILDING SITE.

A MEGA PERIMETER BLOCK !

THE BUILDING WOULD **CURVE AROUND** EXISTING CLUBHOUSES AND FACILITIES...

...AND RESPECT THE **SAFETY DISTANCE** TO SURROUNDING INDUSTRIES.

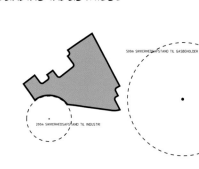

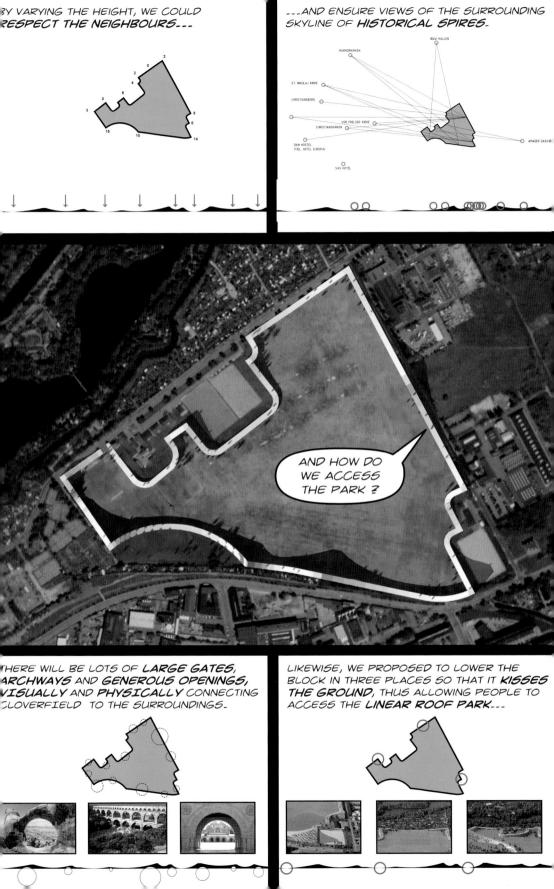

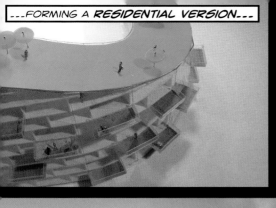

...FORMING A *RESIDENTIAL VERSION*...

...OF THE GREAT WALL OF CHINA !

WE CALCULATED THAT WE COULD CREATE **2000 HOMES, 3 KINDERGARTENS** AND A *PUBLIC SCHOOL*...

WITHOUT SACRIFICING AS MUCH AS A SINGLE FOOTBALL FIELD !

WHY CHOOSE WHEN WE CAN HAVE BOTH !?!

WE SUBMITTED THE PROJECT TO A NEWSPAPER.

TRADITIONALLY *ARCHITECTURE* IS ALWAYS DEALT WITHIN THE CULTURAL SECTION OF THE NEWSPAPER: *SOFT ISSUES* LIKE *ART* OR *ENTERTAINMENT*. IN THIS CASE, HOWEVER, MOST OF THE MORE THAN *300 ARTICLES* APPEARED IN THE FIRST SECTION ALONG WITH POLITICS AND ECONOMY. *ARCHITECTURE* WAS NOW MORE THAN JUST A TIRED *CONTRADICTION* ABOUT *UGLY* OR *BEAUTIFUL*: IT WAS THE *SOLUTION* OF AN OTHERWISE *UNRESOLVABLE POLITICAL CONFLICT*.

THE WEBSITE **WWW.KLOVERKARREEN.DK** INFORMING ABOUT THE **FACTS, POTENTIAL PROBLEMS** AND **POSSIBILITIES** OF THE IDEA, AND GAVE SUPPORTIVE CITIZENS A CHANCE TO SIGN UP FOR THE PROJECT.

KLØVERKARRÉEN

Der er indsamlet i alt 5134 underskrifter:

5134 XCbUIUZDJzcyQi HYcvGGaoICIDzmqXrhn, bbfJnWHmWJSJzpOEShx
5133 Sebastian Ly Serena, 3500 Værløse
5132 Jacob Ørmen, 2200 Kbh. N
5131 Jens albagaard, 2791 Dragør
5130 Thomas Østerby, 2610 Rødovre
5129 YDBjreUSvkEtmZZ mJkLnTZL, gfVESwhAsn
5128 JfozJWepLZVv NUrxiCgaw, sFHrrihsYnvgyJJj
5127 Kjeld Larsen, 2620 Albertslund
5126 Andreas Lange, 2200 København N
5125 aBRmvCCfmZRQNCt OdBVEudrYzWwmoLCMU, jCOLbpEBGFrZsqeh
5124 yRTSQJwjvEliCNS sULawYhpYafwvf, ixUuHwCzxykEU
5123 Søren Olsen, 2650 Hvidovre
5122 Søren Højbjerg Nolsöe, 2400 København Nv.
5121 Magnus Thøgersen, 8600 Silkeborg

APPARENTLY THE FIRST TIME SOMEONE COLLECTED SIGNATURES **FOR** SOMETHING. TRADITIONALLY THE PUBLIC WAS ONLY EVER AGITATED BY **FURY**, NEVER **EXCITEMENT**.

bigstop.dk

Hvem er vi?   Information   Stem imod!   Underskrifter   Forum

Nej til boligbyggeriet...

THE CAMPAIGNERS RESPONDED BY LAUNCHING THEIR OWN SITE: **WWW.BIGSTOP.DK** (NAMED AFTER YOU KNOW WHO !?!)

...relse af Kløvermarken..
...rregaard har planer om at bygge i en af byens folkekære parker – fordi hun ...blemer med nogle grundpriser.

Der er kernen i balladen om Kløvermarken.
Modstanden mod boligbyggeri på Kløvermarken er begrundet fundamentale og i byarkitektoniske argumenter.
På denne side kan du finde en række reelle begrundelse og fakta om projektet, og give din stemme til støtte imod boligbyggeriet på Kløvermarken! Du har mulighed for at bidrage med din mening i vores offentlige debat på siden og være med til at bevare Kløvermarken.

Følgegruppen

Sidste nyt:
...e hvor du her vil kunne læse de sidste nye tiltag,
...i forbindelse med hjemmesiden, eller Kløvermarken.

NEJ TIL BOLIGBYGGERI PÅ KLØVERMARKEN

www.bigstop.dk

IN SEPTEMBER 2006, A PUBLIC OPINION SURVEY DECLARED THAT **64%** OF THE COPENHAGENERS THOUGHT **IT WAS A GOOD IDEA TO BUILD AFFORDABLE HOMES AROUND THE FOOTBALL FIELDS.**

A FEW WEEKS LATER, A BROAD POLITICAL SPECTRUM CONSISTING OF THE SOCIAL DEMOCRATS, THE RADICAL LEFT, THE SOCIALIST PEOPLE'S PARTY AND THE LEFT DECIDED TO **GO AHEAD WITH THE IDEA.**

A YEAR LATER, THE **LOCAL PLANNING PROCESS HAD BEEN INITIATED** AND A PUBLIC PARTICIPATION PROCESS WAS UNDER WAY.

TWO YEARS LATER, THE TECHNICAL MAYOR KLAUS BONDAM OF THE RADICAL LEFT, RETURNED FROM SUMMER HOLIDAYS **WITH SECOND THOUGHTS ABOUT THE PROJECT.**

WITHOUT HIS VOTE, **THE PROJECT FELL**, AND IN A POLITICAL COMPROMISE, IT WAS DECIDED TO ANNOUNCE AN **ARCHITECTURAL COMPETITION.**

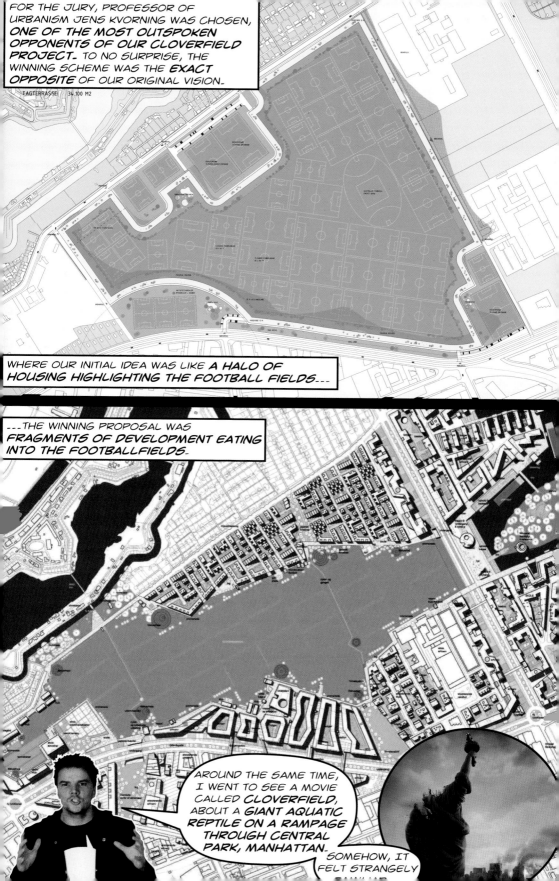

FOR THE JURY, PROFESSOR OF URBANISM JENS KVORNING WAS CHOSEN, **ONE OF THE MOST OUTSPOKEN OPPONENTS OF OUR CLOVERFIELD PROJECT.** TO NO SURPRISE, THE WINNING SCHEME WAS THE **EXACT OPPOSITE** OF OUR ORIGINAL VISION.

WHERE OUR INITIAL IDEA WAS LIKE *A HALO OF HOUSING HIGHLIGHTING THE FOOTBALL FIELDS...*

...THE WINNING PROPOSAL WAS **FRAGMENTS OF DEVELOPMENT EATING INTO THE FOOTBALLFIELDS.**

AROUND THE SAME TIME, I WENT TO SEE A MOVIE CALLED *CLOVERFIELD,* ABOUT A *GIANT AQUATIC REPTILE ON A RAMPAGE THROUGH CENTRAL PARK, MANHATTAN.*

SOMEHOW, IT FELT STRANGELY

BAFFLED BY THE **SCALE** OF THE PARK, WE STARTED TO **COMPARE** IT TO PLACES WE KNEW.

...LIKE **CENTRAL PARK**, NEW YORK...

...THE **FORBIDDEN CITY**, BEIJING...

...OR **GIARDINI BIENNALE**, VENICE.

IT WAS ALMOST **3 TIMES LARGER** THAN **TIVOLI**, THE THEME PARK AT THE HEART OF **COPENHAGEN**...

IT WAS **EXACTLY THE SAME SIZE** AS THE **CLOVERFIELD**...

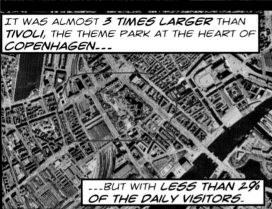

...BUT WITH **LESS THAN 2%** OF THE DAILY VISITORS.

...AND ITS **PERIMETER** WAS **EQUAL** TO SOME OF THE **BIGGEST ROLLER COASTERS IN THE WORLD.**

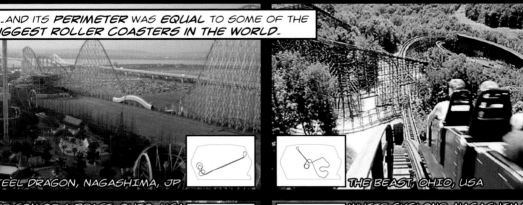

STEEL DRAGON, NAGASHIMA, JP

THE BEAST, OHIO, USA

THE SON OF A BEAST, OHIO, USA

WHITE CYCLONE, NAGASHIMA, JP

TIVOLI IS *UNIQUE*...

CARLSBERG GLYPTOTEK

...BECAUSE IT IS PRACTICALLY THE *CENTRE OF COPENHAGEN*.

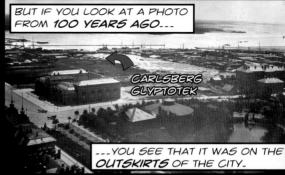

BUT IF YOU LOOK AT A PHOTO FROM *100 YEARS AGO*...

CARLSBERG GLYPTOTEK

...YOU SEE THAT IT WAS ON THE *OUTSKIRTS* OF THE CITY.

WITH ABU DHABI'S CURRENT DEVELOPMENT, *100 YEARS OF GROWTH* WOULD HAPPEN IN *20 YEARS*.

WHAT IF *KHALIFA PARK* COULD BECOME TO *ABU DHABI* WHAT *TIVOLI* IS TO *COPENHAGEN* ?

A *LIVELY OASIS*...

2010

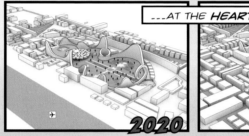

2020

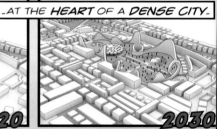

...AT THE *HEART* OF A *DENSE CITY*.

2030

TO CREATE *INSTANT DENSITY*, WE PROPOSED TO CONSOLIDATE THE NEXT THREE YEARS OF COMMERCIAL DEVELOPMENT...

...INTO *A PERIMETER BUILDING* PROTECTING THE PARK FROM THE DESERT WINDS...

...AND ALLOWING LOCAL INHABITANTS TO *POPULATE* THE EMPTY PARK.

 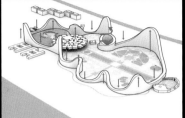 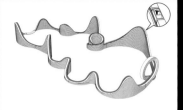

THE ROOFSCAPE OF THE NEW **PERIMETER CITY** WOULD **RISE** AND **FALL** TO ACCOMMODATE THE **WORLD'S LARGEST ROLLER COASTER RIDE.**

WHERE THE **CLOVERFIELD BLOCK** WAS CONCEIVED AS A WAY TO **WEDGE MORE PROGRAM** INTO **A FULL CITY...**

...THE **ROLLER COASTER BLOCK** CREATES A **WAFER-THIN WALL** OF **URBAN DENSITY** IN ANTICIPATION OF **THE CITY TO COME.**

THE CLOVERFIELD BLOCK RESURRECTED AS A **HEDONISTIC MIRAGE** IN THE **EMIRATE SAND DUNES.**

MARBLED BLOCK

HOLY ROAD

HOLY

WHEN ASKED TO DESIGN A **MIXED-USED BUILDING** IN THE ATHENS RED LIGHT DISTRICT, AT THE FOOT OF **ACROPOLIS**, WE FELT LIKE RETURNING TO THE **ROOTS** OF ARCHITECTURE.

SINCE THE **GREEK TEMPLES** WERE THE **CRADLE OF CLASSIC ARCHITECTURE**...

...AND THE **TRADITIONAL GREEK VILLAGES** INSPIRED THE **FLAT ROOFS**...

...AND **WHITE WALLS**...

...OF THE **INTERNATIONAL STYLE**...

...WE THOUGHT IT WOULD BE A **CHALLENGE** TO **REVISIT GREEK VERNACULAR**, TO SEE IF IT ONCE AGAIN COULD INSPIRE A **CONTEMPORARY STYLE**.

THE SITE WAS IN A **SUPER DENSE CONTEXT**...

... BUT FROM THE ROOF, YOU WOULD HAVE **VIEW OF THE ACROPOLIS**.

THE BOTTOM HALF OF THE PROGRAM WOULD BE **SHOPS** AND **GALLERIES**, THE TOP HALF **RESIDENTIAL**.

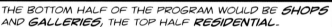

URBAN CIRCULATION   COMPACT HOUSING

ON THE GROUND, IT WOULD BE OBVIOUS TO CREATE AN ALMOST **MEDIEVAL PATTERN** OF **ALLEYS** AND **SHORTCUTS**, MEANDERING THROUGH THE SITE TO CONNECT ALL THE ADJACENT **STREETS** AND **SQUARES**.

FOR THE TOP, WE WOULD HAVE TO STICK TO A **MIESEAN ORTHOGONAL GRID** OF PATIO HOUSES TO ACHIEVE THE **REQUIRED MINIMUM OF SQUARE METERS**.

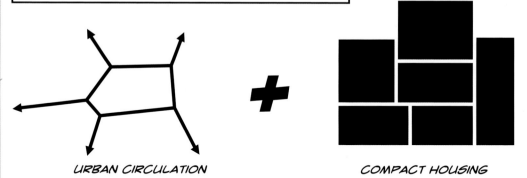

ON OUR FIRST SITE VISIT IN AUGUST, WE WERE OVERWHELMED BY THE **BLAZING HEAT.**

TO **MAXIMIZE** THE **RESIDENTIAL** PROGRAM AS WELL, WE **REDUCED** THE WIDTH OF THE STREETS FROM **4 METERS** AT THE **BOTTOM** TO **1 METER** AT THE **TOP.**

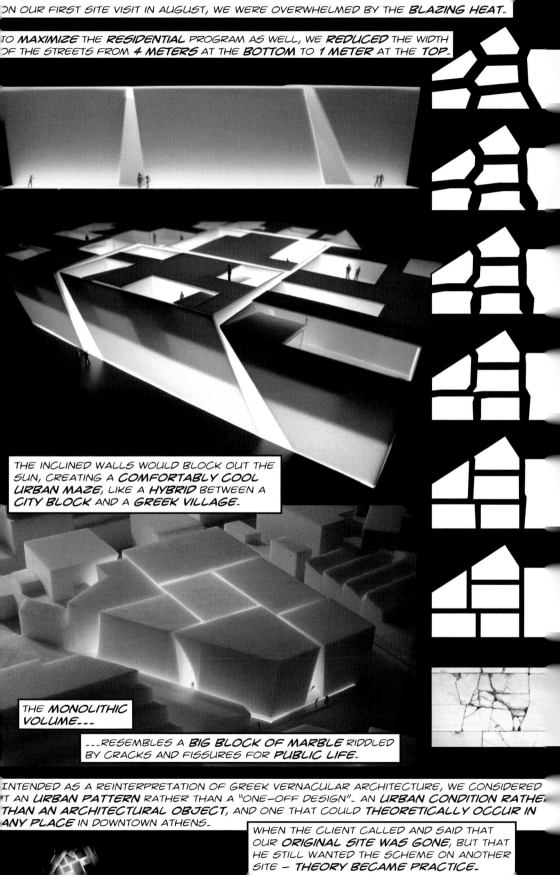

THE INCLINED WALLS WOULD BLOCK OUT THE SUN, CREATING A **COMFORTABLY COOL URBAN MAZE,** LIKE A **HYBRID** BETWEEN A **CITY BLOCK** AND A **GREEK VILLAGE.**

THE **MONOLITHIC VOLUME...**

...RESEMBLES A **BIG BLOCK OF MARBLE** RIDDLED BY CRACKS AND FISSURES FOR **PUBLIC LIFE.**

INTENDED AS A REINTERPRETATION OF GREEK VERNACULAR ARCHITECTURE, WE CONSIDERED IT AN **URBAN PATTERN** RATHER THAN A "ONE–OFF DESIGN". AN **URBAN CONDITION RATHER THAN AN ARCHITECTURAL OBJECT,** AND ONE THAT COULD **THEORETICALLY OCCUR IN ANY PLACE** IN DOWNTOWN ATHENS.

WHEN THE CLIENT CALLED AND SAID THAT OUR **ORIGINAL SITE WAS GONE,** BUT THAT HE STILL WANTED THE SCHEME ON ANOTHER SITE – **THEORY BECAME PRACTICE.**

ART CROSS

INSTANT ICON

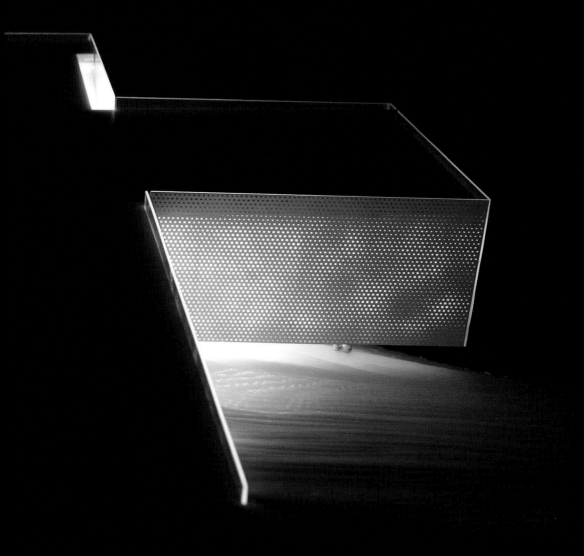

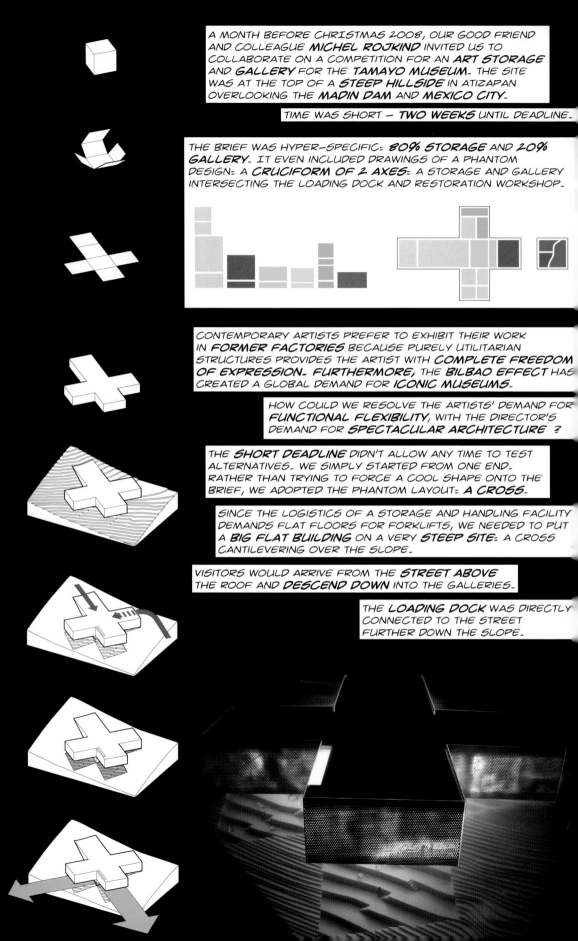

A MONTH BEFORE CHRISTMAS 2008, OUR GOOD FRIEND AND COLLEAGUE **MICHEL ROJKIND** INVITED US TO COLLABORATE ON A COMPETITION FOR AN **ART STORAGE** AND **GALLERY** FOR THE **TAMAYO MUSEUM**. THE SITE WAS AT THE TOP OF A **STEEP HILLSIDE** IN ATIZAPAN OVERLOOKING THE **MADIN DAM** AND **MEXICO CITY**.

TIME WAS SHORT — **TWO WEEKS** UNTIL DEADLINE.

THE BRIEF WAS HYPER–SPECIFIC: **80% STORAGE** AND **20% GALLERY**. IT EVEN INCLUDED DRAWINGS OF A PHANTOM DESIGN: A **CRUCIFORM OF 2 AXES**: A STORAGE AND GALLERY INTERSECTING THE LOADING DOCK AND RESTORATION WORKSHOP.

CONTEMPORARY ARTISTS PREFER TO EXHIBIT THEIR WORK IN **FORMER FACTORIES** BECAUSE PURELY UTILITARIAN STRUCTURES PROVIDES THE ARTIST WITH **COMPLETE FREEDOM OF EXPRESSION**. FURTHERMORE, THE **BILBAO EFFECT** HAS CREATED A GLOBAL DEMAND FOR **ICONIC MUSEUMS**.

HOW COULD WE RESOLVE THE ARTISTS' DEMAND FOR **FUNCTIONAL FLEXIBILITY**, WITH THE DIRECTOR'S DEMAND FOR **SPECTACULAR ARCHITECTURE** ?

THE **SHORT DEADLINE** DIDN'T ALLOW ANY TIME TO TEST ALTERNATIVES. WE SIMPLY STARTED FROM ONE END. RATHER THAN TRYING TO FORCE A COOL SHAPE ONTO THE BRIEF, WE ADOPTED THE PHANTOM LAYOUT: **A CROSS**.

SINCE THE LOGISTICS OF A STORAGE AND HANDLING FACILITY DEMANDS FLAT FLOORS FOR FORKLIFTS, WE NEEDED TO PUT A **BIG FLAT BUILDING** ON A VERY **STEEP SITE**: A CROSS CANTILEVERING OVER THE SLOPE.

VISITORS WOULD ARRIVE FROM THE **STREET ABOVE** THE ROOF AND **DESCEND DOWN** INTO THE GALLERIES.

THE **LOADING DOCK** WAS DIRECTLY CONNECTED TO THE STREET FURTHER DOWN THE SLOPE.

ADDITIONAL PROGRAM FOR VISITORS LIKE A **RESTAURANT** AND **RESTROOMS** WERE NESTED UNDER THE CANTILEVER...

...ENJOYING THE **COOL SHADE** OF THE CROSS ABOVE AND THE **BEAUTIFUL VIEW** OF MEXICO CITY BELOW.

FOR THE FACADES, WE PROPOSED **WHITE PAINTED BRICKS** WITH VARYING GAPS BETWEEN THEM. BY CONTROLLING THE GAP BETWEEN THEM — IN 6 DIFFERENT WIDTHS — WE TURN THE BRICK WALL INTO A LIGHTING AND SHADING DEVICE.

THE DIFFERENT SIZES OF DARK HOLES IN THE WHITE WALL CONSTITUTE A GIANT GRAYSCALE REPRODUCTION OF A **TAMAYO CANVAS**.

THE CANTILEVERING CROSS IS THE **LITERAL MATERIALIZATION** OF THE **FUNCTIONAL DIAGRAM** — DEVOID OF ANY ARTISTIC INTERPRETATION.

PURE FUNCTION AND **PURE SYMBOL** AT THE SAME TIME !

AN INSTANT ICON.

ENGINEERING WITHOUT ENGINES

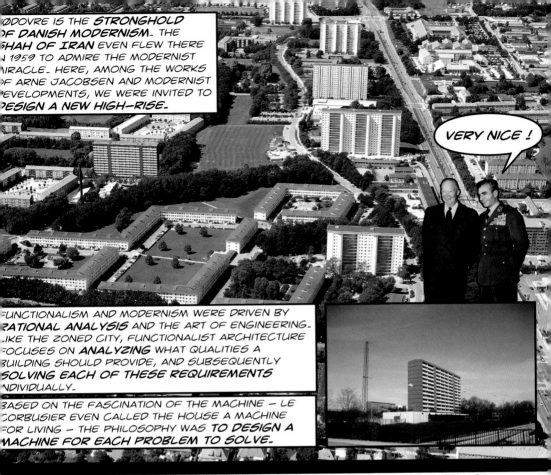

RØDOVRE IS THE **STRONGHOLD OF DANISH MODERNISM.** THE SHAH OF IRAN EVEN FLEW THERE IN 1959 TO ADMIRE THE MODERNIST MIRACLE. HERE, AMONG THE WORKS OF ARNE JACOBSEN AND MODERNIST DEVELOPMENTS, WE WERE INVITED TO **DESIGN A NEW HIGH-RISE.**

VERY NICE !

FUNCTIONALISM AND MODERNISM WERE DRIVEN BY **RATIONAL ANALYSIS** AND THE ART OF ENGINEERING. LIKE THE ZONED CITY, FUNCTIONALIST ARCHITECTURE FOCUSES ON **ANALYZING** WHAT QUALITIES A BUILDING SHOULD PROVIDE, AND SUBSEQUENTLY **SOLVING EACH OF THESE REQUIREMENTS** INDIVIDUALLY.

BASED ON THE FASCINATION OF THE MACHINE — LE CORBUSIER EVEN CALLED THE HOUSE A MACHINE FOR LIVING — THE PHILOSOPHY WAS **TO DESIGN A MACHINE FOR EACH PROBLEM TO SOLVE.**

WHERE YOU WOULD PREVIOUSLY TURN TO DAYLIGHT AS THE PRIMARY LIGHT SOURCE, **ELECTRIC LIGHT** WAS NOW USED. WHERE YOU WOULD PREVIOUSLY TURN TO OPEN WINDOWS FOR FRESH AIR, **MECHANICAL VENTILATION** WAS NOW AVAILABLE. TO SUSTAIN A PLEASANT ROOM TEMPERATURE, YOU NOW USED **AIR CONDITIONING** OR CENTRAL HEATING.

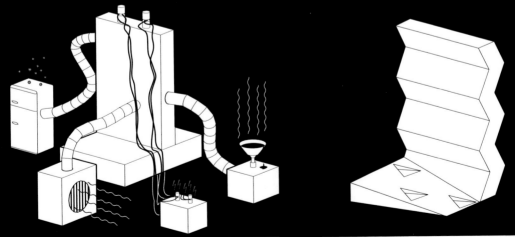

GRADUALLY A LARGER AND LARGER PORTION OF **THE CONSTRUCTION BUDGET WAS SPENT ON INSTALLATIONS,** AND A LARGER AND LARGER BUDGET TO RUN THESE MACHINES.

BORING BOXES WITH BIG ENERGY BILLS.

AN ECONOMICALLY AND ECOLOGICALLY **UNSUSTAINABLE SOLUTION.**

WHAT IF RØDOVRE COULD BE OUR **URBAN LABORATORY** FOR **A NEW WAVE OF FUNCTIONALISM,** NOT BASED ON ACCUMULATING MACHINES BUT RATHER SHAPING BUILDINGS AND CHOOSING MATERIALS SO **THE INHERENT PROPERTIES OF THE ARCHITECTURE WOULD PROVIDE THE NECESSARY QUALITIES ?**

AN ARCHITECTURE WHERE **THE QUALITY DERIVES FROM THE BUILDING'S OVERALL OUTLINE AND SHAPE** RATHER THAN ITS MACHINES.

ENGINEERING WITHOUT **ENGINES !**

THE PROGRAM OF THE TOWER IS DIVIDED INTO **TWO DIFFERENT ACTIVITIES — LIVING AND WORKING.** ACTIVITIES THAT OFTEN **TAKE PLACE IN FAIRLY IDENTICAL SETTINGS,** EVEN THOUGH THEY HAVE **RADICALLY DIFFERENT NEEDS.**

HOUSING SPENDS ENERGY ON HEATING, OFFICES ON COOLING. OFFICES NEED DAYLIGHT, BUT NOT SUNLIGHT. HOUSING LOVES SUN ON THE TERRACE AND THE PASSIVE SOLAR HEAT GAIN IN THE WINTERTIME.

INSTEAD OF CRAMMING ALL THE PROGRAMS INTO THE SAME TEMPLATE, WE SUGGEST TO **TAILOR THE FRAMEWORK TO THE RESPECTIVE ACTIVITIES.**

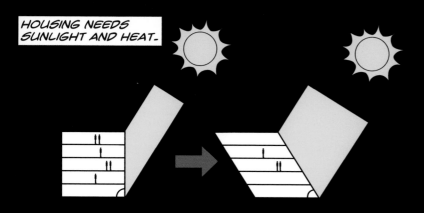

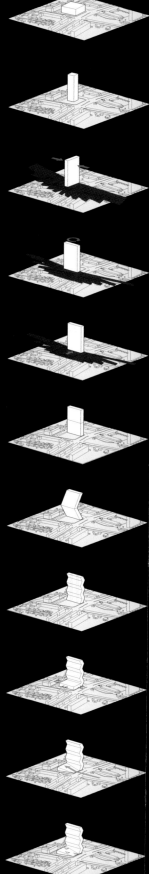

BY *TILTING THE HOUSING* TOWARDS THE NORTH, THEY
ARE OPTIMIZED FOR PASSIVE SOLAR HEAT GAIN. AT THE
SAME TIME SUNLIGHT IS ENSURED FOR THE TERRACES
OF ALL APARTMENTS FROM MORNING TO EVENING.

CONVERSELY, OFFICES NEED DAYLIGHT,
WHILE THEY HATE DIRECT SUN IN THEIR
FACES OR ON THEIR COMPUTER SCREENS.

SO WE HAVE *ATTEMPTED TO CREATE A BUILDING
VOLUME THAT MAXIMIZES DAYLIGHT BUT
MINIMIZES OVERHEATING AND GLARE.* THE OPTIMAL
ORIENTATION OF AN OFFICE BUILDING IS NORTH–SOUTH
SINCE THE BUILDING RECEIVES LOTS OF DIFFUSE LIGHT
FROM THE NORTH AND A MINIMAL AMOUNT OF DIRECT
SUNLIGHT FROM THE SOUTH, WHERE THE SUN SITS HIGH
IN THE SKY COMPARED TO EAST OR WEST.

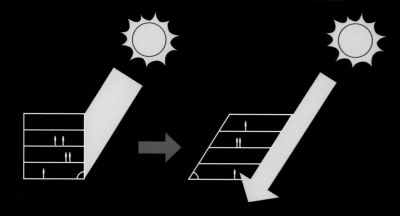

BUT THE NORTH–SOUTH ORIENTATION WILL STILL
ENTAIL A RISK OF CONSIDERABLE OVERHEATING IN THE
WARMER MONTHS — WHEN THE SUN SITS THE HIGHEST
IN THE SKY. SO WE SUGGEST *TO LEAN THE BUILDING
VOLUME TOWARDS THE SOUTH,* SO THE EXPOSURE
TO THE DIFFUSE LIGHT IS MAXIMIZED WHILE THE DIRECT
SUNLIGHT FROM THE SOUTH IS MINIMIZED.

THE NORTH SIDE IS NEVER HIT BY THE SUN WHILE
ON THE SOUTH SIDE *THE DIRECT SUN EXPOSURE
IS REDUCED BY UP TO 50% IN THE SUMMER.* AT
THE SAME TIME, THE *DIFFUSE LIGHT EXPOSURE
FROM THE NORTH IS INCREASED BY ABOUT 40%*
COMPARED TO A STRAIGHT BUILDING.

THE TWO COMPLEMENTARY BUILDING PARTS, TAILORED TO EITHER OFFICE OR HOUSING, **ALTERNATE FROM ONE TO THE OTHER IN A ZIG ZAG MOVEMENT** FROM SKY TO GROUND.

FURTHERMORE, **THE RECIPROCAL SLOPING HELPS STABILIZE THE STRUCTURE** IN SUCH A WAY THAT THE **SCULPTURAL SHAPE** CAN BE ACHIEVED BY MEANS OF A **CONVENTIONAL STRUCTURE.**

THE ZIG ZAG SHAPE IS A **DIRECT CONSEQUENCE OF THE FUNCTIONALITY AND ENERGY DEMANDS,** CREATING A CHARACTERISTIC ICON FOR RØDOVRE'S SKYLINE.

LIKE A POST—EARTHQUAKE *ARNE JACOBSEN !*

SEEN FROM THE EAST OR WEST, THE TOWER STANDS AS **A SLENDER SILHOUETTE OF A LIGHTNING** AGAINST THE SKY. SEEN FROM THE NORTH OR SOUTH THE OPPOSITE SLOPING FACADES WILL REFLECT THE SKY AND THE GROUND RESPECTIVELY — IN **A TRIPLE SANDWICH OF TREE CROWNS AND CLOUDS.**

PS
OUR DEVELOPER IN THE PROJECT WENT **BANKRUPT** DURING THE GREAT FINANCIAL CRUNCH, AND WE WERE DISQUALIFIED FROM THE COMPETITION.

PPS
THE COMPETITION WAS WON BY BRAINSTONES WITH **MVRDV** AND **ADEPT** WITH THEIR PROPOSAL FOR A VERTICAL (LEGO) VILLAGE.

PPPS
TUESDAY, NOVEMBER 4TH 2008, **BRAINSTONES WENT BANKRUPT.**

Rødovre

PPPPS
TUESDAY DECEMBER 16TH AT 6.20 AM, **RØDOVRE EXPERIENCED THE FIRST EARTHQUAKE IN 20 YEARS.**

VMCP HOTEL

ROYAL TREATMENT

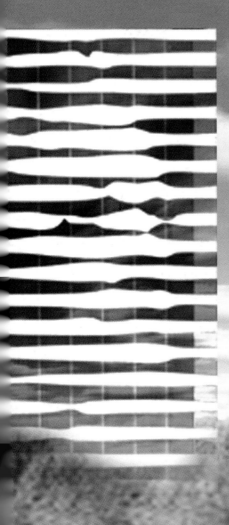

THE LAST GROUP OF PROJECTS SOMEHOW SUM UP THE CONCEPT OF **EVOLUTIONARY ARCHITECTURE**, AND DESCRIBES HOW A SERIES OF SEEMINGLY UNRELATED EVENTS, PLACES AND PROGRAMS CAN COME TO BE INTERTWINED IN **UNANTICIPATED WAYS**. JUST LIKE DARWIN'S IDEA OF EVOLUTION THROUGH NATURAL SELECTION IS AFFECTED BY MIGRATION, ADAPTATION AND CROSSBREEDING, **ARCHITECTURAL EVOLUTION HAPPENS ACROSS BORDERS, CULTURES AND CLIMATES.**

FIRST

IN THIS CASE, CONCEPTS THAT WE HAVE PREVIOUSLY PURSUED – SUCH AS **LITERAL BRANDING** IN A **POST-URBAN CONTEXT, ECOLOMICAL SUSTAINABILITY** AND THE IDEA OF **THE CONTEMPORARY VERNACULAR** – BECAME INTERTWINED IN A CASCADE OF FIRST REJECTED THEN REINVENTED CONCEPTS WITH MULTIPLE LOOPHOLES BACK AND FORTH THROUGH THE DIFFERENT DESIGN PROCESSES.

IT STARTED WHEN OUR CLIENT **ASMUND HAARE** OF FIRST HOTELS COMMISSIONED US TO DESIGN AN **AIRPORT HOTEL** AT OSLO AIRPORT. THE BRIEF WAS RESTRICTIVE – A 70M TALL SLAB OF 600 ROOMS, WITH A HOST OF PUBLIC PROGRAMS INCLUDING A SWIMMING POOL, LOBBY, CONFERENCE ROOMS, AUDITORIA, BANQUET HALL, GYM AND RESTAURANT AT THE BASE.

THE SITE WAS SUBURBAN, SURROUNDED BY HIGHWAY AND HOUSING, BUT BEYOND THE SPRAWL AND INFRASTRUCTURE WERE **ROLLING HILLS AND LUSH NATURE** IN ALL DIRECTIONS.

WE DESIGNED A RATIONAL SLAB THAT UPON ENCOUNTERING THE SURROUNDINGS WOULD GET SHREDDED INTO 6 **SEPARATE BUILDINGS** – ONE FOR EACH PROGRAM REACHING IN ALL DIRECTIONS. THE LANDSCAPE WOULD WEDGE BETWEEN THE PROTRUDING MEMBERS AND REACH ALL THE WAY TO THE GENEROUS LOBBY IN THE MIDDLE.

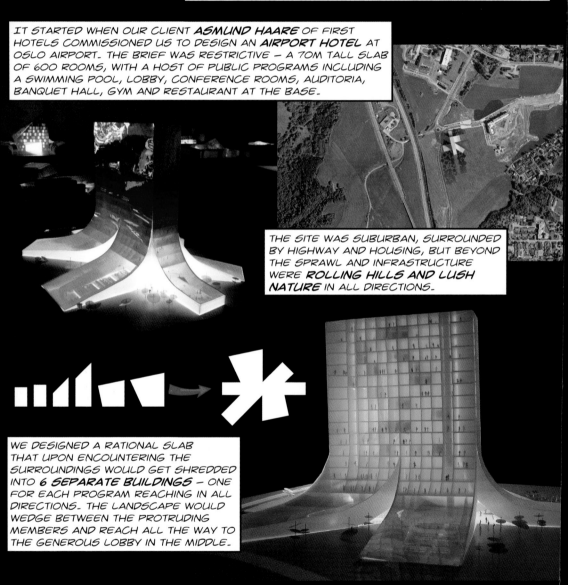

THE FACADES WOULD ALLOW THE GUESTS TO ENJOY THE **SPECTACULAR VIEWS** BEYOND, AND AS THE SLAB PEELED OPEN TOWARDS THE GROUND THE WINDOWS WOULD TURN TO BECOME **SKYLIGHTS,** PROTECTING THE LOWER FLOORS FROM THE **MEDIOCRITY OF THE IMMEDIATE SURROUNDINGS** IN RETURN FOR A VIEW OF THE BEAUTIFUL NORWEGIAN SKY ABOVE.

THE RESULTING ARCHITECTURE — NICKNAMED THE OCTOPUS — WAS A HYPER–RATIONAL HIGHWAY HOTEL TYPOLOGY **THAT TURNED ITS LIMITATIONS INTO POTENTIAL.** ITS TOWERING SILHOUETTE COULD BE SEEN FROM THE HIGHWAY AND ITS RADIAL PLAN BECAME A SORT OF **LAND ART OR LANDMARK** VISIBLE FROM THE INBOUND AIRPLANES. THE CLIENT LIKED THE DESIGN ALMOST AS MUCH AS HE DID THE GROSS/NET FACTOR.

HAVING JUST COMPLETED THE SKETCH DESIGN, HE ACQUIRED A SIMILAR SITE FOR AN **IDENTICAL HOTEL WITH THE EXACT SAME PROGRAM** AT **STOCKHOLM'S AIRPORT.** ADDICTED TO **INNOVATION** AS WE ARE, WE REFUSED TO REDO THE SAME SCHEME.

WHEN WE ARRIVED IN STOCKHOLM'S AIRPORT TO INVESTIGATE THE SITE, WE WERE MET WITH A STRIP OF IMAGES OF FAMOUS SWEDES UNDER THE COMMON THEME: **WELCOME TO MY HOMETOWN.** RANGING FROM ABBA TO ALFRED NOBEL TO KING CARL GUSTAV AND QUEEN SILVIA, *WE FELT WELL—RECEIVED* BY STOCKHOLM'S ELITE AND MONARCHY.

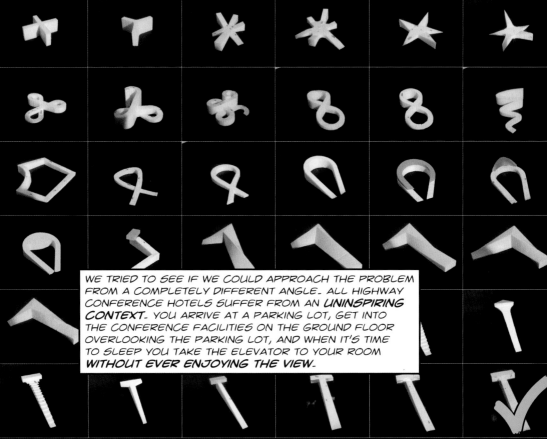

WE TRIED TO SEE IF WE COULD APPROACH THE PROBLEM FROM A COMPLETELY DIFFERENT ANGLE. ALL HIGHWAY CONFERENCE HOTELS SUFFER FROM AN **UNINSPIRING CONTEXT.** YOU ARRIVE AT A PARKING LOT, GET INTO THE CONFERENCE FACILITIES ON THE GROUND FLOOR OVERLOOKING THE PARKING LOT, AND WHEN IT'S TIME TO SLEEP YOU TAKE THE ELEVATOR TO YOUR ROOM *WITHOUT EVER ENJOYING THE VIEW.*

WHAT IF WE COULD *FLIP* THE TRADITIONAL DIAGRAM *UPSIDE DOWN* ?

BY TURNING HOTEL ROOMS AND PARKING INTO A **LONG, GENTLY SLOPING RAMP**, GUESTS COULD DRIVE UP ON THE ROOF TO THE PUBLIC FACILITIES BALANCING ABOVE. HERE THEY WOULD HAVE A **PHENOMENAL 360 DEGREE PANORAMA** OF THE SURROUNDINGS, AND AFTERWARDS THEY COULD TAKE THE ELEVATOR DOWN IN TO THEIR HOTEL ROOMS **RESTING IN THE SWEDISH FOREST.**

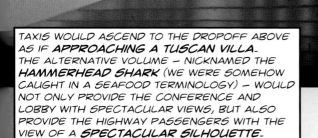

TAXIS WOULD ASCEND TO THE DROPOFF ABOVE AS IF **APPROACHING A TUSCAN VILLA.** THE ALTERNATIVE VOLUME — NICKNAMED THE **HAMMERHEAD SHARK** (WE WERE SOMEHOW CAUGHT IN A SEAFOOD TERMINOLOGY) — WOULD NOT ONLY PROVIDE THE CONFERENCE AND LOBBY WITH SPECTACULAR VIEWS, BUT ALSO PROVIDE THE HIGHWAY PASSENGERS WITH THE VIEW OF A **SPECTACULAR SILHOUETTE.**

WE ALREADY KNEW OUR CLIENT'S CRITERIA, SO WE BUILT ALL HIS STANDARD CRITICISMS INTO THE CONCEPT, **TAKING EVERY POTENTIAL PROBLEM INTO ACCOUNT.** SO AFTER HAVING SPENT MOST OF THE TIME AND THE ENTIRE DESIGN BUDGET, WE PRESENTED THE SCHEME. **HE ABSOLUTELY HATED IT !** HE THOUGHT IT LOOKED LIKE SOMETHING DESIGNED BY DARTH VADER. **IT WAS A DEFINITE NO-GO.**

"THIS IS A MASS MARKET HOTEL — **I NEED EFFICIENCY !** I NEED COMPACTNESS ! **I NEED TO COUNT THE FOOTSTEPS OF EVERY EMPLOYEE.** I WANT A RATIONAL BOX OF 600 ROOMS ON A SINGLE LEVEL PODIUM OF PUBLIC FUNCTIONS BENEATH. **NOTHING MORE, NOTHING LESS !"**

HE INSISTED:

WE THOUGHT: "JESUS, HE ALREADY DESIGNED THE BUILDING — WHAT'S LEFT FOR US TO DO ?"

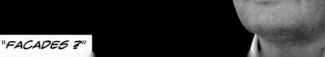

"FACADES ?"

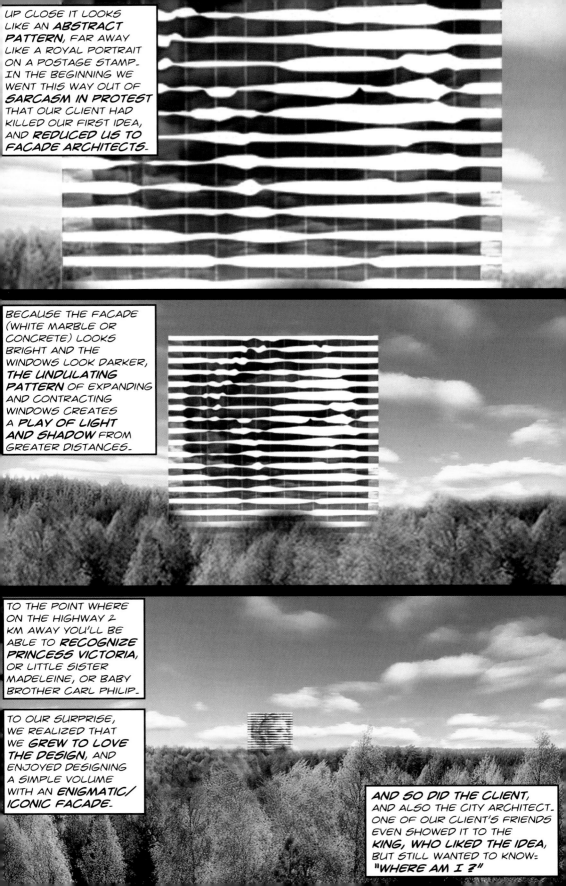

UP CLOSE IT LOOKS LIKE AN **ABSTRACT PATTERN**, FAR AWAY LIKE A ROYAL PORTRAIT ON A POSTAGE STAMP. IN THE BEGINNING WE WENT THIS WAY OUT OF **SARCASM IN PROTEST** THAT OUR CLIENT HAD KILLED OUR FIRST IDEA, AND **REDUCED US TO FACADE ARCHITECTS.**

BECAUSE THE FACADE (WHITE MARBLE OR CONCRETE) LOOKS BRIGHT AND THE WINDOWS LOOK DARKER, **THE UNDULATING PATTERN** OF EXPANDING AND CONTRACTING WINDOWS CREATES A **PLAY OF LIGHT AND SHADOW** FROM GREATER DISTANCES.

TO THE POINT WHERE ON THE HIGHWAY 2 KM AWAY YOU'LL BE ABLE TO **RECOGNIZE PRINCESS VICTORIA,** OR LITTLE SISTER MADELEINE, OR BABY BROTHER CARL PHILIP.

TO OUR SURPRISE, WE REALIZED THAT WE **GREW TO LOVE THE DESIGN,** AND ENJOYED DESIGNING A SIMPLE VOLUME WITH AN **ENIGMATIC/ ICONIC FACADE.**

AND SO DID THE CLIENT, AND ALSO THE CITY ARCHITECT. ONE OF OUR CLIENT'S FRIENDS EVEN SHOWED IT TO THE **KING, WHO LIKED THE IDEA,** BUT STILL WANTED TO KNOW: **"WHERE AM I ?"**

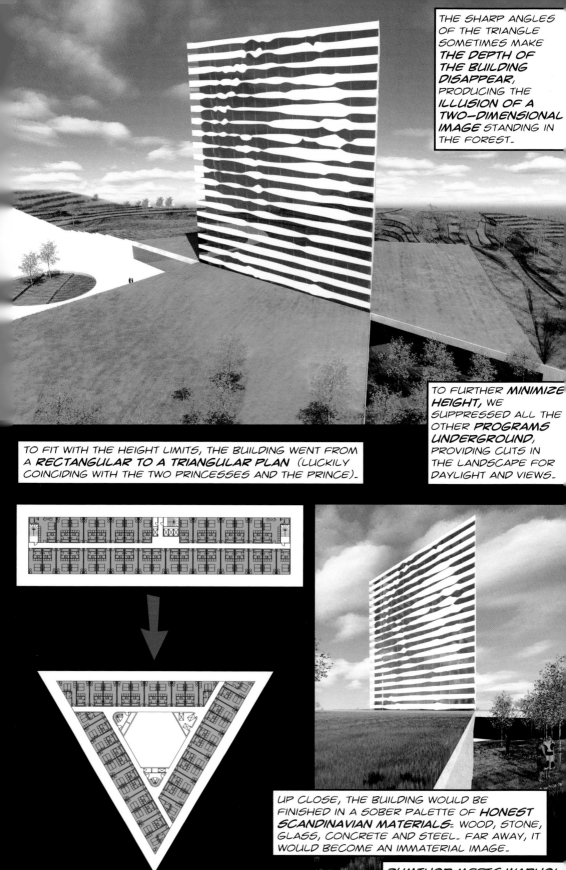

THE SHARP ANGLES OF THE TRIANGLE SOMETIMES MAKE **THE DEPTH OF THE BUILDING DISAPPEAR,** PRODUCING THE **ILLUSION OF A TWO-DIMENSIONAL IMAGE** STANDING IN THE FOREST.

TO FURTHER **MINIMIZE HEIGHT,** WE SUPPRESSED ALL THE OTHER **PROGRAMS UNDERGROUND,** PROVIDING CUTS IN THE LANDSCAPE FOR DAYLIGHT AND VIEWS.

TO FIT WITH THE HEIGHT LIMITS, THE BUILDING WENT FROM A **RECTANGULAR TO A TRIANGULAR PLAN** (LUCKILY COINCIDING WITH THE TWO PRINCESSES AND THE PRINCE).

UP CLOSE, THE BUILDING WOULD BE FINISHED IN A SOBER PALETTE OF **HONEST SCANDINAVIAN MATERIALS:** WOOD, STONE, GLASS, CONCRETE AND STEEL. FAR AWAY, IT WOULD BECOME AN IMMATERIAL IMAGE.

ZUMTHOR MEETS WARHOL.

FIRST HOTEL'S LOGO IS THAT OF A **FLYING ELEPHANT** — TRADITIONALLY ROYALTIES HAVE ANAGRAMS, AND FOR THIS HOTEL WE DESIGNED THE **ANAGRAM OF VMCP INTERTWINED.**

FINALLY, WE REALIZED THAT THE **COLORS OF THE CARPETS** AND WALLPAPERS WOULD COME TO BE REFLECTED IN THE WINDOWS AT NIGHT. SO REVISITING WARHOL, WE CAME UP WITH A **COMBINATION OF COLORS** THAT WOULD ADD A LAYER TO THE ARCHITECTURE'S TRANSFORMATION FROM **DAY TO NIGHT.**

THE **STOCKHOLM AIRPORT HOTEL**, A.K.A. THE VMCP, CONSTITUTES A THIRD ADDITION TO THE TWO AMERICAN VERNACULAR TYPOLOGIES VENTURI DISCOVERED WHEN LEARNING FROM LAS VEGAS. **THE DECORATED SHED** (UTILITARIAN BOX WITH EYE CATCHING APPENDAGE) AND **THE DUCK** (FUNCTIONAL PROGRAMS FORCED INTO ARBITRARY FUNKY SHAPE) ARE NOW SUPPLEMENTED BY **THE PRINCESS**: FUNCTIONAL ELEMENTS THAT INDEPENDENTLY SEEM BENIGN CONSTITUTE A COLLECTIVE ICONIC EXPRESSION OF ANOTHER MAGNITUDE.

SOME MONTHS LATER, OUR FRIEND IN HOLLAND SENT US THIS E-MAIL:

"... **ANYWAY**, I WENT TO SEE A LECTURE BY KELLER EASTERLING AT THE BERLAGE TONIGHT WHERE SHE TALKED ABOUT AN **ALTERNATIVE REPERTOIRE OF ARCHITECTURAL ACTIVISM.** FOR ME, THE MOST NOVEL WEAPON IN HER PROPOSED ARSENAL WAS THE **"PANDA"**, OR "GIFT" (BECAUSE CHINA OFFERED TWO PANDAS TO TAIWAN AS A GIFT, BUT THEIR NAMES MEANT **"UNITY"** IN CHINESE... SNEAKY CHINESE GOVERNMENT).

THE EXAMPLE SHE SEEMED MOST ENTHUSIASTIC ABOUT WAS **THE ARLANDA AIRPORT** , WITH THE SWEDISH ROYAL FAMILY PORTRAIT FACADES **AS THE PHYSICAL MANIFESTATION OF TOTAL-COMPLIANCE-AS-ALTERNATIVE-ACTIVISM.** PRETTY COOL, WHETHER THAT WAS THE INTENTION OR NOT...

THE CENTRAL VOID IS CRISSCROSSED BY MEETING ROOMS AND FINISHED IN A HIGHLY REFLECTIVE MATERIAL, CREATING **A KALEIDOSCOPE OF PIRANESIAN SPACES.**

OUR EVOLUTIONARY APPROACH TO ARCHITECTURE HAD BEEN RECOGNIZED FOR WHAT IT IS: TOTAL-COMPLIANCE-AS-ALTERNATIVE-ACTIVISM – OR IN OTHER WORDS, TURNING PLEASING INTO A RADICAL AGENDA – OR EVEN BETTER: **"YES IS MORE".**

SHEIKH CHIC

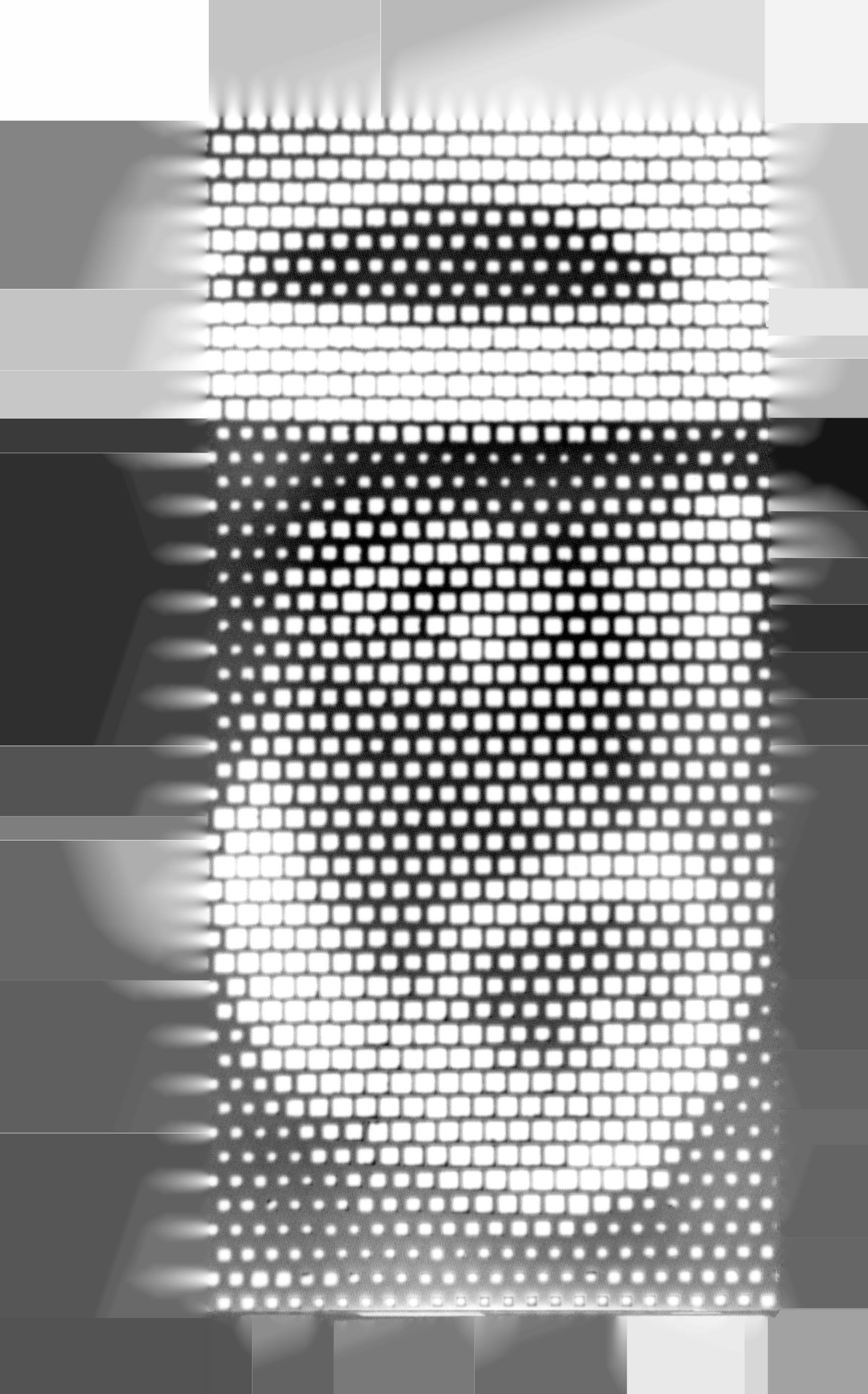

AROUND THE SAME TIME, WE WERE APPROACHED BY A *KUWAITI CLIENT* COMMISSIONING US FOR A GIANT HOTEL IN BAWADI DUBAI.

HE HAD SEEN US ON THE FRENCH/GERMAN *TV CHANNEL ARTE* AND CAME TO COPENHAGEN TO SEE OUR OFFICE AND OUR WORK.

(THE SAME PROGRAM HAD GIVEN US A PROJECT FROM A TEL AVIV REAL ESTATE DEVELOPER, SO SOMEHOW OUR WORK TRANSGRESSED THE TRADITIONAL BOUNDARIES OF CULTURE AND RELIGION.)

THEY INSISTED THAT *THEY WANTED ONE!*

WHEN THEY CAME TO THE OFFICE, THEY SAW THE *VMCP HOTEL.* "WOW ! WE NEED ONE OF THOSE ! *WITH THE SHEIK ON IT !*" WE WERE ENTHUSED THAT THEY LIKED IT, BUT HAD TO EXPLAIN THAT WE WERE ALREADY DOING THIS PROJECT FOR ANOTHER CLIENT.

WE THOUGHT – "WELL, ARTISTS TEND TO DO WORK IN SERIES – SO THEY WILL PURSUE THE *SAME IDEA IN VARIOUS ITERATIONS* UNTIL THEY FEEL THAT THEY HAVE EXHAUSTED THE POTENTIAL OF THAT IDEA, AND MOVE ON."

WE LOOKED INTO THE ARCHIVES AND FOUND A REJECTED STUDY FOR VICTORIA AND MADELEINE'S FACES – SO WE TOUGHT THIS MIGHT WORK...

SO WE DESIGNED A *MONOLITHIC BUILDING:* 300 METERS TALL AND A 100 METERS WIDE. A SUPER–RATIONAL STRUCTURE, IT WOULD BE AN ORGY OF ORTHOGONALITY. THE FACADES WOULD BE FINISHED WITH WHITE MARBLE, AND A *RATIONAL GRID OF SQUARE WINDOWS IN VARYING SIZES* – FROM 1X1 TO 4X4 METERS – WOULD CREATE AN EVEN RASTER OF FENESTRATION ACROSS THE WHITE SLAB OF MARBLE.

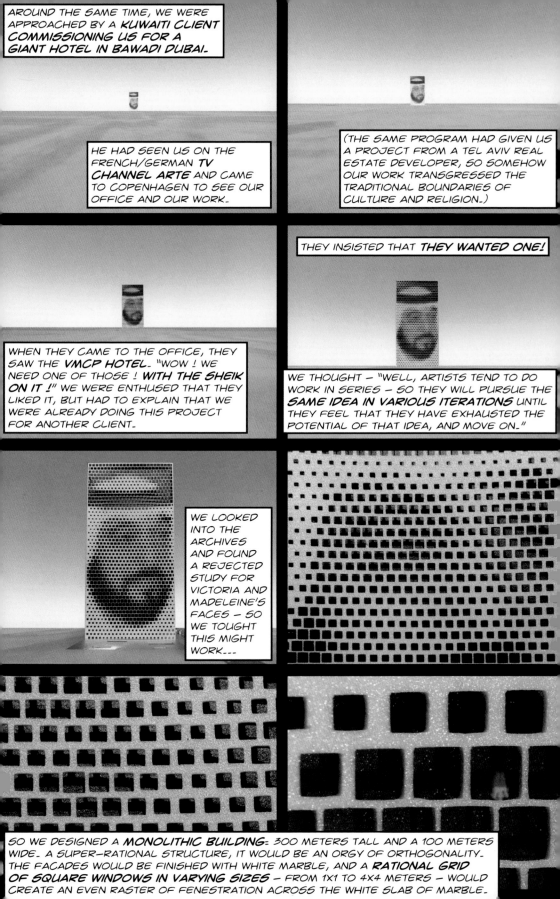

THE **MARBLE FACADE** WOULD
ADDITIONALLY FORM A BRISE-
SOLEIL — **PROTECTING THE
GLASS WINDOWS FROM THE
BLAZING SUN.** A PROGRAM OF
OFFICES, HOTEL AND APARTMENTS
ABOVE WOULD BENEFIT FROM THE
SHADED BALCONIES BETWEEN THE
GLASS AND THE MARBLE.

ALL ADDITIONAL PROGRAMS,
I.E. LOBBY, SPAS, RETAIL
AND RESTAURANTS, WERE
SUBMERGED INTO THE
DESERT SANDS, ILLUMINATED
THROUGH A **SYSTEM OF
SUNKEN COURTYARDS —
LITTLE OASES** PROTECTED
FROM WIND AND WEATHER.

PROPOSED BETWEEN DUBAI AND ABU
DHABI, THE LEADERSHIP TOWER'S
MYRIAD OF **SQUARE HOLES
WOULD MERGE TO FORM THE
PORTRAITS OF THE RESPECTIVE
RULERS.** BOTH OF THEIR FACES
ALREADY DECORATE THE FACES
OF BILLBOARDS AND BUILDINGS
THROUGHOUT THE EMIRATES.

ON THE **LEADERSHIP TOWER** THEY
WOULD APPEAR LIKE A MIRAGE IN
THE DESERT — ONLY **VISIBLE IN THE
MISTY HAZE FROM FAR AWAY** — IN
ORDER TO FADE AWAY AND DISAPPEAR
AS YOU ARRIVE AT YOUR DESTINATION.

5 PILLARS OF BAWADI
BAW

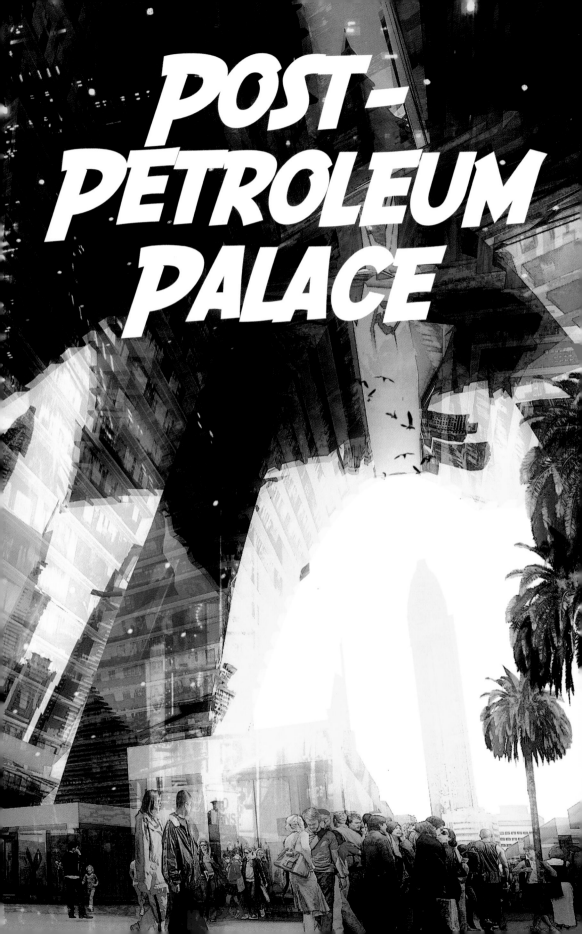

POST-PETROLEUM PALACE

THE LEADERSHIP TOWER WAS ONLY A **SPIN-OFF**. THE REAL CHALLENGE WAS TO DESIGN A 200.000 M² **HOTEL** AND **SHOPPING COMPLEX** IN BAWADI, DUBAI...

PART OF DUBAI-LAND, BAWADI IS PROJECTED TO BECOME THE **LAS VEGAS OF DUBAI** WITH A 6 KM LONG STRIP PACKING MORE THAN 60.000 HOTEL ROOMS, THE LARGEST CONCENTRATION OF HOTEL BEDS IN THE WORLD.

10 YEARS AGO, WE HAD NEVER HEARD ABOUT DUBAI, BUT BECAUSE OF **SPECTACULAR PROJECTS...**

BATTLEFIELD!

...LIKE THE PALM...

...OR THE WORLD...

...DUBAI HAS BECOME A BATTLEFIELD FOR STARCHITECTS AND DEVELOPERS COMPETING TO ATTRACT GLOBAL ATTENTION AND INVESTMENT WITH EVER M**ORE MIND-BLOWING MEGALOMANIACAL MEGA-PROJECTS!**

BUT CONSIDERING THAT DUBAI IS NOW FAMOUS FOR ITS **UNIQUE ARCHITECTURE**, WE WERE SURPRISED AT HOW MUCH IT RESEMBLES ANY **TYPICAL AMERICAN CITY...**

THIS IS **MIAMI**

THIS IS **DUBAI**

...BECAUSE WHAT THEY HAVE DONE SO FAR IS TO SYSTEMATICALLY REPLICATE **AMERICAN SKYSCRAPERS** ALL OVER TOWN.

TO BUILD A GLASS TOWER IN THE MIDDLE OF THE DESERT IS PRACTICALLY THE MOST **UNSUSTAINABLE** THING YOU CAN DO. YOU NEED TO BURN TONS OF OIL TO **KEEP COOL INSIDE**, AND THE GLASS NEEDS TO BE SO TINTED THAT YOU NEED **ELECTRIC LIGHTS EVEN IN THE DAYTIME.**

IT HASN'T ALWAYS BEEN LIKE THAT: IN 1964, BERNARD RUDOFSKY PUT ON THE EXHIBITION **"ARCHITECTURE WITHOUT ARCHITECTS – A SHORT INTRODUCTION TO NON-PEDIGREED ARCHITECTURE"** AT THE MUSEUM OF MODERN ART, NEW YORK.

HE SHOWED HOW PEOPLES ACROSS THE PLANET HAD FOUND WAYS OF BUILDING THEIR CITIES AND BUILDINGS IN SUCH WAYS THAT THEY **OPTIMIZED THE LIVING CONDITIONS IN ALMOST NATURAL WAYS.** HE CALLED IT **VERNACULAR ARCHITECTURE:**

"FOR WANT OF A GENERIC LABEL, WE SHALL CALL IT **VERNACULAR, ANONYMOUS, SPONTANEOUS, INDIGENOUS, RURAL,** AS THE CASE MAY BE."

Architecture Without Architects

A Short Introduction to Non-Pedigreed Architecture

DUBAI HAS ALREADY SUCCESSFULLY PROPELLED ITSELF INTO A **POST-PETROLEUM ECONOMY.** IF WE COULD REINVENT A VERNACULAR ARABIC ARCHITECTURE VERSION 2.0, RATHER THAN COPY-PASTING GENERIC ALIEN TYPOLOGIES, WE COULD TAKE DUBAI ONE STEP FURTHER INTO A **POST-PETROLEUM ECOLOGY !**

SO WE SET OUT TO SEARCH FOR A **NEW VERNACULAR** FOR THE CURRENT URBAN EXPLOSION IN DUE

SINCE BAWADI IS ALL VISION AND NO REALITY (YET), THERE IS **NO CONTEXT** TO RELATE TO. ALL WE HAVE IS THE **SITE,** THE **ORIENTATION** AND THE FUTURE **STREETS AND SQUARES.**

HOW DO YOU BUILD 200.000 M² OF MIXED PROGRAM IN THE **MIDDLE OF THE DESERT ?**

FIRST OF ALL, GET THE GLASS FACADES **OUT OF THE SUN !**

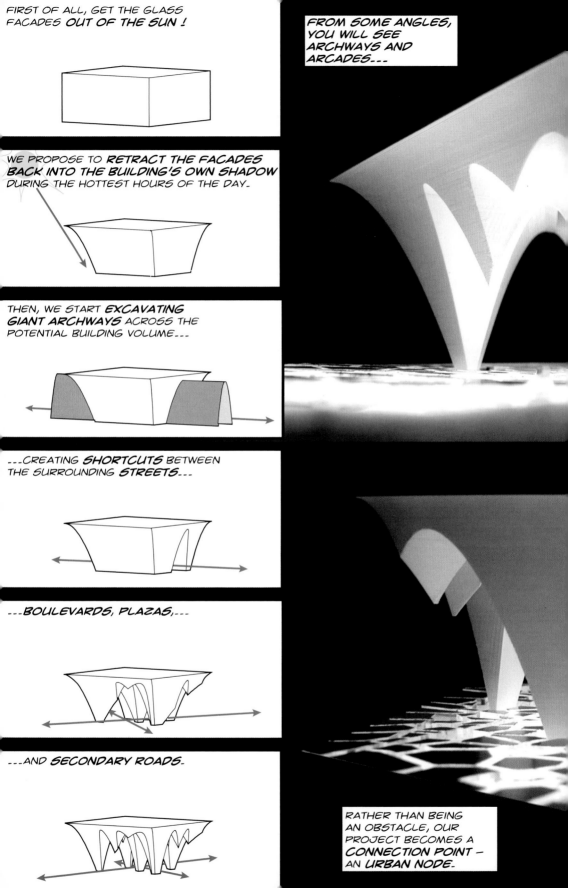

FROM SOME ANGLES, YOU WILL SEE ARCHWAYS AND ARCADES...

WE PROPOSE TO **RETRACT THE FACADES BACK INTO THE BUILDING'S OWN SHADOW** DURING THE HOTTEST HOURS OF THE DAY.

THEN, WE START **EXCAVATING GIANT ARCHWAYS** ACROSS THE POTENTIAL BUILDING VOLUME...

...CREATING **SHORTCUTS** BETWEEN THE SURROUNDING **STREETS**...

...**BOULEVARDS, PLAZAS,**...

...AND **SECONDARY ROADS.**

RATHER THAN BEING AN OBSTACLE, OUR PROJECT BECOMES A **CONNECTION POINT –** AN **URBAN NODE.**

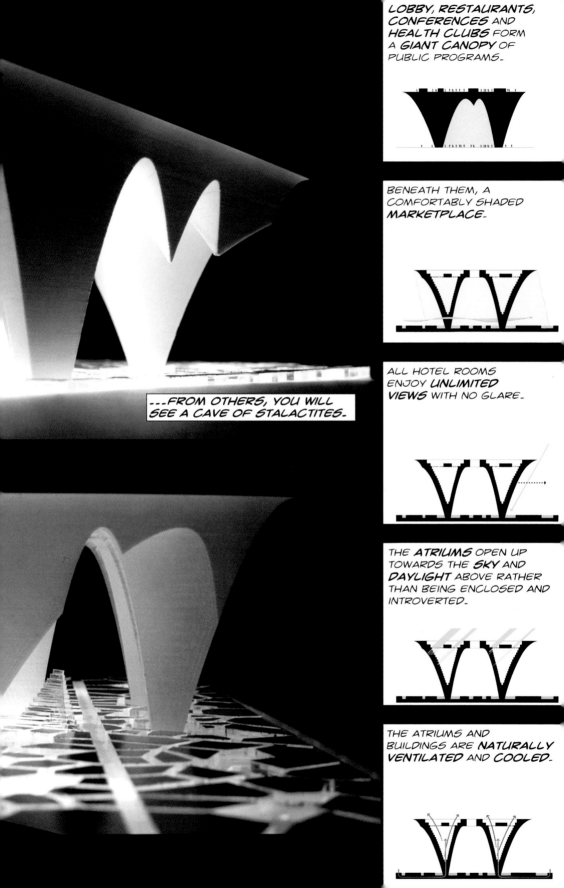

LOBBY, RESTAURANTS, CONFERENCES AND HEALTH CLUBS FORM A GIANT CANOPY OF PUBLIC PROGRAMS.

BENEATH THEM, A COMFORTABLY SHADED MARKETPLACE.

...FROM OTHERS, YOU WILL SEE A CAVE OF STALACTITES.

ALL HOTEL ROOMS ENJOY UNLIMITED VIEWS WITH NO GLARE.

THE ATRIUMS OPEN UP TOWARDS THE SKY AND DAYLIGHT ABOVE RATHER THAN BEING ENCLOSED AND INTROVERTED.

THE ATRIUMS AND BUILDINGS ARE NATURALLY VENTILATED AND COOLED.

AN **OPEN-AIR SOUK** SHADED UNDER THE CANOPY OF THE HOTEL.

AT THE BOTTOM, THE FLOOR PLATES ARE REDUCED TO **STRUCTURE** AND **CIRCULATION**---

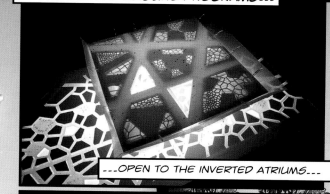

---BUT THEY GET LARGER AND LARGER TO HOST MORE AND MORE HOTEL ROOMS.

AS YOU MOVE UP, YOU ENCOUNTER A LEVEL WITH **RETAIL** AND **LEISURE PROGRAMS**---

---OPEN TO THE INVERTED ATRIUMS---

---BELOW A PUBLIC LEVEL WITH **RESTAURANTS** AND **GARDENS**.

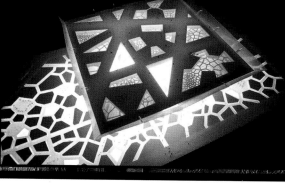

FINALLY, THE UPPER FLOORS ARE THE BIGGEST---

---WITH A SUCCESSION OF **EXCLUSIVE PENTHOUSES**.

WHEN THE CLIENTS CAME FOR A MIDTERM REVIEW, WE PRESENTED OUR **IDEA** AND **EARLY MODELS**. THEY LIKED THE IDEA OF **PROGRESSIVE SUSTAINABILITY**, BUT IT WASN'T UNTIL WE SHOWED THE FIRST SKETCHES THAT **THEY GOT OUT OF THEIR SEATS** !

THEY TOLD US THAT...

... THE ISLAMIC SOCIETY IS FOUNDED ON THE FIVE PILLARS OF ISLAM. EACH PILLAR IS A DUTY INCUMBENT ON EVERY MUSLIM: **SHAHADAH** (PROFESSION OF FAITH), **SALAH** (RITUAL PRAYER), **ZAKAT** (ALMSGIVING), **SAWM** (FASTING DURING RAMADAN) AND **HAJJ** (PILGRIMAGE TO MECCA).

THEY SAW OUR PROPOSAL AS AN ARCHITECTURAL EMBODIMENT OF THIS **HOLY PRINCIPLE – AN ISLAMIC COMMUNITY OF PUBLIC SPACES RESTING ON A FIRMAMENT OF FIVE PILLARS.**

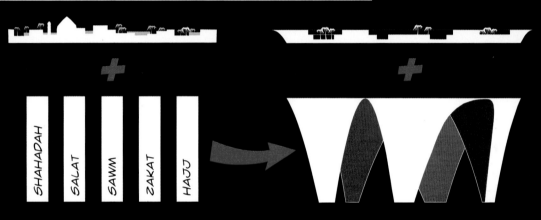

SHAHADAH SALAT SAWM ZAKAT HAJJ

WE ALSO REALIZED THEN THAT WE HAD COME ACROSS **FORMS** AND **SHAPES** RESONATING **TRADITIONAL ISLAMIC ARCHITECTURE.**

ALTHOUGH GENERATED OUT OF CONCERNS FOR THE LOCAL CLIMATE, THEY SEEMED TO STEM FROM **THE LOCAL CULTURE.**

IT SEEMED THAT **ECOLOGY** AND **COSMOLOGY** INTERSECTED IN OUR FIRST DESIGN ATTEMPT.

WE WERE GRADUALLY REALIZING THAT OUR FAILED ATTEMPT AT STOCKHOLM AIRPORT TO TURN THE HOTEL TYPOLOGY *UPSIDE DOWN* APPEARED TO BE THE RIGHT SOLUTION IN DUBAI !

BY TURNING *THE VISION OF BAWADI UPSIDE DOWN---*

---WE CREATED AN *INVERSE SKYLINE OF SPIRES AND TOWERS.*

WHEN WE STARTED TO LOOK INTO STRUCTURE, OUR ENGINEER TOLD US THAT AT THIS SCALE, THE ARCHES COULD EVEN MEAN AN *IMPROVEMENT OF MATERIAL CONSUMPTION---*

MODERN CONSTRUCTION NORMALLY USES A RATIONAL GRID OF BEAMS AND COLUMNS, WHILE IN FACT AN *ARCH IS THE MOST EFFICIENT WAY OF TAKING FORCES DOWN* BECAUSE OF THE *REDUCED BENDING MOMENTS.*

THE CATALAN ARCHITECT *ANTONI GAUDI* KNEW THIS. HE WOULD MODEL THE *OPTIMAL ARCHES* FOR HIS SOPHISTICATED CHURCH DESIGNS BY *HANGING SANDBAGS IN WEBS OF STRING.* GRAVITY WOULD SIMPLY DELINEATE THE *OPTIMAL CURVE* BY PULLING THE STRINGS INTO THEIR NATURAL SHAPE. USING MIRRORS, HE WOULD THEN *FLIP THE MODEL UPSIDE DOWN* AND COPY *IT ONTO DRAWINGS.*

TODAY, YOU DON'T HAVE TO GO THROUGH ALL THIS — YOU SIMPLY ASK YOUR ENGINEER TO *CALCULATE THE OPTIMAL ARCHES.* ONCE AGAIN, WE ENDED UP WITH SEEMINGLY *TRADITIONAL SHAPES* GENERATED BY *CONTEMPORARY INTELLIGENCE.*

BY MOBILIZING ALL OF THE KNOWLEDGE AND PROCESSING POWER AVAILABLE TODAY, WE ENDED UP WITH AN ARCHITECTURE RELYING ON ITS *DESIGN* RATHER THAN ITS **MACHINERY** TO CREATE **OPTIMAL LIVING CONDITIONS** IN THE EMIRATE CLIMATE. **ENGINEERING WITHOUT ENGINES: A NEW VERNACULAR ARCHITECTURE FOR DUBAI.**

NOT ONLY DID IT MEAN AN **INVERSION** OF THE TRADITIONAL AMERICAN SKYLINE OF SKYSCRAPERS, IT ALSO EVOKED FORMS OF FORMER **ISLAMIC SENSIBILITIES.**

BENEATH THE URBAN VAULTS, A NEW FORM OF PUBLIC SPACE APPEARED, REINTRODUCING THE **SHADED OUTDOOR SOUK** AS AN ALTERNATIVE TO THE AIR CONDITIONED INTERIOR ATRIUM.

SEEN FROM A DISTANCE, THE FIVE PILLARS OF BAWADI FORM THE SILHOUETTE OF AN **INVERTED PYRAMID** – THE ULTIMATE SYMBOL OF **INSANITY** CREATED THROUGH **RATIONAL REASONING** AND **COOL CALCULATIONS.**

AMIDST THE EMIRATE ARCHITECTURAL ARMS RACE, OUR QUEST FOR THE **VERNACULAR** RATHER THAN THE **SPECTACULAR** LED US TO A MUCH MORE **EXPRESSIVE ARCHITECTURE** THAN WE COULD EVER HAVE IMAGINED ON OUR OWN...

TO BE CONTINUED...

BIG CITY

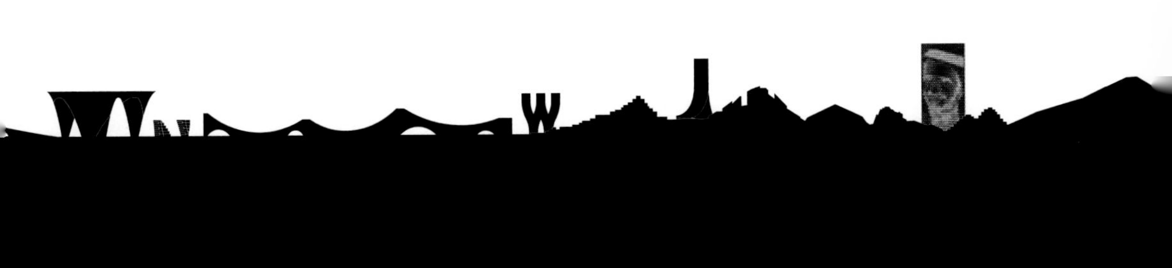

ARCHITECTURAL EVOLUTION

AN ECOSYSTEM OF IDEAS

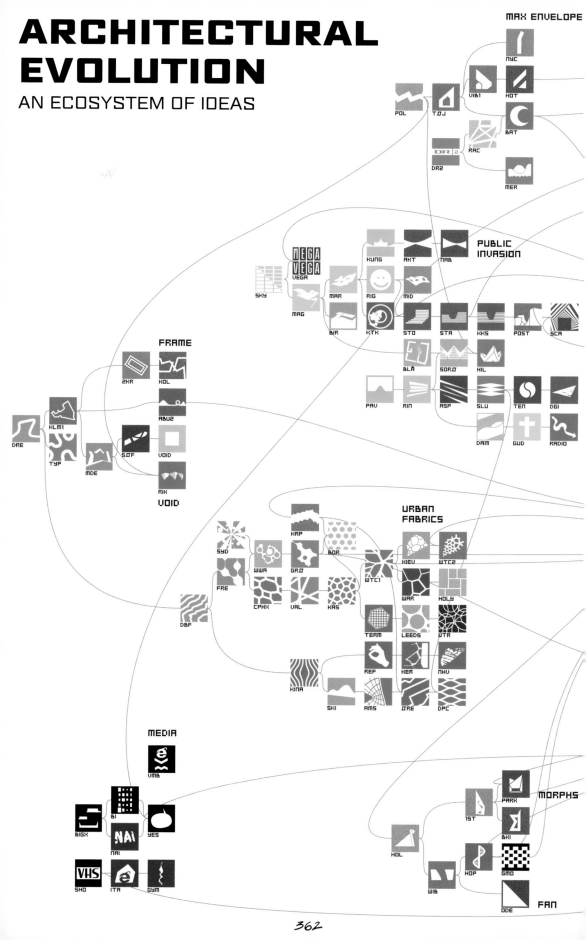

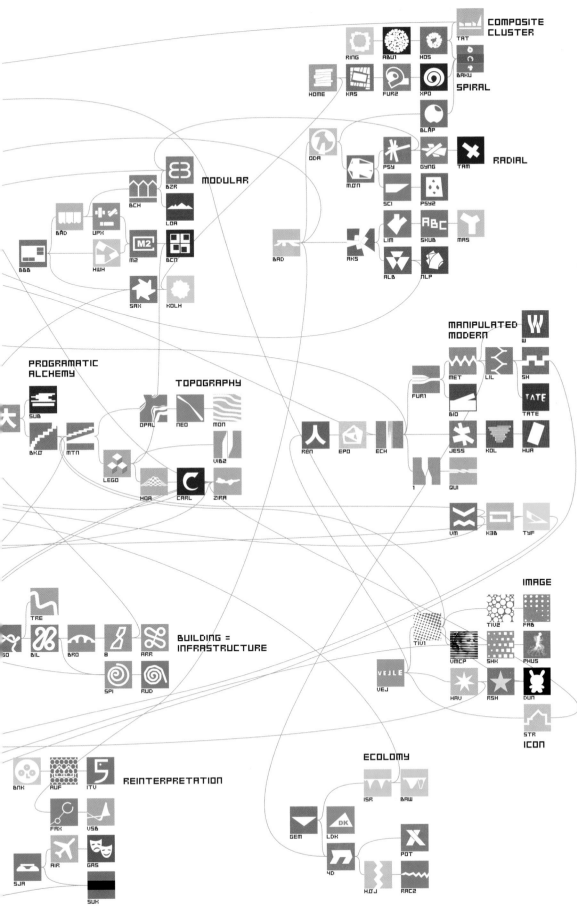

COMPOSITE
CLUSTER

TAT

BAKU

RING   ABU1   HOS

SPIRAL

HOME   KAS   FUR2   XPO

BLAP

MODULAR

B2R

BCH

LOA

ODA

M.ZN

PSY   GYNG   TAM   RADIAL

BAD   UPX

BBB

M2   BCN

HWH

SCI   PSY2

SAX   KOLH

LIM   SKUB   MRS

BAD   AKS   ALB   NLP

MANIPULATED
MODERN   W

PROGRAMATIC
ALCHEMY

TOPOGRAPHY

MET   LIL   SH

FUR1

BIO   TATE

SUB

OPAL   NEO   MON

BKO   MTN

VIB2

REN   EPO   ECH   JESS   KOL   HUA

LEGO

HOA   CARL   ZIRA   1   QUI

VM   K3B   TYF

IMAGE

TRE

TIV2   FAB

TIV1

BUILDING =
INFRASTRUCTURE

GO   BIL   BRO   B   ARR

VMCP   SHK   PHUS

VEJLE

SPI   RUD   VEJ

HAV   RSH   DUN

STR

ICON

BNK   AUF   ITV   REINTERPRETATION

ECOLOMY

ISR   BAW

FAX   VSB

GEM   LDK

AIR   GAS   POT

SJA   4D

SUK   H.OJ   RAC2

363

PROJECT INDEX

BIG PROJECTS 1999 - 2009

 REN

PEOPLE'S BUILDING SHANGHAI
SIZE : 50,000 M2, ADDITIONAL BUILDINGS : 500,000 M2 - LOCATION : WORLD EXPO SITE, SHANGHAI, CN - COLLABORATORS : JDS, AKT

Bjarke Ingels, Andreas Klok Pedersen, Julien De Smedt, Bo Benzon, Jakob Christensen, Jakob Lange, Jan Tanaka, Julie Schmidt-Nielsen, Karsten Hammer Hansen, Andrew Griffen, Christian Dam, Damita Yu, Katrin Betschinger, Kristoffer Harling, Mia Frederiksen, Mia Scheel Kristensen, Nanna Gyldholm Møller, Narisara Ladawal, Sophus Søbye, Thomas Christoffersen

 XPO

THE DANISH EXPO PAVILION 2010
SIZE : 3,000 M2 - LOCATION : SHANGHAI, CN - CLIENT : ERHVERVS- OG BYGGESTYRELSEN - COLLABORATORS : ARUP AGU, 2+1, JEPPE HEIN

Bjarke Ingels, Finn Nørkjær, Niels Lund Petersen, Jan Magasanik, Henrick Villemoes Poulsen, Kamil Szoltysek, Cat Huang, Tobias Hjortdahl, Sonja Reisinger, Klaus Tversted, Anders Ulsted, Jan Borgstrøm, Teis Draiby, Pauline Lavie, Daniel Sundlin, Line Gericke, Armen Menendian, Karsten Hammer Hansen, Martin Mortensen

 LDK

LITTLE DENMARK
SIZE : 100,000 M2 - LOCATION : COPENHAGEN, DK - CLIENT : DANISH ARCHITECTURE CENTER - COLLABORATORS : JDS, JØRGEN LØGSTRUP, NCC, DR, ARUP

Bjarke Ingels, Julien De Smedt, Andreas Klok Pedersen, Dan Stubbergaard, Anne Louise Breiner, Dhairya Sheel Ramesh Powar, Jakob Christensen, Jakob Lange, Julie Schmidt-Nielsen, Mads Birgens, Mia Frederiksen, Nina Ter-Borch, Ole Schrøder, Uffe Topsøe-Jensen

 VM

VM HOUSES
SIZE : 25,000 M2 - LOCATION : COPENHAGEN, DK - CLIENT : HØPFNER A/S, DANSK OLIE KOMPAGNI A/S - COLLABORATORS : JDS, HØPFNER A/S, MOE & BRØDSGAARD

Bjarke Ingels, Julien De Smedt, Thomas Christoffersen, Finn Nørkjær, Henrick Villemoes Poulsen, Alistair Wiliams, Anna Manosa, Anne Louise Breiner, Annette Jensen, Bent Poulsen, Christian Finderup, Claus Tversted, David Zahle, David Vega, Dhairya Sheel Ramesh, Dorte Børresen, Henning Stüben, Ingrid Serritslev, Jakob Christensen, Jakob Lange, Jakob Møller, Jakob Wodschou, Jørn Jensen, Karsten Hammer Hansen, Mads H. Lund, Marc Jay, Maria Yedby Ljungberg, Nadja Cederberg, Nanna Gyldholm Møller, Narisara Ladawal, Ole Elkjær-Larsen, Ole Nannberg, Oliver Grundahl, Sandra Knöbel, Simon Irgens-Møller, Sophus Søbye, Søren Stærmos, Xavier Pavia Pages

 MTN

THE MOUNTAIN
SIZE : 33,000 M2 - LOCATION : COPENHAGEN, DK - CLIENT : HØPFNER A/S, DANSK OLIE KOMPAGNI A/S - COLLABORATORS : JDS, MOE & BRØDSGAARD, SLA, FREDDY MADSEN

Bjarke Ingels, Jakob Lange, Finn Nørkjær, Jan Borgstrøm, Henrick Villemoes Poulsen, Julien De Smedt, Annette Jensen, Dariusz Bojarski, David Vega, Dennis Rasmussen, Eva Hviid-Nielsen, Joao Vieira Costa, Jørn Jensen, Karsten V. Vestergaard, Karsten Hammer Hansen, Leon Rost, Louise Steffensen, Malte Rosenquist, Mia Frederiksen, Ole Elkjær-Larsen, Ole Nannberg, Roberto Rosales Salazar, Rong Bin, Sophus Søbye, Søren Lambertsen, Wataru Tanaka

 B

B HOUSE + 1 TOWER
SIZE : 62,000 M2 - LOCATION : COPENHAGEN, DK - CLIENT : HØPFNER A/S, DANISH OIL COMPANY A/S, STORE FREDERIKSLUND - COLLABORATORS : MOE & BRØDSGAARD, KLAR

Bjarke Ingels, Thomas Christoffersen, Henrik Lund, Rune Hansen, Agustin Perez-Torres, Annette Jensen, Carolien Schippers, Caroline Vogelius Wiener, Claus Tversted, David Duffus, Dennis Rasmussen, Finn Nørkjær, Hans Larsen, Jan Magasanik, Jakob Lange, Jakob Monefeldt, Jeppe Marling Kiib, Joost Van Nes, Kasia Brzusnian, Kasper Brøndum Larsen, Louise Hebøll, Maria Sole Bravo, Ole Elkjær-Larsen, Ole Nannberg, Pablo Labra, Pernille Uglvig Jessen, Peter Rieff, Peter Voigt Albertsen, Rasmus Kragh Bjerregaard, Richard Howis, Søren Lambertsen, Eduardo Perez, Ole Schrøder, Ondrej Tichy, Rune Hansen, Sara Sosio, Karsten Hammer Hansen, Christer Nesvik, Søren Peter Kristensen

 SCA

SCALA TOWER
SIZE : 45,000 M2 - LOCATION : COPENHAGEN, DK - CLIENT : CENTERPLAN - COLLABORATOR : AKT

Bjarke Ingels, Andreas Klok Pedersen, Camilla Hoel Eduardsen, Christian Bratz, Karsten Hammer Hansen, Simon Lyager Poulsen, Ville Haimala, Sara Sosio, Jaulia Szierer, Daichi Takano

 LEGO

LEGO TOWERS
SIZE : 50,000 M2 - LOCATION : COPENHAGEN, DK - CLIENT : KALMTORVET 29 A/S - COLLABORATOR : MOE & BRØDSGAARD

Bjarke Ingels, Andreas Klok Pedersen, Jan Børgstrom, Camilla Hoel Eduardsen, David Vega, Eva Hviid-Nielsen, Tina Lund Højgaard Jensen, Ville Haimala, Doug Stechshulte

ECH

ESCHER TOWER
SIZE : 20,000 M2, HEIGHT: 200 M - LOCATION : COPENHAGEN, DK - CLIENT : FIRST HOTEL

Bjarke Ingels, Niels Lund Petersen, Bo Benzon, Imke Bahlmann, Krestian Ingemann Hansen, Marc Jay, Matias Labarca Clausen, Mikelis Putrams, Wataru Tanaka, Karsten Hammer Hansen

 TØJ

TØJHUS HOUSING
SIZE : 20,000 M2, HEIGHT: 200 M - LOCATION : COPENHAGEN, DK - CLIENT : FIRST HOTEL - COLLABORATORS : JDS, TAKKER

Bjarke Ingels, Niels Lund Petersen, Julien De Smedt, Bo Benzon, Imke Bahlmann, Krestian Ingemann Hansen, Marc Jay, Matias Labarca Clausen, Mikelis Putrams, Roberto Rosales Salazar, Louise Høyer, Jakob Lange, Morten Lomholdt, Nanna Gyldholm Møller, Ole Nannberg

BAT

THE BATTERY
SIZE : 20,000 M2 - LOCATION : COPENHAGEN, DK - COLLABORATORS : JDS, NIRAS A/S, PK3

Bjarke Ingels, Ole Schrøder, Julien De Smedt, Bo Benzon, David Benitez, Eliza Rudkin, Jakob Lange, Joao Vieira Costa, Karsten Hammer Hansen, Kathrin Gimmel, Krestian Ingemann Hansen, Matias Labarca Clausen, Nanna Gyldholm Møller, Simon Herup, Simon Irgens-Møller, Thomas Garvin, Wataru Tanaka, Carina Kurzhals, Christer Nesvik, Jerôme Glay, Lacin Karaöz, Louise Fiil Hansen, Simon Portier, Yuteki Dozono, Michael Ferdinand Eliasen Henriksen, Armen Menendian, Peter Larsson, Henrik Lund, Ondrej Janku

WTC I
VILNIUS WORLD TRADE CENTER I
SIZE : 310,000 M2 - LOCATION : VILNIUS, LT

Bjarke Ingels, Ole Schrøder, Karsten Hammer Hansen, Julie Schmidt Nielsen, Michael Ferdinand Eliasen Henriksen, Jérôme Glay, Simon Potier, Hans Bærholm, Marc Jay, Rie Shiomi, Roberto Rosales Salazar, Eva Hviid-Nielsen

WTC II
VILNIUS WORLD TRADE CENTER II
SIZE : 200,000 M2 - LOCATION : VILNIUS, LT
COLLABORATOR : NIRAS A/S

Bjarke Ingels, Ole Schrøder, Bo Benzon, David Benitez, Eliza Rudkin, Jakob Lange, Joao Vieira Costa, Karsten Hammer Hansen, Kathrin Gimmel, Krestian Ingemann Hansen, Matias Labarca Clausen, Nanna Gyldholm Møller, Simon Herup, Simon Irgens-Møller, Thomas Garvin, Wataru Tanaka, Jérôme Glay, Julie Schmidt-Nielsen, Simon Portier

ZIRA
ZIRA ISLAND
SIZE : 1,000,000 M2 - LOCATION : BAKU, AZERBAIJAN - CLIENT : AVRO-SITI HOLDING - COLLABORATOR : RAMBØLL

Bjarke Ingels, Andreas Klok Pedersen, Kai-Uwe Bergmann, Sylvia Feng, Kinga Rajczykowska, Pål Arnulf Trodahl, Pauline Lavie, Maxime Enrico, Oana Simionescu, Alex Cozma, Molly Price, Ondrej Janku

HAV
SUPERHARBOUR
SIZE : 680 HA - LOCATION : FEMERN BELT, DK - CLIENT : DANISH AND GERMAN PRIVATE AND PUBLIC PARTNERING PROJECT - COLLABORATORS : JDS, BRUCE MAU DESIGN

Bjarke Ingels, Julien De Smedt, Andreas Klok Pedersen, Dan Stubbergaard, Anne Louise Breiner, David Zahle, Mads Birgens, Teis Draiby

VEJ
THE VEJLE HOUSES
SIZE : 15,000 M2 - LOCATION : VEJLE, DK - CLIENT : NCC & KUBEN - COLLABORATOR : JDS

Bjarke Ingels, Julien De Smedt, Dan Stubbergaard, Casper Larsen, Eva Hviid-Nielsen, Henning Stüben, Jakob Christensen, Karsten Hammer Hansen, Nanako Ishizuka, Narisara Ladawal, Nina Ter-Borch, Simon Irgens-Møller, Sophus Søbye, Dan Stubbergaard

W
W TOWERS
SIZE : 38,000M2 - LOCATION : PRAGUE, CZ - COLLABORATOR : AKT

Bjarke Ingels, Niels Lund Petersen, Jan Magasanik, Kamil Szoltysek

HOL
HOLBÆK HOTEL
SIZE : 8,000 M2 - LOCATION : HOLBÆK, DK - CLIENT : BRAINSTONES, CORRELL EJENDOMME - COLLABORATOR : JDS

Bjarke Ingels, Andreas Klok Pedersen, Julien De Smedt, Jan Tanaka

KAS
HOLBÆK KASBA
SIZE : 13,500 M2 - LOCATION : HOLBÆK, DK - CLIENT : BRAINSTONES

Bjarke Ingels, Jakob Christensen, Julie Schmidt-Nielsen

2KR
DOUBLE PERIMETER BLOCK
SIZE : 32,000 M2 - LOCATION : HOLBÆK, DK - CLIENT : BRAINSTONES

Bjarke Ingels, Andreas Klok Pedersen, Jakob Christensen, Julie Schmidt-Nielsen, Mariano Castillo, Roberto Rosales Salazar, Simone Cartier

MET
STRETCH METAL HOUSING
SIZE : 17,000 - LOCATION : HOLBÆK, DK - CLIENT : SCHAUMANN

Bjarke Ingels, Andreas Klok Pedersen, Jakob Christensen, Julie Schmidt-Nielsen, Mariano Castillo, Roberto Rosales Salazar, Simone Cartier

---

WIB
THE FAN BUILDINGS
SIZE : 21,000 M2 - LOCATION : COPENHAGEN, DK - CLIENT : BRYGGEN WATERFRONT APS - COLLABORATORS : JDS, NIRAS A/S

Bjarke Ingels, Jan Borgstrøm, Rasmus Rodam, David Zahle, Thomas Christoffersen, Julien De Smedt, Anders Ulsted, Andreas Ellitsgaard, Christer Nesvik, Christian Brejner, Claus Tversted, Dan Stubberaard, Jan Tanaka, Kai-Uwe Bergmann, Katrin Betschinger, Kristina Loskotova, Kurt Jensen, Merete Andersen, Morten Hansen, Morten Lomholdt, Nanako Ishizuka, Ole Schrøder, Richard Howis, Sophus Søbye, Thomas Zacek, Tina Lund Højgaard Jensen, Tobias Hjortdal, Junhee Jung, Katrin Betschinger, Mikelis Putrams, Mikkel Marcker Stubgaard, Pernille Uglvig Jessen, Rasmus Sørensen, Annette Jensen, Rune Hansen, Henrik Ulsfort

MAR
MARITIME YOUTH HOUSE
SIZE : 2,000 M2 - LOCATION : COPENHAGEN, DK - CLIENT : KVARTERLØFT COPENHAGEN, LOA FUND - COLLABORATORS : JDS, BIRCH & KROGBOE

Bjarke Ingels, Julien De Smedt, Henning Stüben, Annette Jensen, Dorte Børresen, Finn Nørkjær, Jørn Jensen

SØF
THE DANISH MARITIME MUSEUM
SIZE : 17,500 M2 - LOCATION : HELSINGØR, DK - CLIENT : THE DANISH MERCANTILE AND MARITIME MUSEUM - COLLABORATOR : RAMBØLL

Bjarke Ingels, David Zahle, Rune Hansen, Karsten Hammer Hansen, Andy Yu, Pablo Labra, Marc Jay, Kristina Loskotova, Maria Mavrikou, Qianyi Lim, Peter Rieff, Tina Lund Højgaard, Annette Jensen, Johan Cool, Sara Sosio, Todd Bennett

PSY
PSYCHIATRIC HOSPITAL
SIZE : 6,000 M2 - LOCATION : HELSINGØR, DK - CLIENT : FREDERIKSBORG COUNTY, HELSINGØR HOSPITAL - COLLABORATORS : JDS, NCC, MOE & BRDSGGAARD

Bjarke Ingels, Julien De Smedt, David Zahle, Jakob Eggen, Leif Andersen, Anders Drescher, Anna Manosa, Annette Jensen, Ask Hvas, Casper Larsen, Christian Finderup, Dennis Rasmussen, Finn Nørkjær, Hanne Halvorsen, Henrik Juel Nielsen, Ida Marie Nissen, Jakob Møller, Jamie Meunier, Jesper Bo Jensen, Jesper Wichmann, Jørn Jensen, Kasper Brøndum Larsen, Lene Nørgaard, Louise Steffensen, Nanna Gyldholm Møller, Simon Irgens-Møller, Thomas Christoffersen, Xavier Pavia Pages

SJA
SJAKKET YOUTH CLUB
SIZE : 2,000 M2 - LOCATION : COPENHAGEN, DK - CLIENT : SJAKKET YOUTH CENTRE, REALDANIA - COLLABORATORS : JDS, BIRCH & KROGBOE

Bjarke Ingels, Julien De Smedt, Sophus Søbye, Bo Benzon, Christian Dam, David Zahle, Julie Schmidt-Nielsen, Kathrin Gimmel, Louise Steffensen, Mia Frederiksen, Nanna Gyldholm Møller, Nina Ter-Borch, Ole Elkjær-Larsen, Ole Nannberg, Olmo Ahlmann, Søren Lambertsen, Narisara Ladawal

ODA
ODENSE AQUA CENTER
SIZE : 5,000 M2 - LOCATION : ODENSE, DK - CLIENT : ODENSE MUNICIPALITY, REALDANIA FOUNDATION - COLLABORATOR : JDS

Bjarke Ingels, Julien De Smedt, Finn Nørkjær, Kurt Jensen, Annette Jensen, Casper Larsen, Christian Guttler, Christina Garcia Gomez, Eva Hviid-Nielsen, Gianfranco Biagini, Gudjon Kjartansson, Hanne Halvorsen, Hao Li, Helena Kristina Nyholm, Jakob Lange, Jamie Meunier, Jennifer Dahm Petersen, Jørn Jensen, Karsten Hammer Hansen, Lene Nørgaard, Oliver Grundahl, Peter Voigt Allbertsen, Rie Shiomi, Snorre Nash, Thomas Christoffersen, Thomas Tulinius

STA
STAVANGER CONCERT HALL
SIZE : 22,000 M2 - LOCATION : STAVANGER, NO - CLIENT : STAVANGER CITY COUNCIL, STAVANGER ORCHESTRA - COLLABORATOR : JDS

Bjarke Ingels, Julien De Smedt, David Zahle, Alistair Williams, Anders Drescher, Jakob Lange, Karsten Hammer Hansen, Marc Jay, Sandra Knöbel, Sune Nordby, Thomas Christoffersen

BKI
LANDSBANKINN
SIZE : 20,000 M2 HQ + 13,000 M2 DEVELOPMENT - LOCATION : REYKJAVIK, ICELAND - CLIENT : LANDSBANKINN - COLLABORATORS : EINRUM, ARKITEO, ANDRI MAGNASON, VSÓ, AKT, TRANSSOLAR

Bjarke Ingels, Thomas Christoffersen, Agustin Perez-Torres, Catherine Huang, Janghee Yoo, Junehee Jung, Jung IK Kong, Sonja Reisinger, Jan Magasanik, Maria Glez-Cabanellas, Grisha Zotov, Line Gericke, Marcello Cova, Simon Potier

SLU

SLUSSEN
SIZE : 150.000 M2 - LOCATION : STOCKHOLM, SE
CLIENT : STOCKHOLM MUNICIPALITY - COLLABORATORS : AKT, NOD

Bjarke Ingels, Niels Lund Petersen, Jan Magasanik, Daniel Sundlin, Marc Jay, Johan Cool, David Marek, Ole Schrøder, Roberto Rosales Salazar, Maria Mavrikou, Kamil Szoltysek, Ondrej Tichy, Teis Draiby

---

 BRO

HOUSING BRIDGE
SIZE : 100.000 M2 - LOCATION : COPENHAGEN, DK
COLLABORATOR : JDS

Bjarke Ingels, Andreas Klok Pedersen, Julien De Smedt, Jakob Christensen, Julie Schmidt Nielsen, Maxime Enrico, Oana Simionescu

---

KLM

THE KLØVERMARKEN
SIZE : 200.000 M2, 5000 RESIDENCES - LOCATION : COPENHAGEN, DK - CLIENT : KLØVERMARKEN DEVELOPMENT COMPANY COLLABORATOR : JDS

Bjarke Ingels, Andreas Klok Pedersen, Julien De Smedt, Bo Benzon, David Zahle, Jakob Christensen, Julie Schmidt-Nielsen, Ole Schrøder, Stefan Mylleager Frederiksen

---

 HOLY

HOLY ROAD
SIZE : 4.500 M2 - LOCATION : ATHENS, GRE - CLIENT : OLIAROS S.A.

Bjarke Ingels, Andreas Klok Pedersen, Doug Stechschulte, Marie Lancon, Simon Lyager Poulsen, Andy Rah, Kinga Rajczykowska, Ondrej Janku

---

HOJ

RØDOVRE TOWER
SIZE : 27.500 M2 - LOCATION : RØDOVRE, DK - CLIENT : RØDOVRE MUNICIPALITY - COLLABORATOR : RAMBØLL

Bjarke Ingels, Nanna Gyldholm Møller, Frederik Lyng, Pål Arnulf Trodahl, Florian Feddereke, Jacub Chuchlik

---

 ARL

ARLANDA HOTEL
SIZE : 25.000 M2 - LOCATION : ARLANDA, SE - CLIENT : FIRST HOTEL

Bjarke Ingels, Andreas Klok Pedersen, Douglas Stechschulte, Marie Camille Lancon, Simon Lyager Poulsen, Christer Nesvik, Simon Portier, Roberto Rosales, Sara Sosio

---

SHK

THE LEADERSHIP TOWER
SIZE : 100 .000 M2 - LOCATION : DUBAI - CLIENT : SAID ABDUL HADI

Bjarke Ingels, Andreas Klok Pedersen, Jakub Chuchlik

 BAW

THE 5 PILLARS OF BAWADI
SIZE : 80.000 M2 HOTEL, 110.000 M2 RETAIL - LOCATION : DUBAI, UAE - CLIENT : SAID ABDUL HADI - COLLABORATOR : AKT

Bjarke Ingels, Agustin Perez-Torres, Ole Schrøder, Enrico Lau, Catherine Huang, Marcello Cova, Ole Storjohann, Lacin Karaöz, Sonja Reisinger, Karsten Hammer Hansen

---

 BI

ØRESTAD BIOPSY

Bjarke Ingels, Advisor-Jens Thomas Arnfred

ET STYKKE ØRESTAD

 SHO

SHORTCUT

Bjarke Ingels, Julien De Smedt - Collaborator: JDS

 ITA

INFORMATION TECHNOLOGY AND ARCHITECTURE

Bjarke Ingels, Julien De Smedt - Collaborators: JDS, E-Tect

 SUB

THE NEW SUBURBS

Bjarke Ingels, Julien De Smedt - Collaborator: JDS

 DRE

DREJEN RESIDENTIAL CITY

Bjarke Ingels, Julien De Smedt - Collaborator: JDS

BBB

BETTER AND AFFORDABLE HOUSING

Bjarke Ingels, Julien De Smedt, Søren Stærmose, Christina Garcia Gomez, Annette Jensen, Casper Larsen, Claus Tversted, Dan Stubbergaard, David Zahle, Dhairya S. Ramesh Powar, Finn Nørkjær, Gudjon Kjartansson, Hanne Halvorsen, Kasper Brøndum Larsen, Lene Nørgaard, Narisara Ladawal, Nina Ter-Borch, Oliver Grundahl, Thomas Christoffersen, Thomas Tulinius - Collaborator: JDS

 KTK

THE ROYAL DANISH THEATER

Bjarke Ingels, Julien De Smedt, Benedicte Erritzøe, Cristina Garcia Gomez, Finn Nørkjær, Gudjon Kjartansson. Jakob Ohm Laursen, Kristain Sejer, Laszlo Fecske, Oliver Grundahl, Thomas Christoffersen, Thomas Tulinius - Collaborators: JDS, Dr. Dante

---

 MON

GEOLOGY MUSEUM AND VISITORS CENTER

Bjarke Ingels, Julien De Smedt, David Zahle, Annette Jensen, Finn Nørkjær, Gudjon Kjartansson, Henrik Juul Nielsen, Lene Nørgaard, Oliver Grundahl, Thomas Tulinius - Collaborator: JDS

 DBF

DEUTSCHE BAHN FRANKFURT HOUSING QUARTER

Bjarke Ingels, Julien De Smedt, Gudjon Kjartansson, Henning Stüben, Henrik Juul Nielsen, Ida Marie Nissen, Jamie Meunier, Jesper Reiter, Jeppe Kjærsgaard Jørgensen, Lene Nørgaard, Oliver Grundahl, Thomas Tulinius, Viviana Vidal Iversen - Collaborators: JDS, Ramboll Nyvig

---

 BKO

BIKUBEN STUDENT HOUSING

Bjarke Ingels, Julien De Smedt, Annette Jensen, Gudjon Kjartansson, Henrik Juul Nielsen, Ida Marie Nissen, Jeppe Kjærsgaard, Lene Nørgaard, Oliver Grundahl, Dhairya Sheel Ramesh Powar, Snorre Nash - Collaborators: JDS, Birch & Krogboe

---

GYM

HIGH SCHOOL OF THE FUTURE

Bjarke Ingels, Julien De Smedt, David Zahle, David Rahle, Henrik Juul Nielsen - Collaborators: JDS, Kant, Dorte Mandrup

---

GEM

GRAND EGYPTIAN MUSEUM

Bjarke Ingels, Julien De Smedt, Barbara Wolff, Dorte Børresen, Henning Stüben, Henrik Juul Nielsen - Collaborators: JDS, Reed Kram, Moe & Brødsgaard

SYD COPENHAGEN SOUTH HARBOUR

Bjarke Ingels, Julien De Smedt, Dorte Børresen, Henning Stüben, Henrik Juul Nielsen, Jeppe Kjærsgaard Jørgensen, Laszlo Fecske – Collaborator: JDS

 BLÅ SPORT AND COMMUNITY CENTER IN NØRREBRO

Bjarke Ingels, Julien De Smedt, Dorte Børresen, Ingrid Serritslev, Mads H. Lund, Marc Jay, Thomas Christoffersen – Collaborator: JDS

 FRE FREJA PROPERTY'S ESTATE IN HERSTEDVESTER

Bjarke Ingels, Julien De Smedt, Annette Jensen, Dorte Børresen, Henning Stüben, Jamie Meunier, Thomas Christoffersen, Xavier Pavia Pages – Collaborator: JDS

 BÅD PREFABRICATED HOUSEBOATS

Bjarke Ingels, Julien De Smedt, Lars Larsen, Annette Jensen, Jakob Lange, Jesper Bo Jensen, Jørn Jensen, Nanna Gyldholm Møller, Sune Nordby, Thomas Christoffersen, Karsten Hammer Hansen – Collaborators: JDS, CC-Design

 SKY SKY LOUNGE

Bjarke Ingels, Julien De Smedt – Collaborator: JDS

 RSH RED STAR HARBOUR

Bjarke Ingels, Julien De Smedt, Andreas Klok Pedersen, Anne Louise Breiner, Dan Stubbergaard, Mads Birgens, Teis Draiby Collaborator: JDS

 HWH HARDWOOD HOUSES

Bjarke Ingels, Julien De Smedt, David Zahle, Dhairya Sheel Ramesh Powar, Kasper Brøndum Larsen, Mads H. Lund, Morten Diediskis, Ole Elkjær-Larsen, Ole Nannberg, Peter Voigt Allbertsen, Rikke Møller Andersen, Søren Lambertsen, Thomas Christoffersen – Collaborators: JDS, Moe & Brødsgaard

 RIG DAUGAVA EMBANKMENT

Bjarke Ingels, Julien De Smedt, Jakob Lange – Collaborator: JDS

 PAV PRAGSBOULEVARD PAVILION

Bjarke Ingels, Julien De Smedt, David Zahle – Collaborator: JDS

 SAX YOUTH HOUSING IN GLADSAXE

Bjarke Ingels, Julien De Smedt, Lars Larsen, Jakob Lange, Jørn Jensen, Sune Nordby – Collaborator: JDS

 MAG HIGH SQUARE MAGASIN DU NORD

Bjarke Ingels, Julien De Smedt, Thomas Christoffersen, Finn Nørkjær, Henrik Juul Nielsen, Jesper Wichmann, Xavier Pavia Pages – Collaborators: JDS, Birch & Krogboe

 AKS ARCTIC CULTURAL CENTER

Bjarke Ingels, Julien De Smedt, Thomas Christoffersen, Dorte Børresen, Karsten Hammer Hansen, Sandra Knöbel – Collaborators: JDS, Moe & Brødsgaard

 BAD COPENHAGEN HARBOUR BATH

Bjarke Ingels, Julien De Smedt, Jakob Møller, Finn Nørkjær, Christian Finderup, Henning Stüben, Ingrid Serritslev, Marc Jay – Collaborators: JDS, Birch & Krogboe, CC-Design

 FAX HOUSEBOAT DOCK IN FAKSE LADEPLADS

Bjarke Ingels, Julien De Smedt, Thomas Christoffersen, Karsten Hammer Hansen – Collaborators: JDS, CC-Design

 SCI COPENHAGEN SCIENCE HOUSE

Bjarke Ingels, Julien De Smedt – Collaborator: JDS

 BIR ROOFTOP TERRACES IN BIRKEGADE

Bjarke Ingels, Julien De Smedt, Thomas Christoffersen, Eva Hviid-Nielsen, Mia Frederiksen, Morten Lomholdt, Nanako Ishizuka – Collaborator: JDS

 BNK COPENHAGEN BUNKERS

Bjarke Ingels, Julien De Smedt, Dorte Børresen – Collaborator: JDS

 VSB BATHING FACILITIES AND BEACH

Bjarke Ingels, Julien De Smedt, Thomas Christoffersen, Candice Enderlé, Mia Frederiksen, Sophus Søbye – Collaborator: JDS

 STO STOCKHOLM CONTEMPORARY DANCE THEATER

Bjarke Ingels, Julien De Smedt, Thomas Christoffersen, Francois Blanciak, Ingrid Serritslev – Collaborator: JDS

 LIM THE IRISH WORLD PERFORMING ART VILLAGE

Bjarke Ingels, Julien De Smedt, Thomas Christoffersen, Anders Drescher, Narisara Ladawal, Nina Ter-Borch, Olmo Ahlmann Collaborator: JDS

WWA WHITE WATER ADVENTURE PARK

Bjarke Ingels, Julien De Smedt, Thomas Christoffersen, Narisara Ladawal – Collaborator: JDS

 EPO EUROPEAN PATENT OFFICE

Bjarke Ingels, Julien De Smedt, David Zahle, Annette Jensen, Karsten Hammer Hansen, Nanna Gyldholm Møller, Narisara Ladawal, Nina Ter-Borch – Collaborators: JDS, Arup

 PSY2 TRONDHEIM PSYCHIATRIC HOSPITAL

Bjarke Ingels, Julien De Smedt, David Zahle, Christian Dam, Jan Tanaka, Karsten Hammer Hansen – Collaborators: JDS, White

 ESSO STAVANGER HOUSING AND PARK

Bjarke Ingels, Julien De Smedt, Andreas Klok Pedersen, Jan Tanaka, Karsten Hammer Hansen, Nanna Gyldholm Møller, Nicola Schiaffano – Collaborators: JDS, BDA

 AIR COPENHAGEN AIRPORT

Bjarke Ingels, David Zahle, Julien De Smedt, Candice Enderlé, Christian Dam, Louise Hebøll, Nanako Ishizuka, Niels Brockenhuus, Niels Lund Petersen, Ole Elkjær-Larsen, Peter Larson, Peter Voigt Allbertsen, Simon Herup, Thomas Garvin – Collaborator: JDS

 K3B ØRESTAD CITY HOUSING

Bjarke Ingels, Julien De Smedt, Thomas Christoffersen, Annette Jensen, Damita Yu, Karsten Hammer Hansen, Mia Frederiksen, Nanna Gyldholm Møller, Sophus Søbye, Tina Kortmann – Collaborator: JDS

 POL HAMBROGSGADE OFFICE BUILDING

Bjarke Ingels, Julien De Smedt, Andreas Klok Pedersen, Candice Erderlé, Christian Dam, Jan Tanaka, Katrin Betschinger, Mia Frederiksen, Nanna Gyldholm Møller – Collaborators: JDS, Moe & Brødsgaard

 RIN RINGKØBING CULTURAL WATERFRONT

Bjarke Ingels, Julien De Smedt, Thomas Christoffersen, Jan Tanaka, Karsten Hammer Hansen, Tina Kortmann – Collaborator: JDS

 TIV1 TIVOLI CONCERT HOUSE

Bjarke Ingels, Julien De Smedt, Nanna Gyldholm Møller, Nanako Ishizuka – Collaborator: JDS

 DÆM THE FUTURE OF DAMMING

Bjarke Ingels, Julien De Smedt, Dan Stubbergaard, Jakob Christensen, Tove Fogelström – Collaborator: JDS

 VAL VALBY URBAN PLAN

Bjarke Ingels, Julien De Smedt, Andreas Klok Pedersen, Christian Dam, Dhairya Sheel Ramesh Powar, Jan Tanaka, Mia Frederiksen, Nanna Gyldholm Møller – Collaborator: JDS

 KKS KRISTIANSAND THEATER- OG CONCERTHOUSE

Bjarke Ingels, Thomas Christoffersen, David Zahle, Julien De Smedt, Jan Tanaka – Collaborator: JDS

 HOME HOTEL IN CHRISTIANSHAVN

Bjarke Ingels, Julien De Smedt, Andreas Klok Pedersen, Jakob Christensen, Jan Tanaka, Kathrin Gimmel, Simon Irgens-Møller – Collaborators: JDS, Moe & Brødsgaard

 BCH REHABILITATION CENTER IN CHARLOTTENLUND

Bjarke Ingels, Julien De Smedt, Christina Garcia Gomez, Annette Jensen, Casper Larsen, Claus Tversted, Dan Stubbergaard, David Zahle, Dhairya Sheel Ramesh Powar, Finn Nørkjær, Gudjon Kjartansson, Hanne Halvorsen, Kasper Brøndum Larsen, Lene Nørgaard, Narisara Ladawal, Nina Ter-Borch, Oliver Grundahl, Søren Stærmos, Thomas Christoffersen, Thomas Tulinius – Collaborator: JDS

 B2R BRUUNS BAZAAR SCANDINAVIAN STORES

Bjarke Ingels, Julien De Smedt, Ole Schrøder, Ali Tabatabai, Bo Benzon, Candice Enderlé, Christian Dam, Joao Vieira Costa, Karsten Hammer Hansen, Peter Larson, Stefan Mylleager Frederiksen – Collaborator: JDS

 AUF AALBORG UNIVERSITET

Bjarke Ingels, Julien De Smedt, Karsten Hammer Hansen, Peter Berg – Collaborator: JDS

 SKUB CULTURE CENTER IN ORDRUP

Bjarke Ingels, Julien De Smedt, Andreas Klok Pedersen, Jakob Lange – Collaborators: JDS, Nord

1ST 1ST HOTEL AND CONFERENCE CENTER

Bjarke Ingels, Andreas Klok Pedersen, Julien De Smedt, Bo Benzon, Christian Bay, Damita Yu, Enrico Lau, Jakob Christensen, Jan Tanaka, Julie Schmidt-Nielsen, Karla Spennrath, Karsten Hammer Hansen, Kathrin Gimmel, Peter Larson, Simon Irgens, Qianyi Lim, Søren Lambertsen, Thomas Garvin – Collaborator: JDS

 TYP DRAGON HOUSING

Bjarke Ingels, Julien De Smedt, Morten Lumholdt, Bo Benzon, Ole Nannberg – Collaborator: JDS

 KUNG UMEÅ CITY HALL SQUARE

Bjarke Ingels, Andreas Klok Pedersen, Julien De Smedt, Jakob Christensen, Jan Tanaka – Collaborators: JDS, White A/S

RAC — STATE ADMINISTRATIVE CITY

Bjarke Ingels, Julien De Smedt, Simon Irgens, Catherine Huang, Enrico Lau, Jerôme Glay, Jonas Lehmann, Nanna Gyldholm Møller, Ondrej Tichy, Sebastian Frerichs, Kathrin Gimmel, Karsten Hammer Hansen – Collaborator: JDS

LOA — SPORTS CENTER

Bjarke Ingels, Julien De Smedt, Ole Schrøder, Jakob Lange, Jakob Christensen, Jan Tanaka - Collaborator: JDS

MER — DOLPHINARIUM AND WELLNESS CENTRE

Bjarke Ingels, Julien De Smedt, Simon Herup, David Benitz, Jakob Lange, Joao Vieira Costa, Julie Schmidt-Nielsen, Karla Spennrath, Karsten Hammer Hansen, Kathrin Gimmel, Leon Rost, Yooju Yooju – Collaborator: JDS

KRI — KRISTIANSAND AQUA CENTER

Bjarke Ingels, Jennifer Dahm Petersen, Rikke Møller Andersen, Jakob Christensen, David Benitez, Julie Schmidt-Nielsen, Christian Dam – Collaborator: JDS

AKT — CULTURE PAVILION

Bjarke Ingels, Julien De Smedt, Ole Schrøder, Jakob Lange, Jan Tanaka, Mia Frederiksen - Collaborators: JDS, Pihl A/S, Tækker A/S

BIL — CAR PARK AND HOUSING

Bjarke Ingels, Julien De Smedt, Jennifer Dahm Petersen, Louise Hebøll, Peter Larson, Thomas Garvin, David Benitez - Collaborator: JDS

DR2 — DR2

Bjarke Ingels, Julien De Smedt, Andreas Klok Pedersen, Jakob Lange – Collaborator: JDS

KRP — KRØYERS PLADS

Bjarke Ingels, Julien De Smedt, David Zahle, Bo Benzon, David Vega, Jakob Christensen, Jennifer Dahm Petersen, Kathrin Gimmel, Marc Jay, Peter Larson, Peter Gavin Kornerup, Peter Voigt Albertsen, Simon Irgens-Møller - Collaborators; JDS, NCC, Carlyle Group

POST — STAVANGER POST OFFICE

Bjarke Ingels, Julien De Smedt, Jakob Christensen, Kathrin Gimmel – Collaborator: JDS

UPX — UPPER TEN TYPEHOUSES

Bjarke Ingels, Julien De Smedt, Nanna Gyldholm Møller, Morten Lomholdt, Ole Nannberg - Collaborator: JDS

MID — BANK HEADQUARTERS IN MIDDELFART

Bjarke Ingels, Julien De Smedt, Karsten Hammer Hansen, Louise Hebøll – Collaborator: JDS

NAB — NORTH ATLANTIC CULTURE HOUSE

Bjarke Ingels, Julien De Smedt, Andreas Klok Pedersen, Jakob Christensen, Jan Tanaka, Simon Irgens-Møller – Collaborator: JDS

M2 — M2 TYPE HOUSES

Bjarke Ingels, Julien De Smedt, Kurt Jensen, Bo Benzon, Casper Larsen, David Vega, David Zahle, Hao Li, Jeppe Ecklon, Karsten Hammer Hansen, Kasper Brøndum Larsen, Livia Paula Zanelli De Morais, Nanna Gyldholm Møller, Ole Elkjær-Larsen, Ole Nannberg, Peter Voigt Albertsen, Sophus Søbye, Tina Lund Højgaard Jensen – Collaborator: JDS

MAS — MULTI-PURPOSE HALLS IN ASSENS

Bjarke Ingels, Julien De Smedt, Eva Hviid-Nielsen, Katrin Betschinger – Collaborator: JDS

SKI — TRYSIL SKI RESORT

Bjarke Ingels, Jakob Lange, Benny Jepsen, Jakob Christensen, Jørgen Smeby, Kathrin Gimmel, Nina Soppelsa, Sara Almstrup

NYC — HOTEL, RESTAURANT AND CLUB

Bjarke Ingels, Jakob Lange, Thomas Christoffersen, Bo Benzon, David Zahle, Maria Sole Bravo

FUR I — VILLA FUR

Bjarke Ingels, Bo Benzon, Sophus Søbye, Ondrej Tichy, Roberto Rosales Salazar, Jeppe Ecklon, Karin Björsmo

FUR II — VILLA FUR II

Bjarke Ingels, Thomas Christoffersen, Junhee Jung, Catherine Huang, Marie Glez-Caballas

GAS — INTERNAL EXPANSION OF OSTRE GASVARRK THEATER

Bjarke Ingels, Simon Irgens, Henrik Schafranek, Lorenzo Pannot

MDE — MARINA DEL ESTE HOTEL

Bjarke Ingels, Andreas Klok Pedersen, Julie Schmidt-Nielsen, Eva Hviid-Nielsen, Jakob Christensen, Bo Benzon, Peter Gavin Kornerup

MGS MARGRETHESTADEN

Bjarke Ingels, Andreas Klok Pedersen, Daichi Takano, Julie Schmidt-Nielsen, Peter Larson, Simone Cartier

 TIV II TIVOLI RETAIL SHOP

Bjarke Ingels, Niels Lund Petersen, Julien De Smedt, Karsten Hammer Hansen, Louise Høyer, Nanako Ishizuka, Nanna Gyldholm Møller, Rie Shiomi, Stefan Mylleager

 VIB I VIBENHUS OFFICE BUILDING

Bjarke Ingels, Thomas Christoffersen, Marc Jay, Andy Yu, David Marek, Qianyi Lim, Roberto Rosales Salazar, Simone Cartier, Wataru Tanaka, Jakob Henke

 NLP NATIONAL LIBRARY OF THE CZECH REPUBLIC

Bjarke Ingels, Kathrin Gimmel, David Vega, Henrik Schafranek, Jan Magasanik, Kai-Uwe Bergmann, Krestian Ingemann Hansen, Marc Jay, Mariano Castillo, Matias Labarca Clausen, Ondrej Tichy, Simone Cartier

 VIB II VIBENHUS HIGH-RISE

Bjarke Ingels, Marc Jay, Andy Yu, Qianyi Lim

 ASP ASPLUND LIBRARY EXTENSION

Bjarke Ingels, Krestian Ingemann Hansen, Christer Nesvik, David Zahle, Jan Magasanik, Kai-Uwe Bergmann, Kathrin Gimmel, Nanna Gyldholm Møller, Ondrej Tichy

 ALB HERSTEDLUND COMMUNITY TOWER

Bjarke Ingels, Mark Jay, Roberto Rosales Salazar

 ISR ISRAEL'S SQUARE

Bjarke Ingels, Niels Lund Petersen, Mikelis Putrams, Nanna Gyldholm Møller, Rie Shiomi, Andy Yu

 DUN THE DUNNY SHOW

Bjarke Ingels, Andreas Klok Pedersen, David Vega

 JESS JESSHEIM HOTEL

Bjarke Ingels, Marc Jay, Rasmus Rodam, Andy Yu, Christian Brejner, David Vega, Eva Hviid-Nielsen, Jan Borgstrøm, Kristoffer Harling, Matias Labarca Clausen, Martin Hjejl, Jin Kyung Park, Masatoshi Oka, Maria Glez-Cabanellas, Armen Menendian

 HIL HILLERØD

Bjarke Ingels, Ole Schrøder, Andy Yu, David Vega, Jakob Lange, Kristoffer Harling, Roberto Rosales Salazar, Ville Haimala

 NAI NEW FACES IN EUROPEAN ARCHITECTURE

Bjarke Ingels, Eva Hviid-Nielsen, Joshua Petrie, Mikelis Putrams

 GRO GRØNTTORVET HILLS

Bjarke Ingels, Jakob Lange, David Vega, David Zahle, Hans Bærholm, Louise Høyer, Peter Gavin Kornerup, Rie Shiomi

 LIL HAFJELL SKI RESORT

Bjarke Ingels, Jakob Lange, Andy Yu, Camilla Hoel Eduardsen, Dariusz Bojarski, David Marek, David Vega, Merete Kinnerup Andersen, Pablo Ladra

 BIO MOVIE THEATER IN NYKØBING

Bjarke Ingels, Krestian Ingemann Hansen, Mikelis Putrams, Joshua Petrie, Roberto Rosales Salazar

 BCN BARCELONA PROTOTYPE

Bjarke Ingels, Maria Sole Bravo, Christian Bratz, Jeppe Ecklon, Louise Fiil Hansen, Michael Ferdinand Eliasen Henriksen, Teis Draiby

 ITU IT INCUBATOR

Morten Lomholdt, Rie Shiomi, Peter Kornerup

 TRE TRETORN RESIDENCES

Bjarke Ingels, Andreas Klok Pedersen, Agustin Perez Torres, Camilla Hoel Eduardsen, David Vega, Jakob Lange, Rasmus Rodam

 KINA YANCHENG + PIZHOU

Bjarke Ingels, Niels Lund Petersen, Nanna Gyldholm Møller, David Vega, Roberto Rosales Salazar

   **OPAL** OPALTORGET URBAN STUDY

Bjarke Ingels, Rasmus Rodam, Niels Lund Petersen, David Marek, Maria Mavrikou, Roberto Rosales Salazar, Sonja Reisinger, Helene Käschel, Jin Kyung Park

BI BIG IDEAS EXHIBITION

Bjarke Ingels, Jan Magasanik, Ondrej Tichy, Henrik Schafranek, Jakon Monefeldt, Peter Rieff, Jonas Bülow-Olsen Wolffbrandt

 VEGA **MEGA VEGA**

Bjarke Ingels, Jakob Lange, Andreas Klok Pedersen, Lenka Lesso, Maria Sole Bravo, Pablo Labra, Peter Rieff, Tina Lund Højgaard Jensen, Yuteki Dozono

 NEO NEOPOLIS TECHNOPARK

Bjarke Ingels, Eva Hviid-Nielsen, Nanna Gyldholm Møller, Ondrej Tichy, Teis Draiby

 TYF TYPHOON

Bjarke Ingels, Marc Jay, Andy Yu, Armen Menendian, Carina Kurzhals, Enrico Lau, Jeppe Marling Kiib, Julie Schmidt-Nielsen, Karsten Hammer Hansen, Luis Felipe González Delgado, Martin Hejl, Masatoshi Oka, Sigurd Elling

 WAR WARSAW MUSEUM OF MODERN ART

Bjarke Ingels, David Zahle, Agustin Perez Torres, Andy Yu, David Vega, Jan Magasanik, Kai-Uwe Bergmann, Kristina Loskotova, Louise Hansen, Marc Jay, Pablo Ladra, Peter Larson, Peter Rieff, Simon Lyager Poulsen, Tina Lund Højgaard Jensen

 PARK PARKEN NEW SPORTS ARENA

Bjarke Ingels, Niels Lund Petersen, Nanna Gyldholm Møller, Cat Huang, Jonas Lehmann, Ondrej Tichy, Brian Yang

 SORØ HOUSING, RETAIL AND PARKING IN SORØ

Bjarke Ingels, Nanna Gyldholm Møller, Byungki Kim, Eva Hviid-Nielsen, Niels Lund Pedersen, Julie Schmidt-Nielsen, Ondrej Tichy, David Marek, Liva Paula Zanelli De Morais, Maria Mavrikov

 RUD RUDKØBING LANGELAND MASTERPLAN

Bjarke Ingels, Peter Larsson, Jakob Lange, Joost Van Nes, Yuteki Dozono

 CARL CARLSBERG CAMPUS

Bjarke Ingels, Ole Schrøder, David Marek, Kai-Uwe Bergmann, Louise Fiil Hansen, Michael Ferdinand Eliasen Henriksen, Ondrej Tichy – Collaborators: Cobe, e-Types, Cowi, SLA, Gallery V1

 BOR BORGERGADE HOUSING

Bjarke Ingels, Marc Jay, David Zahle, Martin Hejl, Jennifer Myers, Masatoshi Oka, Jan Borgstrøm

REF REFSHALEØEN STUDY

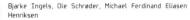
Bjarke Ingels, Ole Schrøder, Michael Ferdinand Eliasen Henriksen

 RADIO RADIOHUSET

Bjarke Ingels, Niels Lund Petersen, Andy Yu, Carina Kurzhals, Daichi Takano, Kamil Szoltysek, Julia Szierer, Daniel Sundlin, Joanna Gasparski.

 KIEV HOUSING, RETAIL AND PARKING IN KIEV

Bjarke Ingels, Nanna Gyldholm Møller, Ondrej Tichy, David Marek, Liva Paula Zanelli De Morais, Eva Hviid-Nielsen, Julie Schmidt-Nielsen, Teis Draiby, Lenka Lesso, Daichi Takano – Collaborator: Zotov & Co

 TATE TATE MOBILE

Bjarke Ingels, Niels Lund Petersen, Brian Yang, Cat Huang, Yuteki Dozono, Andreas Klok Pedersen

 GUD SDR. TRANDERS

Bjarke Ingels, Jeppe Ecklon, Peter Larsson

 BIGX COPENHAGEN EXPERIMENTS, STOREFRONT

Bjarke Ingels, Kai-Uwe Bergmann, Jan Magasanik, Doug Stechshulte, Lacin Karaöz, Marie Camille Lancon, Toke Nielsen, Wayne Congar

 HOA HANDBALL ARENA AND HOUSING

Bjarke Ingels, David Zahle, Andy Yu, Pablo Lebra

KERT KERTEMINDE HARBOUR FRONT

Bjarke Ingels, Julie Schmidt-Nielsen, Simon Portier – Collaborator: KLAR

 TERM SANTA CESAREA TERME

Bjarke Ingels, Julie Schmidt-Nielsen, Ole Schrøder, Peter Larson, Sara Sosio, Martin Hejl, Qianyi Lim – Collaborator: SLA

 VOID VOID HOUSE

Bjarke Ingels, Jakob Lange, Merete Kinnerup Andersen, David Zahle, Sonja Reisinger, Po Yuan Lin, Line Gericke, Annette Jensen, Anders Ulsted, Helene Käschel, Alexandru Marian Cozma, Hanna Johanson

RING RING HOUSE

Bjarke Ingels, Jakob Lange, Merete Kinnerup Andersen, David Zahle, Sonja Reisinger, Po Yuan Lin, Line Gericke, Annette Jensen, Anders Ulsted, Helene Käschel, Alexandru Marian Cozma, Hanna Johanson

 ØRE ØRESUNDSPARKEN

Bjarke Ingels, Ole Schrøder, David Zahle, Jeremo Glay, Simon Potier, Nanna Gyldholm Møller, Marcello Cova, Lacin Karaöz, Marcello Cova, Ole Storjohan, Frederik Lyng, Pål Arnulf Trodahl, Joanna Gasparski, Jonas Lehmann, Joao Albuquerque, Alexandru Marian Cozma

 SUK SUPERKILEN

Bjarke Ingels, Nanna Gyldholm-Møller, Mikkel Stubgaard, Jonas Lehmann, Lacin Karaöz, Ondrej Tichy, Jan Borgstrøm, Jonas Barre, Nicklas Antoni Rasch – Collaborators: Topotek1, Superflex, Help PR & Communication, Lemming Eriksson

 MONT MONTENEGRO RESIDENCES

Bjarke Ingels, Rune Hansen, Armen Menendian, Grisha Zotov, Sebastian Frerichs, Brian Yang, Morten Wulff

 **TEN** TIANJIN TENNIS CENTER

Bjarke Ingels, Andreas Klok Pedersen, Christer Nesvik, Doug Stechshulte, Grisha Zotov, Marie Camille Lancon, Simon Lyager Poulsen

 BLÅP THE BLUE PLANET

Bjarke Ingels, David Zahle, Karsten Hammer Hansen, Cat Huang, Enrico Lau, Frederik Lyng, Pål Arnulf Trodahl, Line Gericke – Collaborators: Arup Agu, Vogt, Battle Maccarthy

 4D ZIG ZAG HOUSING AND OFFICES

Bjarke Ingels, Niels Lund Petersen, Brian Yang, Catherine Huang, Enrico Lau – Collaborator: AKT

 HOT HOTEL STAVANGER

Bjarke Ingels, Nanna Gyldholm Møller, Pål Arnulf Trodahl, Jonas Lehmann, Luis Delgado, Frederik Lyng, Morten Wulff, Line Gericke, Niels Lund Petersen, Armen David Menendian

 SH SOUTH HARBOUR OFFICE AND HOUSING

Bjarke Ingels, Marc Jay, Masatoshi Oka, Sigurd Elling, Jennifer Myers

 STR STRANDPROMENADEN

Bjarke Ingels, Andreas Klok Pedersen, Marie Camille Lancon, Doug Stechshulte, Andy Rah, Tobias Hjortdal, Jan Borgstrøm, Kinga Rajczykowska

 LEEDS LEEDS SHOPPING AND HOUSING

Bjarke Ingels, Jakob Lange, Bo Benzon, Jerôme Glay, Merete Kinnerup Andersen – Collaborator: Heatherwich Studio

 ARR ARRIVA

Bjarke Ingels, Thomas Christoffersen, Janghee Yoo, Junhee Jung

 RAC2 RAC2 BRUXELLES

Bjarke Ingels, Nanna Gyldholm Møller, Jonas Lehmann, Brian Yang, Cat Huang, Enrico Lau, Jerome Glay, Sebastian Frerichs

 KOL MOTEL KOLDING

Bjarke Ingels, Rune Hansen, Armen Menendian, Sebastian Frerichs, Grisha Zotov, Morten Wulff

 FAB FABRIKKEN OFFICES

Bjarke Ingels, Kai-Uwe Bergmann, Marc Jay, Louis Filipe González Delag, Tobias Hjortdal, Bo Benzon, Rasmus Rodam, Armen Menendian, Kinga Rajczykowska, John Clark, Masatoshi Oka, SIigurd Elling, Jennifer Myer, Enrico Lau, Jan Borgstrøm

 ODE ODENPLAN OFFICES

Bjarke Ingels, Rasmus Rodam, Sonja Reisinger, Maria Glez-Cabanellas, Masatoshi Oka, Jung Ik Hong, Morten Wulff, Armen Menendian, Jin Kyung Park, Daniel Sundlin

 KOLH STUDENT HOUSING FOR HØPFNER

Bjarke Ingels, David Zahle, Julie Schmidt-Nielsen, Jonas Lehmann, Pål Arnulf Trodahl, Armen Menendian, Enrico Lau, Luis Delgado, Jakob Lange, Pauline Lavie, Simon Potier, Kamil Szoltysek

 BAKU BAKU VILLAS

Bjarke Ingels, Doug Stechschulte, Kai-Uwe Bergmann, Jakob Lange, Sonja Reisinger, John Clark, Todd Bennett – Collaborator: Rambøll

 POT POTSDAMER PLATZ BERLIN

Bjarke Ingels, Jakob Lange, Carolien Schippers, Merete Kinnerup Andersen, Sebastian Frerichs

 ABU1 ABU DHABI EXHIBITION CENTER

Bjarke Ingels, Kai-Uwe Bergmann, Ole Storjohann, Marcello Cova, Andy Rah, Sonja Reisinger, Sara Sosio, Helene Käschel – Collaborators: AKT, Realities United

ABUZ KHALIFA PARK

 Bjarke Ingels, Kai-Uwe Bergmann, Andreas Klok
Pedersen, Marie Camille Lancon, Jung Ik Hong, Morten
Wulff, Andy Rah, Ole Storjohann, Marcello Cova,
Helene Käschel – Collaborators: AKT, Realities United

 UTR UTRECHT LIBRARY

 Bjarke Ingels, Andreas Klok Pedersen, Doug
Stechshulte, Marie Camille Lancon, Jung Ik Hong,
Maria Glez-Cabanellas

 DGI DGI HOLBÆK

 Bjarke Ingels, Thomas Christoffersen, Janghee Yoo,
Junhee Jung, Marie Camille Lancon, Doug Stechshulte,
Frederik Lyng, Nanna Gyldholm Møller

 HUA HUAXI

 Bjarke Ingels, Niels Lund Petersen, Andy Rah, Ole
Storjohann, Daniel Sundlin, Kinga Rajczykowska, Sylvia
Feng

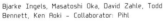 **QUI** QUINGDAO BRIDGE

 Bjarke Ingels, Masatoshi Oka, Jung Ik Hong, Maria
Glez-Cabanellas, Daniel Sundlin, Rasmus Rodam

 GYNG GYNGEMOSEHALLEN

 Bjarke Ingels, Masatoshi Oka, David Zahle, Todd
Bennett, Ken Aoki – Collaborator: Pihl

 NHU NORTH HARBOUR MASTERPLAN

 Bjarke Ingels, Ole Schrøder, Michael F. Eliasen
Henriksen, Hanna Johanson, Joanna Gasparski, Joao
Albuquerque, Kai-Uwe Bergmann, Karsten Hammer
Hansen – Collaborators: PK3, Cowi

 PHUS PARKING HOUSE KOLDING

Bjarke Ingels, Rune Hansen, Armen Menendian, Jakub
Chuchlik, Morten Wulff, Grisha Zotov

 DPC DANUBIA PARK

 Bjarke Ingels, Nanna Gyldholm Møller, David Zahle,
Gabrielle Nadeau, Frederik Lyng

 HOS HOSPICE SØNDERGÅRD

Bjarke Ingels, Nanna Gyldholm Møller, Jan Borgstrøm,
Frederik Lyng, Gabrielle Nadeau, Rune Hansen

 KOLH HOTEL KOLDING

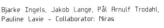 Bjarke Ingels, Jakob Lange, Pål Arnulf Trodahl,
Pauline Lavie – Collaborator: Niras

 RIK MARIEBERG STOCKHOLM

 Bjarke Ingels, Nanna Gyldholm Møller, Jakob Lange,
Pauline Lavie, Armen Menendian, Frederik Lyng,
Gabrielle Nadeau, Alexandru Marian Cozma, Oana
Simionescu

  GMO GMOMA EXHIBITION

Bjarke Ingels, Thomas Christoffersen, Jakob Henke

 TAT TALLINN TOWN HALL

Bjarke Ingels, Jakob Lange, Ondrej Janku, Hanna
Johansson, Daniel Sundlin, Harry Wei, Alex Cozma,
Jin-Kyung Park – Collaborators: AKT, Grontmij-Carl
Bro, Ramboll, Allianss Arhitektid Du

 TAM TAMAYO CULTURAL CENTER

BIG & Rojkind Arquitectos – Team BIG: Bjarke
Ingels, Andreas Klok Pedersen with Pauline Lavie,
Maxime Enrico, Pål Arnulf Trodahl. Team Rojkind
Arquitectos: Michel Rojkind with Agustín Pereyra,
Monica Orozco, Ma. Fernanda Gómez, Tere Levy, Isaac
Smeke, Juan José, Barrios, Roberto Gil Will, Joe Tarr
– Collaborators: Romo y Asociados, ENTORNO, Ernesto
Moncada, Glessner Group

 YES YES IS MORE

Bjarke Ingels, Bo Benzon, Joanna Gasparski, Ken Aoki,
Sebastian Latz, Gabrielle Nadeau, Frederik Lyng, Jakob
Lange, Jonas Barre, Jin Kyung Park, Todd Bennett,
Johan Cool, Pauline Lavie, Thomas Christoffersen,
Kai-Uwe Bergman, Darja Pahhota, Hanna Johansson,
Andreas Pedersen, Elisabeth Ginsberg, David Zahle,
Armen Menendian

YES IS MORE @ DAC

Exhibition: 20. February - 31. May 2009
Location: DAC - Danish Architecture Center
Strandgade 27B
DK-1401 Copenhagen K
Projects: 34
Models: 30
Podiums: 30
Podium material: MDF, painted black, light tubes
Acrylic plates: 45; 2050 x 2592 mm with print
Total length of backlit wall structure: 118 m
Wood and alu construction
Light tubes: 400
Screens: 19

1m

YES IS MORE
EXHIBITION PLAN
1:100

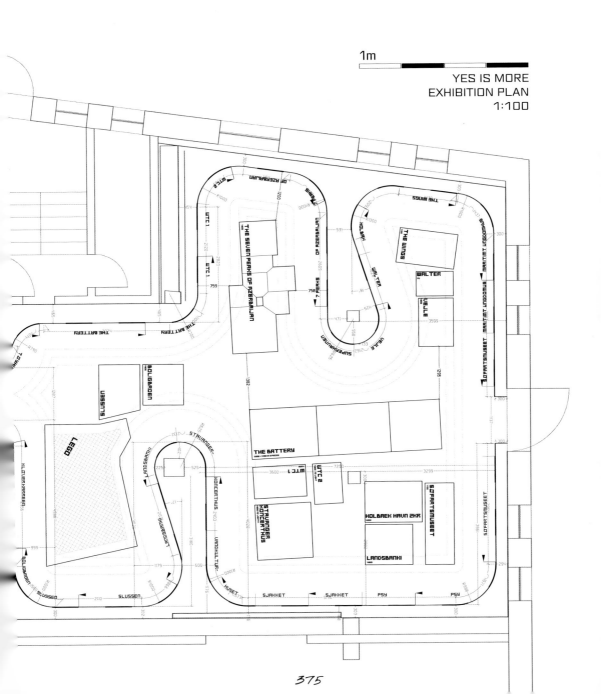

375

An Interactive 360° tour
to the Yes Is More exhibition
can be experienced
in fullscreen by visiting:
www.virtualworks.dk

Production and copyright
virtualworks.dk by architect
MAA IVRPA John F. Kroll

interactive panoramic images | www.big.dk/projects/yim

MY PLAYGROUND
TEAM JIYO @ MTN

Kaspar Astrup Schrøder's film about
Team Jiyo interests us for two rea-
sons.The first has to do with how to
communicate architecture. Where
photography is perfect for portray-
ing objects - film is the ultimate way
to show movement through space.
The slow pans, the easy turns, the
gentle zooms all give you a sense
of the space and its continuity. You
experience the ride with the funicu-
lar and the vertigo of walking up the
long façade stair.

As an architectural film alone, it would be boring. Slow. Empty. But with the two guys jumping around, testing all the surfaces, expanding the space – you perceive the architecture as it really is: the framework for human life. Architecture is a means, life is its purpose.

Secondly, because what Team Jiyo does - through exercise and acrobatics - is what we try to do through models, drawings, wood, steel and cement: They expand the public realm within the city. By climbing higher and jumping farther, they reclaim territory that is normally lost in the city, inaccessible to human occupation - an unexploited resource. For them parking garages, rooftops, alleys, containers, façades are all accessible surfaces, part of their playground.

When we work we always have a client, a need to fulfill or a demand to meet. But we try to look beyond, and see if there are any hidden resources or any latent potential that can be activated.

With the Maritime Youth House we turned walls and roofs into a dune landscape of wood.
With the Harbour Bath we turned the harbour into a giant swimming pool.
With the Mountain we turned the roof of the parking garage into a hundred gardens, and the parking garage itself into a cathedral of car culture, the façade into a promenade and the stair core into a climbing wall.
With the 8-house we are turning a Copenhagen city block into a mountain path extending the public realm for bicycles and baby strollers all the way from the ground floor to the 10th storey penthouse.

All are elements that would have to be there anyway, built and paid for. They would just be off limits and inaccessible. Bit by bit we are expanding our world, and are gradually turning our cities into our playground.

...Team Jiyo just doesn't have the patience to wait for it.

YES MAN

BJARKE INGELS
interviewed by JEFFREY INABA
for VOLUME MAGAZINE

The term Yes Man once referred to the spineless corporate crony, but today it means something else. Bjarke Ingels is a Yes Man. He says 'yes' to just about any demand, reasonable or otherwise. It fuels his ambition to accept all the political interests surrounding a project and absorb them into back-bending forms that disarm the opposition and that eventually populate large areas of Scandanavia (and beyond).

JEFFREY INABA Let's discuss your idea of evolution.
For you, revolution assumes being against something. It means being the contrarian. The first act of revolution is to say 'no', whereas the first move of evolution is to say 'yes' – 'yes' to all the requirements and demands of a project. Saying 'yes' to the client, politicians, the public requires you to process a project's often conflicting interests and to respond in an acrobatic way to find a solution suitable for all.

BJARKE INGELS I think that there is something contradictory in the fact that radicality is normally associated with reacting in opposition to somebody else's agenda. Your entire agenda is defined as being against something, rather than finding your own thing and pushing it. Secondly, it is interesting that the bad-boy is the icon of the radical. Instead, the 'good guy' could be a recipe.
If you're informed, if you're obliged to incorporate a lot of different intentions besides your own into a project, then you have a much more complex range of material to operate with and to manipulate. What we're basically trying is to say that by in-

corporating many good concerns instead of reducing them all to the lowest common denominator, you avoid compromise. Instead of meeting halfway, you oblige yourself to solve everything – to keep looking until you find that impossible move that takes into account all of the concerns of a project's constituents. Then suddenly the functional
and the fantastic become collaborators, and you as an architect don't have to refer to French philosophy, the Kaballah, or whatever source of energy an architect may use. You can just refer to the really pragmatic concerns that all the decision makers and public opinion makers are already dealing with. So architecture becomes a consequence of and the answer to a lot of problems in society. In that sense, we are much more interested in this Gesamtkunstwerk, that things are changing. And as they change, we try to observe those changes and incorporate them into the work, and to constantly gain new territory.
JI You talk about architects accepting the circumstances that they find themselves in, and responding to them by shaping the world. Can you talk more about that?

BI I think it's funny, because it relates a lot to the debate in the U.S. about 'intelligent design' – the Creationists versus the Darwinists. For Creationists, the human eye is so brilliantly engineered that it is evident some intelligent designer was behind it. They can't imagine that it evolved through this extensive process of perpetual refinement, excess, and selection. The city, just like the human species, is the way it is now because it evolved to its current state, and because we created it. And if we don't like it, we can't blame God, we can only blame ourselves. Therefore we should constantly be aware of that power and that responsibility. If it doesn't fit the way that we want to live, if the city doesn't fit the way that we want it to be, then we have to change it. I think you should always remember that we created the city, we created architecture, so therefore we can re-create it, change it, evolve it.

POLITICIAN AND THE GREAT WALL
JI You're not only an architect, you're a politician. You get involved in the political process and as a result, you are able to make your projects viable within the dynamics of political give and take. Can you talk about your experiences with the Great Wall of Housing project in Copenhagen?
BI What we are realizing is that increasingly the people we communicate with when we do projects are not our architecture colleagues. Our projects increasingly address issues that pertain to others. For instance, we did a project on our own initiative around a football field in Copenhagen. We responded to the fact that politicians wanted affordable housing because the city is fully built and people are being forced out. We wanted to create housing without cannibalizing the limited amount of the city's free space The Great Wall

of Housing is an architectural idea to circumvent a political conflict. By doing an impossible political tightrope walk, we actually made it possible to keep the football fields and have new housing.
Architecture was a means to short-circuit an irresolvable political debate. This is where architecture can operate very differently from politics. Politics is based on conflict. If you want to get press coverage you create conflict. If want to brand yourself as a politician you have to seek opposition, whereas in our understanding of design, you incorporate conflicts and resolve them. Your project is only going to survive if it tries to either navigate around the conflict or incorporate a lot of the concerns.
JI You have the skill to define the key problem of a conflict. You define what the conflict is, in this case between football fields and housing, and you use that as a starting point to generate a solution. You are able to articulate the political problem and use that as the basis to give value to the architectural proposal.
BI What you're saying is true, in that often you hear a politician being asked a question, and then he or she will respond by saying, 'I don't think that's the question. I think the question is...' And then they answer the question they want to answer. Of course, the entire idea of reframing the angle of the project is that you set the terms of the debate by defining what will be the key issues. Our statement was: who said that we had to choose between football fields and affordable homes?
The notion of proactive architecture has become a great field of interest, because we can just see the time we've invested in doing competitions where 400 people submit proposals and then it turns out that all that is wanted in the end is, like, a really sad scheme. You realize that you've

spent so much of your resources on something that could never have made it, regardless of how good it was. We realized that the few times we did a project that nobody asked us to do, we had a much better chance of success because we formulated the problem and its solution before anyone else. They say there's no good architecture without a good client – well then you should at least become the guys who formulate the commission, and get somebody else to want it.

JI Can you talk a little bit about the political give-and-take process between the different parties, and how the Great Wall project functioned as a political football in a set of larger power negotiations between parties?

BI The kind of politics that can actually inform a project is the acrobatic quest that incorporates everybody's concerns, where each parameter becomes something that gives shape to the project. In the Great Wall of China, normally you would just make as simple a perimeter block as possible, but it needed to walk this tightrope between the neighbors on one side and football fields on the other side. But then, the people living in the allotment gardens nearby were afraid that others would be able look into their gardens. So we pushed down the buildings to stop people looking in. Then, people were complaining that we were occupying too much space. But then we made the roof into a public promenade to create more public space, and so forth. You can say it became this aikido response where you constantly take criticism, incorporate it, and turn it into an architectural asset. In the end, without having designed anything, the building looked kind of cool.

We sent the proposal to all the newspapers, then we sent it to all the mayoral candidates, and it got quite positive responses. Then when the Social Democratic candidate for mayor got elected, we met with her and she endorsed it in the press. We discovered that suddenly our project had become a component of an overall political negotiation. Normally architecture is handled in the cultural section of the paper, along with cinema, music, and other forms of entertainment, but all the articles about the project were in the first section: what I normally refer to as the 'adult section', which is about the economy and politics.

We were the initiators, but it was now the mayor's project. Suddenly, we had a really powerful alliance in which a possible downfall wouldn't be ours alone. And she really has balls. I mean, I've never met a politician who was so concerned about ideas. So often you can lose yourself in the tactics, whereas she's really a great strategic mind.

So we were called to try to explain the project to her political party. It is a little like alchemy, in that you take a field with 40 football fields, you create 2,000 homes on the field and there's still 40 football fields! So we needed to explain that in detail. Once her political party was convinced, we were invited to talk to one of the support parties, the Socialist People's Party. They raved about it, but the party leader also knew that this would be the mayor's first major political battle and that she couldn't afford to lose. So he wanted to sell his vote as expensively as possible. Then we got invited to another secret meeting with the Liberals to convince them to support it. In the end, we realized that there was this cabala that needed to be settled that had to do with negotiating the city's overall budget. Finally, both the Socialist People's Party and the Liberals supported the project, but leveraged their support in exchange for negotiating their particular interests with the city's budget. The sub-headline of the articles that came out said that the three parties had approved the mayor's budget – and this meant that there would be affordable homes around the Klovermarken football fields. Even though the Socialist People's Party, and the Liberals were basically for it from the start, because it was the Mayor's project they didn't want to give her an easy victory. I was convinced it was just a question of getting access to these guys, showing the project, taking all the potential critique, and incorporating it. But I realized later it was all part of a much bigger bargain.

MASTER PLAN AND MASTERPIECE

JI Has your design process changed as your projects have become more entangled in politics?
Your projects have been super-compelling up until now for their fiscal or structural rationale, but now that projects are entering the public realm as part of a political debate, does that impact the way that you design?
BI I think two things have changed. As we went from being PLOT into being BIG, the office has grown bigger and our projects have grown bigger, meaning that in terms of the design process it is no longer this small group of people who practically do it themselves. It's more like this big collective of a lot of different people with a lot of different motivations doing a lot of different things. And there the design evolution has become a lot more evident. There's an incredible production, really an excess of ideas and models and materials and the sort of natural selection that you see in nature has turned into architectural selection.
And now a lot of our projects operate on a scale between urbanism and architecture. What ten years ago would have been considered a master plan, having different lots

that would grow over ten or twenty years, is now the basis for a masterpiece that you have to make into a single project. On one hand it needs to have the integrity of a single architectural project and at the same time, it needs to contain the complexity and variety of an urban neighborhood. It means that with many our architectural projects the key issues are urban concerns, or speculations about what the city should be, what we want from our neighborhoods, and so on. All of these concerns that are actually about urbanism, now result directly in architecture.
JI A lot of architects accept the idea that the city is so complex now that it's beyond the ability of the architect to define the city to any significant degree. And as a result, they're resigned to focusing on projects of a limited scale to explore the complexity of form itself, whereas you embrace the urban complexities that exist on political, fiscal, and public levels, and synthesize those imperatives into large-scale but deceptively simple forms.
BI We've been working with this idea of pragmatic utopia. We have tried to reinstate the modernist ambition to have big ideas. It's not just a question of personal fulfillment. It's actually a tool that the world can use to constantly refurbish itself. And as an architect you're the midwife of this continual rebirth of the world as you want to live in it. But in order to not become dreamers who always collide with all the limitations of real life, we try to realize this utopian ambition within the confines of an operational unit: to think big, and to think in terms of urbanism, but to do it within a unit over which you actually have power. Once a project in that unit is materialized it will bleed out and influence its surroundings.

JI What do you mean when you say 'masterpiece'? You don't mean an artistic masterpiece of personal expression, but rather it seems like you intend to make a distinction between the responsibility of designing a master plan and the impossible requirements of producing a building that is super-large in scale and required to have the complexities of an urban district.

BI The meaning of the word 'master' in the two terms is extremely different. The master plan is sort of a strategic guidebook for an area to evolve into a complex urban neighborhood, whereas now the building itself has to be the strategic plan. So you enter this twilight zone between a master plan and a masterpiece, where a single project is required to have an identity, but like that of a neighborhood rather than a single architectural building. It used to be quite clear. First someone made the master plan, and then some others inserted their little masterpieces. Now the two merge. You might say that the impotence of the master planner is that there is no way of knowing what will happen, because as soon as the architects come in and start working with their assigned lots there might be new demands and new ideas. Every time an architect is given a master plan, he or she spends fifty percent of the time bitching about how lame it is, and how inconsiderate all the restrictions are, how they completely eliminate the possibility of creative action, blah, blah, blah. But suddenly you have both responsibilities in one go, and you can't blame the lameness of the master-planner, because you are both planner and architect at the same time.

HUMOR

JI Humor plays a role in your work. You've said that a good joke and a good idea are similar because they are both surprising, and they make immediate sense. Can you talk a little bit more about that?

BI A joke is funny when it really sort of takes you from behind, but you get it, you know? And it's the same thing with a really brilliant idea. It's also a major part of our collective creation. In order to have this Darwinist evolution happening in our office we materialize things: we make diagrams, we make statements, and we make lots of models. Then we sit around and discuss them. The fear that the new guy in the office might have of saying something lame is eliminated if every second comment someone is cracking a joke. These jokes are often caused by someone turning things upside down, or twisting things inside out, or making unexpected combinations, or having something that looks profoundly ugly respond to a situation, and stuff like that. Quite often we might spend half a day making a model that we know is primarily funny to double check if could really work.

The thing about a really good joke is that you don't get tired of it. For instance, for the People's Building we hired a Feng Shui master as a joke. We don't really believe in Feng Shui but after a while, we started digging it. In the end, I presented the project with a smile on my face, but I also liked the fact that these Feng Shui elements are embedded in the architecture. We reference things like that as raw material for inspiration. And it makes it more fun to go to work. _

IMAGE CREDITS

INTRO: Portrait,Ludwig Mies van der Rohe, Photographer:Frank Scherschel; Portrait, Robert Venturi, Photographer: Michael Ahearn 02/XPO - A WELFAIRYTALE: Hai Bao, Photo: Matthew J. Stinson; Liang Kai: "Li Bai Strolling"; Cycler in Copenhagen (City of Copenhagen - Bicycle Account 2006), Photo: Troels Helen; Harbourbath Copenhagen, Photo: Julien de Smedt; Render: BIG / Labtop 03/LITTLE DENMARK - LEARNING FROM LOMBORG: Copenhagen Consensus/ Bjørn Lomborg, Photo: Copenhagen Consensus Center; Dlr, Deutsches Zentrum Fuer Luft- Und Raumfahrttechnik, Photo: Segs 04/VM HOUSES - URBAN TETRIS: Photos: Nicholai Moeller, Nils Lund, Esben Bruun, Jimmy Cohrssen, Johan Fowelin, Tobias Toyberg, Jasper Carlberg 05/MOUNTAIN DWELLINGS - VERTICAL SUBURBIA: Photos: Ulrik Jantzen, Jakob Boserup, Jens Lindhe, Carli Bauzá 07/ SCALA TOWER - SP(O)ANISH STEPS: Erick van Egeraat, Associated Architects: Housing, Kroyers Plads, Copenhagen, DK; Lagoons - Towers, Dubai, Thompson, Ventulett, Stainback & Associates (Tvdesign); Ateliers - Jean Nouvel New York - Tower, New York; Rem Koolhaas, OMA-Office for Metropolitan Architecture: CCTV Building, Bejing China; Photo: Khanjan Mohta 08/LEGO TOWERS - MODULAR MANIA: Maya Lin, Systematic Landscapes, 2006 09/ESCHER TOWER - SCANDINAVIAN SKYSCRAPER: M.C. Escher's "Belvedere" © 2009 The M.C. Escher Company-Holland. All Rights Reserved. www.mcescher.com 11/THE BATTERY - URBAN INTEGRATION: Tower Of Babel, Abel Grimmer (1570-1619)12/WTC - BAROQUE NETWORK: Hilbersheimer, Ludwig Karl, Project for a Skyscraper City, 1924; St. Anne Church in Vinius; Minoru Yamasaki, Emery Roth & Sons, World Trade Center, Manhattan, New York, 1972; Frank Gehry, Guggenheim Museum, BIlbao, Spain, 1997; Photo: Steve Double 14/7 PEAKS OF AZERBAIJAN - ZIRA ZERO: Render: BIG/ Oceanpic 17/W TOWERS - SPLIT PERSONALITY: Render: BIG/ Labtop 20/MARITIME YOUTHHOUSE - SWEPT UNDER THE CARPET: Photos: Paolo Rosselli, Mads Hilmer, Matias Labarca, Julien de Smedt 21/MARITIME MUSEUM - TO BE AND NOT TO BE: William Hogarth, "Columbus Breaking the Egg", 1752, Engraving 22/HELSINGØR PSYCHIATRIC HOSPITAL - COLOR THERAPY: Photo: Esben Bruun, Vegar Moen, Rikke Guldberg Hansen, Peter Sørensen; Vincent Van Gogh, Sunflowers, 1887; Vincent Van Gogh, Autoportrait, 1889 23/SJAKKET - RE-SQUAT: Photos: Vegar Moen, Matias Labarca 25/STAVANGER CONCERT HALL - PUBLIC PROSCENIUM: Frank Gehry, Guggenheim Museum, Bilbao, Spain, 1997; Rem Koolhaas, OMA-Office For Metropolitan Architecture: Casa da Musica, Porto, Portugal, 2004; Henning Larsen Architects, Opera, Copenhagen, 2004; Snøhetta, Oslo Opera House, 2008; Jørn Utzon, Opera House, Sidney, 1973; Medplan Architects: Stavanger Concert Hall, Stavanger, Norway 26/LANDSBANKI - NATIONAL ~~BANK~~ STAGE OF ICELAND: Render: BIG/ Luxigon 27/SLUSSEN - SOCIAL INFRASTRUCTURE: Render: Big/ Labtop, Luxigon; Photo: Frank Chmura 29/THE CLOVERFIELD - BATTLEFIELD: Tegnestuen Vandkunsten, Project: "Kløvermarken - 'The Green River'"; Rollercoaster, Photo: Joel Rogers 31/RØDOVRE TOWER - ENGINEERING WITHOUT ENGINES: Render: Labtop 32/ARLANDA - ROYAL TREATMENT: Logo: First Hotel 34/BAWADI - POST-PETROLIUM PALACE: Bernhard Rudolfsky, "Architecture Without Architects", 1964; Great Mosque Of Cordoba "Mezquita"; Alhambra, Granada; Antonio Gaudi, Sand Bag Model, Sagrada Familia; Render: BIG/ Labtop

CREDITS

EDITOR
Bjarke Ingels

PROJECT LEADERS
Bo Benzon and Joanna Gasparski

PROJECT TEAM
Ken Aoki, Sebastian Latz, Gabrielle Nadeau, Frederik Lyng, Jakob Lange, Jonas Barre,
Jin Kyung Park, Todd Bennett, Johan Cool, Pauline Lavie, Thomas Christoffersen

TEXT
Bjarke Ingels

IDEA
Bjarke Ingels, Andreas Pedersen, Ken Aoki, Bo Benzon, Joanna Gasparski

GRAPHIC CONCEPT
BIG
E-Types; Jens Kajus, Michael Thouber

TRANSLATION
Ulla Benzon Malmmose
Signe Lyng
Mads Hebsgaard

TEXT EDITING
Boris Brorman Jensen, Elisabeth Ginsberg, Darja Pahhota, David Zahle, Hanna Johansson, Andreas Pedersen, Kai-Uwe Bergman, Armen Menendian, Todd Bennett, Jennifer Dahm Petersen, Lea Hjort

FUNDRAISING AND PR
Jennifer Dahm Petersen, Darja Pahhota, Kai-Uwe Bergmann, Beate Bernhoft

OFFICE ADMINISTRATION
Sheela Maini Søgaard, Kristine Lorenzen, Kit Nielsen, Kristian Palsmar, Leah Løffler, Esther Løffler

PHOTOGRAPHERS
BIG ApS, PLOT A/S, Jakob Boserup, Esben Bruun, Jasper Carlberg, Jimmy Cohrssen, Johan Fowelin, Rikke Guldberg Hansen, Mads Hilmer, Ulrik Jantzen, Matias Labarca, Jens Lindhe, Nils Lund, Vegar Moen, Nicholai Møller, Paolo Rosselli, Ty Stange, Tobias Toyberg

DAC
Anne Nørgaard Pagh, Fredrik Gyllenhoff, Lonnie Hansen PR / MARKETING Line Juul Greisen, Kari Haugan Engberg, Andreas Spinner Nielsen GRAPHIC DESIGN Naja Tolsing, Nicolai Fontain, Jane Stub Kirchhoff

Pedersen PRODUCTION Ulrik Bliss, Marie Ortving Westh, Michael Gahrn, Nicolas Hjorth, Kim Vedsted, Kenneth Skovby

VOLUME
Jeffrey Inaba

THANKS TO Kent Martinussen, Jeffrey Inaba, Bruce Mau, Boris Brorman Jensen, Sarah Herda, Joseph Grima, Stefano Boeri, Robert E. Somol, Rem Koolhaas, Jens Thomas Arnfred, Shohei Shigematsu, Joshua Ramus, Christian Madsberg, Niels Reiff Koggersbøl, Flemming Andersen, Vibeke Windeløv, Jesper Elg, Thomas Busch, Andreas and Ilka Ruby, Shumon Basar, Beatrice Galilee, Fay Cheah, Michael Kubo, Beat Schenk, Fredrik Fritzson, Friedrich Nietzche, Frank Miller and Charles Darwin for their inspiration and input.

THANKS TO my partners Andreas Pedersen, Finn Nørkjær, David Zahle, Niels Lund Petersen, Jakob Lange, Thomas Christoffersen and all of the BIG team.

THANKS TO Hanif Kara, Andy Murray, Daniel Bosa, Michael Kwok, Martin Rein-Cano, Christian Saabye, Alex Fraenkel, Lars Ostenfeld Riemann, Dan Stubbergaard, Lars Holme Larsen, Rolf Hay, Victor Ash, Kaspar Astrup Schrøder, Team Jiyo, Lars Holme Larsen, Henning Stüben, Dorte Børresen, Malene Krüger, Stig Lennart Anderson, Petter Haufmann, Torben Schønherr, Jakob, Bjørnstjerne and Rasmus aka Superflex, Mads Byder, Einar Ólafsson, Kristin Brynja, Andri Snær, Steffan Iwersen, Jeffrey Inaba, Jan and Tim Edler, Yanson Ma, Minsuk Cho, Michel Rojkind and Julien De Smedt for the collaboration

THANKS TO Per Høpfner, Axel Frederiksen, Frank Hansen, Dan Poulsen, Peter Poulsen, John Hansen, Finn Bach, Anders Bo Bach og Lene Kristensen, Asmund Haare, Torben Frølich, Anders Knudsen and Dan Petersen, Hans Peter Svendler and Flemming Borreskov, Ritt Bjerregaard, Jens Kramer Mikkelsen, Zeid Abdul-Hadi, Ulla-Britt Wikstrøm, Martin Schrøder, Per Söderberg, Ingela Lindh, Peter Sextus, Johnny Laursen, Jan Lehrmann, Iasson Tsakonas, Morten Hemmingsen, Claus Jeppesen, Alfred Dam, Khosrow Bayat, Peter Trøjfeldt, Torben Frøhlich, Jørn Christoffersen, Anders Juhl, Casper Moltke-Leth, Hans Peter Jensen, Kenan Khudaverdiyev and Nazim Ibrahimov, Colin Glover, Jørn Tækker and Thomas Fiellau, Christian Correll, Frugtkarl and Kill Bill, Lars Heilesen, Rolandas Balcikonis, Carsten Leveau, Anna Vos and Antoon Jorna, for entrusting us with your projects.

A BIG THANKS TO:

Høpfner A/S

dreyersfond

RAMBØLL

DANISH HARDWOOD A/s

FOAMGLAS
Building

Grontmij | Carl Bro

Bach
GRUPPEN A/S

pihl
THE JOY OF CREATING

LEGO

akt
ADAMS KARA TAYLOR
A WYG Group Company

© 2009 for this edition:
EVERGREEN GmbH, Köln

Original title: Yes Is More.
An Archicomic on Architectural Evolution
Copyright © 2009 BIG A/S
www.big.dk
Published by BIG A/S on the occasion of the YES IS MORE
exhibition - Close up: BIG at Danish Architecture Center in
Copenhagen, Denmark, 21 February - 31 May 2009
Drawings, renderings and illustrations © BIG A/S

Printed in China

ISBN 978-3-8365-2010-2